The

Left-Leaning Antenna

JOSEPH KEELEY

THE

LEFT-LEANING

ANTENNA

Political Bias in Television

ARLINGTON HOUSE   *New Rochelle, N.Y.*

SECOND PRINTING OCTOBER 1971

Library of Congress Catalog Card Number 70-139888

ISBN 0-87000-115-9

MANUFACTURED IN THE UNITED STATES OF AMERICA

Contents

Preface

═══════════════

Television viewers are accustomed to seeing certain symbols and stereotypes on their picture tubes, and one of the most familiar is the mushroom cloud that signifies The End. They have watched it blossom time and again, as the climax of lurid motion pictures that show what happens when mad militarists or hate-filled anti-Communists are given access to The Bomb. It has been used to underscore the imperative need for complete and immediate U.S. disarmament, regardless of what any other nation does, and it has proved highly effective in politics, as witness its use in the Presidential campaign of 1964 when many voters got the idea that they had to choose between Senator Goldwater and little girls who picked daisies.

Today few people believe everything they see on the aptly named boob tube, but let us assume some truth in one of those Strangelove-type movies. Suppose a demented member of the "military-industrial complex" or a nutty extremist actually did push the button that set off the "nuclear holocaust" we have heard so much about. Man and his works might indeed disappear in a mushroom cloud, and a charred Earth would hurtle, lifeless, through space.

Until, say, the year 3000. Then intrepid beings from some distant galaxy would alight from their spacecraft to probe this strange, dead sphere. The Galaxians would surely be amazed at the ruins around them, but clues concerning Earth's ancient civilization would soon be disclosed through videotapes of ancient telecasts. Those visual records, preserved through the centuries, would give the Galaxians a picture of the world that was, and the visitors would get some strange impressions indeed.

They would learn that while most earthlings must have worked hard to build and maintain their complex civilization, the real leaders, the ones who got the most attention, were furry-headed characters who obviously hated the society in which they found themselves and the people who had created it. Repeatedly the faces of these barbarians would appear on the tapes, making strident demands and vowing destruction if their demands were not met. These were not idle threats either, since there was destruction, and often the same hate-filled faces could be seen in the midst of riots, urging their followers to burn, loot and kill. Amazingly, such people were allowed to move about freely, creating havoc. Little wonder, Galaxians thought, that the ancient civilization of Earth was no more.

Conflict was a dominant theme of much of the tape that was brought from Earth. Men were shown in many different places, waging warfare, but as though this was not enough, violence seemed to be a way of life in the streets and in the home. Countless tapes showed men and women settling disputes or seizing the possessions of others in individual combat, usually in the most brutal fashion. Portrayals of violence were even presented in animated drawings, obviously intended to train the young.

Another theme would run through much of the tape, one that would puzzle Galaxian scholars. This dealt with what Earth people referred to as sex. This apparently was the normal attraction between male and female, but earthlings seemed to be utterly obsessed with it. Much of what was found on the tapes seemed to aim at stimulating greater interest in sex, and this interest was then exploited by people with things to sell. Their merchandise, they promised, would make anyone sexually irresistible.

Certain aspects of the tapes would prove incomprehensible to the Galaxians who studied them. The home life of earthlings, as depicted in extended portrayals called serials, was so difficult and frustrating as to be unbearable. So plagued were Earth people by insurmountable problems that most earthlings became physical, mental and moral wrecks. And here again Galaxians found a theory to explain the end of Earth's civilization. Life on Earth was obviously too much for the human species to cope with.

Despite the evidence that many earthlings, or at least those on the tapes, were of a low mental order, preoccupied and even obsessed with inconsequential things, the planet must have been a pleasant place in many respects. Many scholars expressed regret over what they said were serious omissions in the story told by the tapes. The scholars said they would have liked to know more about the people who had built and directed that great civilization. Questions arose about their history since so little was found to indicate that they had any pride in their past. And why was so much laudatory attention paid to the criminal element? Why indeed were these people not properly punished and shut away from decent earthlings?

Surely, it was felt, many of Earth's people must have had interests other than sex or pastimes which consisted of watching athletic men toss or kick spheres to each other in huge stadia. And was that now-dead world really as violent as it was pictured? The way it ended would indicate that Earth had more than its share of violence, but surely there were other and finer aspects. Why was there so little emphasis on more admirable matters?

Perhaps there was, and maybe it just so happened that the men from Galaxy picked an assortment of tapes that gave a distorted picture of life on Earth.

* * * * * * *

Maybe. But today many earthlings are getting the same impressions from television that mythical Galaxians or Martians of a thousand years hence would get from those same electronic records, and they are beginning to wonder about them. So a close, hard look at television may be in order, as Vice President Spiro T. Agnew suggested in his now-famous speech at Des Moines, Iowa, on November 13, 1969. The Vice President was certainly not the first to raise questions about television and accuse the medium of distortion or downright dishonesty. Such accusations have become commonplace, so much so that networks either ignore them or ridicule them. However, this was impossible with Mr. Agnew, not because he was the

Vice President of the United States but because his remarks were resoundingly echoed by hundreds of thousands of Americans.

When the people speak in such numbers, even television executives have to listen.

The

Left-Leaning Antenna

CHAPTER ONE

The Medium and the Media

WHEN Vice President Spiro Agnew complained about biased news and the way in which television and influential newspapers distorted the facts, he was echoing a complaint that is centuries old. Not long after William Caxton brought the art of printing to England, the Privy Council of King Henry VIII moved against purveyors of the printed word who, it said, were disturbing the tranquility of the realm by publishing "unfitting worrdes." Early in our own country's history George Washington complained, "We have some infamous papers, calculated for disturbing, if not absolutely intended to disturb, the peace."

President Lincoln had reason to feel bitter about press attacks that threatened to abort the Civil War, and more recently another political leader complained about dishonest reporting and unfair editorials that, he said, "have created confusion in the minds of the American people and in several instances have bordered on treason."

This was not Spiro Agnew speaking, but Adlai Stevenson, at the time of World War II, in 1942.

Partisanship in the press is nothing new. In fact it was customary and even expected in the early days of the Republic. Newspapers often labeled themselves for what they were—Whig, Federalist, Republican, Democrat—and readers would have felt betrayed if the various editors attempted to be objective in their presentation of the news and in their editorial comments.

Readers then, as they do today, subscribed to journals that reinforced their own prejudices and beliefs. However, there has been a marked change in this respect. Publications, particularly those of large general circulation, are less openly partisan, and usually they try to give the semblance of objectivity. If a newspaper or magazine aims at a huge circulation, the kind that will permit it to charge lucrative advertising rates, it cannot be restrictive. It must cater to all kinds of people—liberal and conservative, black and white, Protestant, Catholic and Jew. While it cannot exclude the poor, it prefers people with good incomes, since advertisers like to invest their money where they will find affluent customers.

In any case, with the multi-million-circulation publications there is an inevitable blurring of political and other lines so as not to antagonize any sizeable segment of the readership. Indeed, to be successful in the large-circulation communications media, an executive in that field must have some of the attributes of a John V. Lindsay, enabling him to be all things to enough people to keep his job.

Radio, and then television, called for even greater talent in the art of pleasing everybody. Entrepreneurs who moved into radio broadcasting as a commercial venture found themselves catering to a large ready-made audience, and with the advent of network broadcasting those audiences ballooned, becoming far greater than those of the nation's biggest newspapers and magazines. The main problem of radio's masters was how to provide all those people with enough entertainment to keep them happily diverted without irritating them in any manner. This task was particularly important since advertisers have a preference for listeners who are as contented as well-fed cows.

So, to a far greater extent than did purveyors of the printed word, who are accustomed to dealing with *selected* audiences, broadcasters had to learn how to cater to a mass audience covering the entire spectrum of America. Not only did this audience represent all shades of political thought, it also included rich and poor; young and old; every race, religion and nationality; management and every kind of worker. Broadcasters quickly learned about the diversity that exists in our United States because any real or fancied slight to any group brought a quick and sometimes violent reaction.

Broadcasters also came to realize the awesome power of their medium. There was a frightening demonstration of this and of the ease with which people can be misled, electronically, on October 30, 1938. On that Halloween night, Orson Welles and his *Mercury Theatre on the Air* dramatized H.G. Wells' *War of the Worlds* over CBS. Even though the broadcast was clearly presented as fiction, it created panic when vast numbers of listeners accepted as fact the story it told about an invasion by strange creatures from Mars. The script told how New Jersey was being subjugated by these monsters, who had arrived in spaceships, and more than a million listeners were deluded by the broadcast. Many of these people rushed into the streets and scurried about in panic to notify others that doom was at hand.

The Orson Welles halloween prank was not the first of this genre. I was involved in one which was perpetrated two and a half years before the Wells-Welles hoax. I was then employed by the advertising agency that produced the *Crime Clues* broadcasts, popular whodunits of the time. Early in 1936 the British Broadcasting Company announced that it was going to broadcast a program from a haunted house outside London, and I suggested something similar for *Crime Clues.* We would find a haunted house in this country and present a specially written broadcast from it, one with ghostly overtones.

This was done on March 10, 1936, and the *Crime Clues* program emanated from an old stone mansion on Staten Island, reputed to be haunted. Listeners were informed of the background of our haunted house, and a cordial invitation was extended to any resident ghosts to participate in the broadcast. Everything went smoothly until the very end, when the heroine uttered a piercing shriek. The program ended on that note, without explanation. An announcer then calmly told listeners of the merits of the sponsor's product.

The sales pitch was still being given when a phone rang and I was called to it. The editor of a Staten Island newspaper wanted to know if a member of the cast had been murdered, as he had been told. Then there were more calls. Before the evening was over Radio City had been deluged with upwards of six hundred telephone queries about the spooky "murder." Every station on the network wired complaints and subsequently agency and sponsor were called on the carpet by the network.

I might add that the unorthodox ending which caused the trouble was strictly the idea of the script writer, a last-minute revision in the nature of a personal joke. I plead innocent to having been an accomplice in the deception.

The point is that radio and, to a greater extent, television induce an almost hypnotic influence over many listeners and viewers, and under this influence the real and the unreal often blend together. One sees this in the way so many millions of people identify with the strange, tortured souls who daily roam the purgatory of soap operas. Historically, consider the way in which such dictators as Hitler and Castro were aided to power by the electronic media.

Today anyone who wants to reach and persuade large numbers of people knows that no medium can compare with television. This is true whether the item being offered is a bottle of mouthwash or a revolutionary idea. Because of this, people with causes to huckster have long made radio microphones and television cameras a major objective. The radical left has a particular affinity for electronic media, possibly because of tradition. One of the first objectives of Lenin's Bolsheviks is said to have been the wireless station in Moscow.

In the climate of the New Deal and the Fair Deal, a highly liberal coterie of commentators moved into network broadcasting and flourished there during and after World War II. Then when the Soviet Union turned out to be somewhat less than the noble ally those people consistently lauded, there was a reaction from the public and many of them were eased out. This brought a cry of outrage from one Bryce Oliver, who, writing in the *New Republic* of January 13, 1947, complained that "last year more than two dozen broadcasters —all Left of Center—have been dropped or had their air time slashed."

Among those he named were John W. Vandercook, Robert St.

John, Johannes Steele, Frank Kingdon, Don Hollenbeck, Don Goddard, William S. Gailmore and Sam Balter.

Oliver demanded the Federal Communications Commission "ensure that a commentator who talks liberalism gets as good a deal on the air as a commentator who talks conservatism."

In the light of what has happened since that time it would appear that, somehow, the electronic media have moved 180 degrees from that position. Today one may well wonder what ever happened to the conservatives.

When television was getting started commercially after World War II, it was looked upon by many as a reflecting medium, one that would disseminate truth because it would mirror faithfully the people, places and events that passed before it. However, it soon became apparent that this was not quite so. The truth was there but quite often it was seen through a glass, darkly. Marshall McLuhan presented another concept in his catch phrase "the medium is the message," but it is probably more accurate to say that television is a reflecting medium much like those distorting mirrors one finds at amusement parks and penny arcades. Stand in front of one and you appear to be a cadaverous giant, eight feet tall. Move to the next one and you become a bloated midget, with a ridiculous resemblance to a pumpkin. It all depends on where you stand.

This is not to say that television always presents a distorted image. When the medium plays it straight, as it often does, it turns in a superb job, one that cannot be approached, let alone surpassed, by any other medium. Who could possibly complain about the way in which television portrayed the moon landings, which made all Americans, and all mankind, spectators of that epic achievement? Or the way it presented the miraculous return of the astronauts of Apollo XIII? What other medium can approach it in its portrayal of pomp and solemnity, as when a Winston Churchill, a John F. Kennedy or a Dwight D. Eisenhower is laid to rest? What other medium could so awaken Americans to the danger they faced from Communist aggression when President Kennedy issued his warning to Khrushchev at the time of the Cuban missile crisis? Who can ever forget its impact when it brought to shocked millions the dramatic shooting of Lee Harvey Oswald by Jack Ruby, not to mention the details it provided of both Kennedy assassinations, at the time and at the scene?

Television was magnificent then, when it acted as a reflecting medium without embellishments. Unfortunately, though, even in the course of reporting some of those events television was being manipulated in the manner of a distorting mirror. As viewers were being shown the tragic aftermath of President Kennedy's assassination they were being assured by certain experts that this was the diabolical work of right-wing extremists operating in a hate-filled Texas atmosphere. Overlooked almost completely was Oswald's Communist background—his work with Castro's Fair Play for Cuba Committee, his Russian sojourn, his long dalliance with Communism from the time he had been in service and his obvious hatred of his native land.

Likewise, when Sirhan Sirhan cut down Robert S. Kennedy there was the same irrational reluctance to report that the young Arab, who was not even an American citizen, was an ardent and self-professed Communist. It took Mayor Samuel Yorty of Los Angeles to register that strangely overlooked fact by leaking Sirhan's diary at a press conference carried live by NBC. Yorty's disclosure was not greeted kindly by the newsmen, who questioned him sharply concerning it. Immediately afterwards, Edwin Newman, of NBC, attempted to play down the significance of the mayor's contribution.

Trying to understand this almost emotional reaction from supposedly objective newsmen, one can only assume that the truth can be troublesome when it conflicts with preconceived notions. And the notions being widely circulated by the experts of press and television attempted to establish the myth that the two Kennedys were the victims of an America that was sick, violent and obsessed with hatred —right-wing hatred. To those with this fixation, Communist fanaticism could not possibly have entered into it.

This compulsion to absolve Communism of any of our woes is virtually an article of faith with the liberal element. Following is an excellent example of the way the assassinations are explained in the *New York Times Encyclopedic Almanac 1970:*

"These seemingly unmotivated killers do not fit the roseate American dream of life as advertised by the Legionnaires and Elks, the Daughters of the American Revolution, and the Birchers; the babbitts and haters engaged in putting down reality in the home of the brave. But they are kin."

The author of this intelligence, which brackets Legionnaires, Elks, the ladies of the DAR and Birchers as babbitts and haters, then worked his way through some tortuous prose to offer this conclusion: "This is assassination, American style . . ."

Is it indeed? Rather, this kind of nonsense may be considered typical of *Times*-style interpretive reporting, which has no compunction whatever about "putting down reality" when it is attempting to make a point.

While the subject of this book is television and its various wayward ways, it is impossible to deal with the medium without recognizing its relationship with other media—newspapers, magazines, motion pictures and book publishing. This is something that Vice President Agnew learned when he made his now-famous speech criticizing the bias in television news. The nation's broadcasters and publishers fight viciously among themselves for the billions spent in advertising, but they quickly close ranks in a united front if anyone speaks unkindly of them. Criticism is denounced not merely as unwarranted but also as un-American and unconstitutional. Anyone who dares to criticize the media, for any reason, is castigated as a monster, another Hitler, who is trying to destroy freedom of the press, impose censorship and through such censorship establish a dictatorship.

In some of their counterattacks to the Agnew charges, certain gentlemen of the media made themselves look ridiculous. The reaction was somewhat reminiscent of the 1950s during the so-called McCarthy era. At that time, it will be recalled, there was a deafening uproar from liberal commentators, professors, clergymen and others who protested loudly and vehemently that freedom of expression had been completely stifled in this country. No one, bellowed the distraught liberals, dared to open his mouth.

In much the same way, though a bit more restrained, network officials and commentators deplored Agnew's criticism of the press.

Joining them at the wailing wall were the *New York Times,* the *Washington Post,* the *New Republic* and the *New Yorker,* to name just a few. Norman Isaacs, president of the American Society of Newspaper Editors, rushed about like a modern Paul Revere, warning of Agnewism, and Herbert Block dashed off some of the cartoons for which he is held in regard in some quarters. These Herblockisms, which originate in the arch-liberal *Washington Post,* are widely syndicated.

As the nation's most enterprising newspaper in such matters, the *New York Times* unquestionably did more to belittle Spiro Agnew than any other bearer of the printed word, and may even have outdone the networks. It published editorials, editorial features and letters to the editor denouncing the Vice President. Under the guise of "interpretive reporting," barbs against Mr. Agnew were insinuated into news copy.

Times hysteria reached a ridiculous crescendo when the paper's music critic Harold C. Schonberg penned an essay that took the Vice President to task. Mr. Agnew had not presented a concert of bouzouki music at the Lincoln Center or at Carnegie Hall, an event which might have merited Mr. Schonberg's attention and disdain. Mr. Schonberg was wroth because, he said, the Vice President was "acting like a producer when his show is panned." This idea rated considerable space in the widely circulated *Sunday Times* drama section, in line with *Times* standards of news value.

The behavior of the press, or at least the powerful Eastern liberal organs, brings to mind a speech that was quoted in *Editor & Publisher* for August 31, 1968. Addressing a group at Lawrence, Kansas, Roscoe E. Born of the *National Observer* discussed what he called "wolf pack journalism." This is a practice, he said, in which the gentlemen of the press pick a victim and then gang up on him. "Readers," he explained, "or at least the more perceptive readers know that somehow the leaders of the pack have picked a victim and that the pack members are already in full cry after the quarry." Mr. Born was talking primarily about reporters but it is not difficult to figure out where such reporters get their examples, not to mention their ethics.

If the coordinated assault against Mr. Agnew did nothing else it probably convinced the Silent Majority that the Vice President was right in his criticism of Big Media. To use a term favored by the New Left, the attacks probably "polarized" millions.

Ties of a professional nature bind the communications media in an *entente cordiale* when their mutual interests are involved, but there are other interactions and interreactions. One of these is the obvious influence that one medium exerts on another, as illustrated by an item that appeared in *Time* in March 1969. It dealt with David Brinkley, the NBC newscaster, and told how he started every day with a careful reading of the *New York Times* and the *Washington Post.* Since Mr. Brinkley is said to be the only major newscaster who writes his own copy, it is quite possible that what he finds in those liberal newspapers may crop up, albeit unconsciously, in his NBC news. Which fact in turn may explain why, in a poll of congressmen conducted by the University of Missouri School of Journalism late in 1969, David Brinkley was voted "least fair."

A more dramatic example of the way in which a newspaper can influence television—not to mention a nation's foreign policy—was demonstrated at the time the famous Herbert Matthews articles on Castro were prominently featured by the *New York Times* in February 1957. The "Latin American expert" of the newspaper in three lengthy articles told of his meetings with fascinating Fidel Castro, virtually unknown in this country till that time. Castro was presented glowingly, as a great and glorious leader, incredibly brave and full of ideals, a veritable Robin Hood who was dedicated to the overthrow of Batista, Cuba's legitimate leader. Once Castro overthrew Batista, according to Matthews, the Cuban people would be given a new deal.

The widely circulated *Times* pitch for the great and noble Castro was obviously noted in television circles, for soon a CBS camera crew was following Matthews' trail to Castro's hideout in the Sierra Maestra. Heading this crew, incidentally, was one Robert Tabor who, it was later learned, was an ex-felon who had served time for kidnaping, armed robbery and automobile theft. Tabor later became executive secretary of the Fair Play for Cuba Committee, an outfit financed with Castro money. Edward R. Murrow also contributed to Castro's buildup over CBS, as did Ed Sullivan (who later apologized for the disservice he had done). NBC viewers learned about the Cuban miracle man through Jack Paar, who was mightily impressed by him.

Five years after this propaganda buildup, whose end result was a Communist Cuba, the news media were able to report that we were at the brink of war over the missiles the Soviet Union had emplaced in a nation only ninety miles from our shores.

However, if television and other news media learned any lessons from this deadly miscalculation, there is little indication of it. They are doing the same thing all over again, only this time the job is not being done in behalf of a revolutionary leader ninety miles from us, in the Caribbean. Today the media busy themselves in glorifying home-grown counterparts of Castro and Guevara, guerrilla fighters who are turning our nation's streets and campuses into battle-grounds.

Because television is now looked upon by most Americans as their primary source of news and entertainment, and because of its tremendous impact, it has played a leading role in creating the Frankenstein monsters who candidly tell us that they intend to overthrow "the system" and run it in some vague way that only they seem to comprehend.

Certainly television is not the only medium that is aiding and abetting our militants, black and white. They are all contributing to the dangerous buildup. Even the normally gentle field of book publishing has become a center for the manufacture and distribution of literature promoting revolution in this country and glorifying the criminals who are fomenting it. Some of these books are indeed written by the criminals themselves. Recent books, some of them of a highly inflammatory nature, are being turned out not by sleazy underground concerns but by some of our most prestigious publishing houses. They get an inordinate amount of attention in influential book-reviewing publications and as a result you will find considerable revolutionary material on display in bookstores and public libraries.

Possibly because they like and thrive on the excitement that conflict provides, the communications media are doing little to avert it. Quite often they contribute to it. At the time of the Democratic National Convention in Chicago, Richard L. Strout, writing in the *Christian Science Monitor,* said: "The news media in this city may be indicted for inciting to violence. The mildest parade of young people brings a TV camera crew like a hook-and-ladder truck to a three-alarm fire. Any youngster who will denounce the authorities finds himself surrounded by a ring of extended microphones. The press has talked so much about violence that it has a vested interest in violence. It will look silly if it doesn't get it. This is a case where 'the medium is the message.' "

Television adds another element to news coverage that can be explosive. The appearance of a newspaper reporter at the scene of a demonstration is not likely to have much impact on what is taking place. As long as he remains unobtrusive the participants will continue to do whatever it was they were doing. But when a TV crew arrives on the scene, with cameras and lights, the situation changes. It becomes show business, and the participants become performers acting certain roles and usually "hamming it up." People who had been sitting around doing nothing will spring up, grab their picket signs, start screaming, give the clenched-fist salute and otherwise emote while the cameras grind away. Thus, all too often, television "tells it like it ain't."

Television has been accused of many errors of malfeasance, misfeasance and nonfeasance. It has been charged with slanting the news, sabotaging the war being fought in Vietnam and contributing to crime, juvenile delinquency and sexual promiscuity by presenting a warped kind of ethics.

Some of these charges may be overdrawn, but it is not exaggerating to say that television has often shown little responsibility except to its stockholders. And the medium certainly has earned criticism for its glorification of revolutionaries and demagogues who are destroying democracy by inciting mob violence.

Apologists for the medium say that these people are newsworthy and the American people should be made aware of them and what they are doing. Unfortunately, in making the American people aware of such characters, television presented them in such a way that it transformed them from nobodies into Very Important Persons indeed, able to attract followers and create deadly disturbances. Even more reprehensible, however, is the way in which TV continues its buildup of these people and continues to bring new revolutionary types to the fore.

It is sometimes argued that in the marketplace of ideas the stuff that these people offer is quickly shown up for the shoddy it is, but this too is fallacious. The sad fact is that television seems to have few people capable of coping with our revolutionaries, to show up their errors. This takes someone like William F. Buckley, Jr., who knows the score. But almost invariably the job is handled, with singular ineptness, by people who have only a superficial knowledge of the issues or whose liberal outlook makes it impossible for them to take a stand in opposition to people who should be set down hard.

What is back of this and other aspects of television that trouble many Americans? A suspicious person might suspect a monstrous conspiracy on the part of the communications industry to subvert the country. As proof he could point to the unending parade of TV programs that make a mockery of what used to be considered right, proper and good. Is it by chance, he might ask, that television constantly accents hedonistic concepts, stresses self-indulgence, throws an aura of glamour around sex and violence and presents our nation and its leaders in the worst possible light?

Television does many things that merit criticism but its officials are certainly not conspirators. They are doing only what they consider to be perfectly proper and necessary to succeed in this branch of show business. Unfortunately, what is considered necessary to build large viewing audiences that can produce large advertising revenues is often the sort of thing that can do the country and individual Americans irreparable harm.

It is axiomatic that the more violence you can pack into a television program—news or fiction—the higher the rating the program is likely to get. And the more sex you can work in, and get away with, the better you are likely to score with Nielsen. So, while the networks do not aim at corrupting and contributing to the crime rate, increasing delinquency, sexual permissiveness, alcoholism, pot-smoking and other evils, these are the end results when such evils are given so much attention—often as *"in*-things"—in a medium that has such a profound influence on viewers.

But there is something else that explains much of the stuff that pours out of the tube. This was set forth by Aldous Huxley in his *Brave New World Revisited:*

> In regard to propaganda the early advocates of universal literacy and a free press envisaged only two possibilities: the propaganda might be good or it might be false. They did not foresee what in fact has happened, above all in our Western capitalistic democracies—the development of a vast communications industry, concerned in the main neither with the true nor the false but the unreal, the more or less totally irrelevant. In a word, they failed to take into account man's almost infinite appetite for distractions.

Television, catering to that appetite, gives us, hour after hour and day after day, a constant diet of the unreal and the irrelevant.

One of this country's best-known military leaders, General Albert C. Wedemeyer, told me much the same thing, as it applied to the way many journalists covered the Far Eastern theater during World War II.

"Many of the correspondents," he said,

> were openly biased and were interested only in information that supported conclusions long since arrived at. Others had little intellectual background to equip them for the work they were trying to do. Many more concentrated on the offbeat and dramatic, and showed little interest in news that was truly significant. And there was some reason for this sort of journalism because this was what their employers wanted. Supplying those wants meant pay increases.

What about the people in television who gather and disseminate the news? Are they essentially the same as those left of center news casters whose propagandizing made them so unpopular with the Silent Majority of the late 1940s?

An interesting answer to those questions was provided by a television news official with a major network. For obvious reasons he cannot be identified. "Today," he said,

> there is a different breed from those who moved into radio at the time of World War II. Many of those people were openly pro-Communist but few people objected because Russia was looked upon as an ally, and all we were really worried about was Hitlerism. But when the war ended and the Soviet Union made it clear that it considered the United States as much of an enemy as Nazi Germany had been, those commentators kept plugging the Communist line until listeners demanded their removal.
>
> Those newscasters and commentators were not innocent liberals, in my opinion. They knew what they were doing and in that respect they differ from their successors. Today's commentators often promote people and causes they shouldn't but this is usually because they don't know any better. To tell the truth, many of them are not nearly as well informed about what is going on in the world as people have been led to believe.

The fact is, there is no need for them to have a profound knowledge of the many subjects they discuss because their material is usually handed to them, pre-cooked by network news staffs and ready for serving to millions of viewers. Still, if many of our highly publicized news experts are not much more knowledgeable than other readers of the *New York Times,* the *Washington Post, Time* and *Newsweek,* no one can question their liberal credentials, for liberal they are with few exceptions.

Those who believe they detect a liberal bias in network news are not mistaken, for the bias is there. Indeed, it is bound to be when most of the people responsible for presenting the news are liberals. This point was made by Frank Shakespeare at a Sigma Delta Chi dinner on March 25, 1970. However, the former CBS senior vice president, now director of the United States Information Agency, disagreed with the idea that the news is twisted in some sort of Machiavellian way:

That's a lot of nonsense. I know the people in television news at least and they sweat blood trying to be fair, and they believe they're fair. Now in my judgment they're not. But when you say that they're not they immediately get uptight because they're trying hard to be fair and they believe that they're fair, and so they're just saying what they believe when they say you're wrong. It stems from this problem of a preponderance of one type of political thinking.

The printed press, he said, does much better since newspapers try to give some sort of balance by presenting such conservative columnists as John Chamberlain, William F. Buckley, Victor Riesel and others. Television, on the other hand, does not even make an attempt at such objectivity.

"I wonder if anyone in this room," Shakespeare continued, "could name a nationally prominent television newscaster or commentator that he feels would be proud to stand up and say: 'I'm a conservative. I'm not a liberal.' "

This one-sidedness of television is so obvious that it is creating an immense credibility gap between networks and millions of conservative viewers. Writing in *National Observer* for December 8, 1969, Edwin A. Robert, Jr., made this telling point in discussing the medium's bias:

"Over all, it does appear that the three major networks put a distinct slant on their news products. It is not so much the idea of slanted news that is worrisome, but rather that most broadcasters on all three networks give the impression that they are all working the same side of the street."

However, all the television people who are "working the same side of the street" are not in the news departments, by any means. And many of *those* do not even make an attempt to be objective.

CHAPTER TWO

News and Stuff

MOST of the criticism directed at television in recent months has protested the bias that is evident in the news. After considerable discussion, much of it heated, there is now general agreement that there is bias in television news and different reasons have been advanced to explain it.

David Brinkley of NBC concedes some bias, saying that "objectivity is impossible to human nature."

Howard K. Smith of ABC, in an article in *TV Guide,* blamed the bias on liberal conformists and said they followed an inflexible "party line." In so doing, he said, "They're pleasing Walter Lippmann, they're pleasing the *Washington Post,* they're pleasing *The New York Times,* they're pleasing one another."

Frank Reynolds, Mr. Smith's erstwhile colleague on ABC, is reported to be unhappy about some of Smith's remarks about TV bias, but speaking on the national public television network on December 22, 1968 *(The Whole World Is Watching),* he said: "Sure, I suppose there is an Eastern Establishment, left-wing bias. But that just happens to be because the people who are in feel that way."

Eric Sevareid of CBS attributed the trouble to "militant young men and women, in both newspapers and broadcasting, who argue that even the quest for objectivity is a myth, that the prime purpose of the press is not to report the world but to reform it, and in the direction of their ideas."

And Frank Shakespeare stated that the bias was the result of a concentration of liberals in network news departments, with virtually no representation given to the conservative viewpoint.

Today most Americans are getting their news from commercial television. According to a Louis Harris poll, taken for *Time* late in 1969, nine out of ten watch TV news regularly. Most of them, 70 percent, watched NBC and CBS, while ABC got 12 percent of the viewers, and non-network stations got the remainder. Obviously, what the news staffs of the networks decide to put on the air can have a profound effect on the thinking of millions, and can exert a tremendous influence on what is done at home and abroad.

Because of this, most of the criticism of television bias has concentrated on news disseminated by the networks. There is indeed bias in TV news but actually there are other and far more important reasons why so many people are so badly misled by the medium.

For one thing, the networks devote much less time to news than is generally realized. There are news programs in the morning, but here the news is often interspersed with entertainment and interviews. There are early evening news programs which in big cities may run to an hour or more, but which are much briefer in most other places. As bedtime approaches there is another newscast, and for insomniacs late news bulletins may follow the late show.

In its study of broadcast journalism the Alfred I. du Pont–Columbia University survey criticized the overall dearth of news on television. The allotment of prime time to the network journalist, it said, figures out to about 5 percent, while "of the eight-plus hours a day that represents the schedule of the average television station, he [the network journalist] is lucky if he gets 10 percent."

These figures underscore the fact that commercial television is not a news medium at all but an entertainment medium. This concept is apparent in the touches of show business that the medium employs even in straight news programs, to make the news palatable to a mass audience. News headlines, and usually little more, are orated by beneficiaries of a star system that makes them better known than any Pulitzer Prize winner. To provide the necessary drama, television does its best with on-the-spot coverage of the big warehouse fire, the wreckage of a plane, strikers overturning a car at a factory gate, members of the academic proletariat expressing their hatred of the Establishment, and other standard fare.

The war in the Middle East will be explained with the inevitable flashing map showing the latest strikes. The war in Vietnam and Cambodia will of course be scrutinized, and on occasion it gets considerable attention, often with an apparent bias. One of the most flagrant examples of this occurred when President Nixon returned from a visit to Saigon and to American troops of the 1st Infantry Division at Dian, Vietnam. The President praised the sacrifice and heroism of our GIs and referred to their part in this difficult war as "one of America's finest hours." These remarks were carried by NBC on the July 30, 1969, early evening news, but immediately after the President spoke, the network trotted out Senators Frank Church, Albert Gore and Edmund Muskie who obliged with some highly critical comment. No Republican or less-dovish Democrat was called on for his views, and thus the deck was stacked three to one against the President. Probably the only unusual aspect of this, however, was that Senator Fulbright was not a member of the anvil chorus.

As part of the news fare, television often presents the equivalent of the newspaper human-interest story, and here viewers are likely to get some sort of message. There was a good example of this on the *Huntley-Brinkley Report* on NBC, February 6, 1970. It should be kept in mind that this program is on prime time, each second of which is valuable. In a half-hour, actually seven or eight minutes less than that because of commercials, Messrs. Huntley and Brinkley are expected to cover for many millions of Americans the important things happening in the world.

On this occasion Mr. Brinkley announced a special news report and the next scene showed John Chancellor standing on a college campus. He explained that this was Chadron State College in the northwest corner of Nebraska. He further explained that this was a very conservative college in conservative country where there had been no student troubles. The rules at Chadron called on students to behave themselves and keep themselves tidy and the rules up to now had been obeyed. However, Mr. Chancellor went on, the winds of change had started to blow even on this conservative campus. The college had a rebel and the rebel, sporting long hair, sideburns and a moustache, was brought to the microphone. The newscaster established the fact that the young rebel intended to keep all that hair as a matter of principle, even though the college was determined to see that the rules were obeyed. One got the idea that the hirsute student intended to stand firm even if the authorities tortured him at the rack. Mr. Chancellor seemed very sympathetic and understanding.

One might well wonder just what Mr. Chancellor was trying to prove, and why someone thought it was necessary for him to go all the way to northwest Nebraska to locate and interview a student dissenter. And what dictated the allocation of considerable precious prime time to such arrant nonsense?

The only rational explanation of this is that maybe somebody in NBC would like to see even more rebels on the nation's campuses, as though we do not already have a vast surplus. Certainly this is an excellent way to encourage students to rebel. If a kid in Nebraska can make it on a national network by thumbing his nose at the rules, why can't Sam Snood at Four-Square State and Fanny Floose at Country College make the scene by throwing a tantrum against the Establishment?

Supplementing such news is television's equivalent of the newspaper feature story, the so-called special which deals with such timely matters as dope addiction, sex on campus, sex off campus, the generation gap, the Pill, abortion, the prevalence of pot, the plight of the blacks, the plight of senior citizens, crime in the ghettoes, pollution, women's liberation, America's starving millions and so on. Some of these are well done and interesting, but for the most part they are neither newsy nor entertaining.

An example of such treatment was a recent Metromedia feature on nudity. This presented various aspects of people without clothes, as they appear on stage, in photographic studios, in nudist colonies, in the movies and in *Playboy* magazine. It was all discreetly done with the censor in mind. Scenes that implied nudity were interspersed with participants, promoters and the general public. Viewers learned some fascinating facts: a) some people in show business don't mind taking off their clothes for art's sake if they are paid for it, b) while others, probably a small minority, who can afford to keep their clothes on, prefer to do so. Otto Preminger, making another of his frequent TV appearances, offered some ideas in dialect, and then there was the inevitable psychiatrist. This offering did not tell TV viewers, even the residents of disadvantaged Dogpatch, anything they did not know, nor could it be called entertaining. It did, however, get some press attention and that may have been the purpose.

Closely related to such news features are the big Sunday press sessions in which VIPs discuss the big issues. These often generate significant news that rates front-page position in Monday's newspapers. Among those who appeared on such major programs as *Meet the Press, Face the Nation, Issues and Answers* and *Direct Line* during the first part of 1970 were men of a wide range of political beliefs—Birch Bayh, Jacob Javits, Spiro Agnew, Charles Goodell, Nelson Rockefeller, Edmund Muskie, George Wallace, Melvin Laird, Fred Harris, Hugh Scott and William Rogers.

In view of this lineup, it would appear that some effort was made to keep a balance. However, this is not always done, for reasons that can only be guessed. At the height of the controversy over President Nixon's Cambodian move, the following names were listed for TV appearances on the big Sunday shows of May 17: Charles Goodell, J. William Fulbright, Pete Seeger, Paul O'Dwyer, John V. Lindsay, Theodore Sorensen, Mike Mansfield and Richard Ottinger. Not one guest was scheduled who might have been expected to advance any arguments in favor of the President's position. And if anyone that night still felt any doubts about our move into Cambodia, there was a capper to this long, lopsided day. David Susskind brought up the rear with a group of disillusioned young people performing in a two-hour passion play titled "Cambodia Was the Last Straw—Students Demand Peace Now!"

Anyone writing to the networks to criticize them for this Greek chorus would probably be told that television presents all shades of opinion, as it does. However, timing is important, as television programmers know. The time to sell snowmobiles is when snow is falling.

That is one way in which television takes care of the big issues. Another way is to ignore those whose views are opposed to those of network arbiters. Senator Robert Griffin said that when he was opposing the elevation of Associate Justice Abe Fortas to Chief Justice, he "had considerable trouble getting national exposure. I was never invited on any network shows . . . and seldom was asked about it by network reporters." The situation changed abruptly when the senator made it known that he opposed naming Judge Haynsworth to the Supreme Court: "I have had no difficulty getting my message before the public."

The liberal pitch is not hard to detect in many of the big specials and documentaries that the networks present with pride and fanfare. Since these so often echo the sentiments of other liberal media, they are likely to win considerable acclaim, before they are presented and afterwards. Here, for example, is how a CBS feature was described in the *New York Times Encyclopedia Almanac 1970,* telling of the 1968–69 television season:

"In the realm of public affairs programing the Columbia Broadcasting System's documentary on 'Hunger in America' had the strongest national impact, reminding viewers of the paradox of dire want amid affluence."

A favorite cliché of leftists is that millions of people in the United States are starving in the midst of plenty. Ergo, the system is rotten and must be replaced with one that provides "to each according to his needs," in the Marxian way.

Certainly CBS was not trying to overthrow the government by presenting "Hunger in America," but it did provide powerful ammunition to many who are, and the show aroused a storm of protest from many who so interpreted it. A House of Representatives Agriculture Appropriations subcommittee, chaired by Jamie L. Whitten of Mississippi, conducted a probe of the CBS film with startling results. Testimony covering 84 pages showed a succession of distortions and misrepresentations. (See Appendix E.)

A high school boy was portrayed as a hunger victim because of a niggardly government, but investigation disclosed that his family was not eligible for food stamps because his father had a job and was buying two houses. Some of the alleged victims were actually products of broken homes where the basic problems were actually alcoholism, mental retardation and other matters. This was so in the case of an 11-year-old girl, presented to viewers in a pitiful way as a child who had to resort to prostitution in order to live. The investigation disclosed that this little girl and an older sister had run away from home, with reason. Their mother was dead and the father, described as "illiterate, mentally retarded, and addicted to liquor," was suspected of making his living by stealing.

A callous remark, "You'll always have hunger," was attributed to a county commissioner who bitterly complained that this was quoted completely out of context, making him appear as an enemy of the poor. The director of a surplus commodity distribution center was asked by the CBS crew to close the place to allow a line to form for filming. Not realizing that the purpose was to discredit the program, he did so. An hour and 45 minutes later, with a line of 20 people outside, the crew was ready to start recording.

"Probably the most touching portion of the film," said the investigators, and one which CBS later said "moved the nation to tears," was the scene of a baby being given resuscitation in the hospital, after which it appeared motionless. The CBS narrator, Charles Kuralt, made the following statement with respect to the scene:

" 'Hunger is easy to recognize when it looks like this. This baby is dying of starvation. He was an American. Now he is dead.' "

The congressional report said that there was no evidence of malnutrition, let alone starvation. Jack E. Coughlin, director of community relations, Bexar County Hospital District, made an investigation which stated: "The male baby involved was born in the hospital at 8:15 a.m. on October 24, 1967, and expired at 3 p.m. on October 29, 1967, in the premature nursery. The baby's weight at birth was 2 pounds, 12 ounces, and the gestation period was 28 weeks (approximately 7 months). The hospital records disclosed that Dr. Luis Rey Montemayor, the doctor on duty, recorded on the baby's chart that the child had a cardiac arrest and respiratory arrest on October 27, 1967, and two additional attacks on October 29, 1967, the last when he was pronounced dead. The death certificate, filed by the hospital, disclosed the baby died from septicemia, meningitis, and peritonitis, with the underlying cause being 'prematurity.' "

When a CBS representative tried to get Dr. Montemayor to say that a contributing factor to a premature birth was malnutrition, the physician said he told CBS there was no evidence of this in the case of the baby used in the film.

Going on to Hale County, Alabama, the CBS hunger crusaders came up with some more of the same. CBS narrator Charles Kuralt strongly suggested that a baby born to Mrs. Louise Zanders had also died of malnutrition. Not only did Mrs. Zanders deny it, but also Dr. William Standeffer, who had tried to deliver the baby through a Cesarean section, claimed it was untrue. The doctor said that Mrs. Zanders did not show any signs of being malnourished herself, and the size of her stillborn child was a hefty 12 pounds, 5 ounces. Death, according to the death certificate on file at the Bureau of Vital Statistics, Montgomery, Alabama, had been caused by prolonged labor.

Despite the evidence compiled by congressional investigators, CBS still endorsed the film. Richard S. Salant, president of CBS news, has responded to the probe with the customary, the network "stands behind its 'Hunger in America' broadcast." Nevertheless, the information uncovered by the Whitten Subcommittee has jolted many members of Congress. Congressman Whitten himself said:

> I point out again, as a lawyer, I am a strong believer in freedom of speech. It is essential. We don't want government control, nor do we want control by government threat. But we also have about reached the point, in my judgment, where there must be some way found to get the news media to accept responsibility for the objectivity and the soundness of that which they publish for public consumption.
>
> This is a rather strong statement—but someone has said that we are rapidly reaching the place where we could have government by public clamor, and television is an instrument that could well create public clamor.

CBS's aggressiveness in "dramatizing" the news has earned it considerable criticism. One of its escapades was a staged "pot party" at Northwestern University, presented over CBS-owned and -operated Chicago station WBBM-TV as an actual student happening. This aroused considerable controversy, but a tolerant FCC merely reproached CBS. Considerably more elaborate was a CBS project that involved an invasion of Haiti. The project started as a story on arms smuggling, but this burgeoned into something more ambitious, an armed invasion. CBS was in on the ground floor of this and took considerable footage of gun-running and men being trained for the overthrow of Papa Duvalier's regime. The CBS crew even acquired a boat, the *Poor Richard,* presumably to serve as a communications center. The story was blown into the open through various lawsuits. CBS adamantly denies any wrongdoing but certain members of Congress have interested themselves in the matter. Representative Anchor Nelson of Minnesota said, "The network is playing with dynamite. If the allegations are true this is manufactured news."

A desired point can be made in other ways, and very simply. Doubt can be raised in many minds by something that does not even show in a newscaster's script—a raised eyebrow, or an inflection of the voice. Or there may be an aside, a caustic comment about a government policy or a well-known person.

This can be done electronically, too. Years ago Edward R. Murrow demonstrated this in one of his *See It Now* programs; the program portrayed a dispute between an American Legion post and members of the American Civil Liberties Union. Harsh lighting made the Legionnaires look ghastly, and their voices came through sounding harsh and unpleasant. The camera focused on a member of the color guard who had a small moustache, and when the colors were advanced, one sensed a disturbing resemblance to Hitler leading a corporal's guard of storm troopers—possibly because the sound of heels was amplified. When the cameras switched to the ACLU people in another part of the city, there was a tremendous difference. Soft lighting flattered the facial features. All these people looked like solid citizens, thoughtful and concerned about The Important

Things. When they discussed these, their voices came through well modulated. However, what both groups said did not matter greatly. One could make up one's mind by the way they looked.

Such reporting did not end with the passing of Mr. Murrow. In an interview with Theodore H. White in the *Columbia Journalism Review,* White described a more recent incident of this general nature:

> I did the movie version of *The Making of the President 1968.* We had two crews on the road all the time. They were young and wonderful cameramen. I was busy writing my book and reporting and I couldn't direct the film crews, so about nine months later when I finally got to Hollywood to put the film together, I found that these young people absolutely adored Eugene McCarthy and Robert Kennedy, and there was not a bad shot of either Gene McCarthy or Bobby Kennedy in the thousands and thousands of feet that we took. The images were glowing. On the other hand, these people who worked with me did not bring back one human shot of Hubert Humphrey. Everything that was taken looked sinister. He has an angular face, a pointed chin, and if you want to shoot Hubert badly, it's the easiest thing in the world. I have a personal fondness for Hubert Humphrey. I have known him for fifteen years. But I had to work with film that showed Hubert Humphrey only as a sinister character. Such problems are even more pointed when you come to the daily TV shows. You're in the hands of the hundreds of people who are feeding material to you. No single person controls television.

In a category different from the various news shows and specials are the funfests presided over by Dick Cavett, David Frost, Merv Griffin, Johnny Carson and others. Here, in the sparkling repartee of the avant garde, the liberal pitch frequently comes through as clear as a bell. Guests are often the beautiful people, the jet-setters who fly from Rome, Hollywood, Paris or London to talk of their new play, plug their latest movie, describe or model the see-through bikini they've just designed or peddle political pap. When asked about the way the country is being run, they are usually uninhibited in expressing their opinions about such gauche upstarts as Nixon, Agnew and

Mrs. Martha Mitchell. Watching some of these people in action, one can better appreciate the Vice President's term "effete snobs."

Combat, a lively newsletter which details the activities of leftists at work, in its February 1, 1970, issue cited an example to show how the struggle is waged by ideologists who can gain access to television's more popular gabfests:

> While the Silent Majority has been stop-watching each news show, exploring each report for its nuances, over on the other great gateway into the American home—the TV desk-and-sofa shows overseen by the Great Interviewers—the left has been having a field day. On a single evening last month (Jan. 12) a late-night viewer had to choose between the following: On the Metromedia station, Britain's gift to gab, David Frost, was interviewing Vietnam War critics Robert Vaughn and Lee Remick whose foreign policy expertise flows from their innumerable trips to overseas film locations. CBS's Merv Griffin was chatting with ex-CBS newsman David Schoenbrun (now a Columbia University lecturer), an outspoken opponent of U.S. action in Vietnam. Over on the Dick Cavett show (ABC) leftist pamphleteer I. F. Stone, another abrasive critic of the Vietnam War, was guest of honor. Stone has just reissued one of his old books which "proves" that the U.S. and South Korea attacked North Korea in 1950 igniting the Korean War. On the Johnny Carson show (NBC), meanwhile, one of the guests was actor Jimmy Stewart. Stewart is an authentic war hero (25 bombing missions over Germany), a retired Air Force general and a strong supporter of U.S. actions in Southeast Asia. What did Carson ask Stewart about? Hey, Jimmy, you used to be a cheerleader at Princeton; show us some of those old cheers, like lo-co-mo-tive. Stewart, plainly, was side-tracked.

Such shows provide wonderful bazaars for the display and hucksting of books. However, only certain books and certain authors rate the valuable free plugs. Take Joe McGinniss and his *The Selling of the President 1968,* which is a sustained sneer at Richard Nixon the candidate. That subject obviously rated considerable attention and the McGinniss book was rapidly boosted to the top of the bestseller list by cooperative gabfesters all over the country. The author appeared on hundreds of network and local shows where he employed some of the selling techniques he may have picked up as an apprentice image-maker. On one occasion he told of having his TV makeup applied by the same expert who had worked on Richard Nixon's makeup. In his book McGinniss had found this sort of flummery amusing if not demeaning.

If you write a torrid sex novel or think up a good title for a book that deals with sex, TV exposure is almost assured. This of course permits the interviewers to discuss sex on a high, literary plane while providing the opportunity for a few blue remarks. Dr. David Reuben, a psychiatrist, turned out a book on sex with the inspired title, *Everything You Always Wanted to Know About Sex But Were Afraid to Ask.* For weeks the doctor was kept so busy appearing before television cameras that the springs in his office couch must have come back to normal. As of May 1970, more than 350,000 copies of his book had been sold.

It would be cruel and inhuman punishment to force anyone to listen to all the repartee bandied about by the clever people who squat and talk with the Great Interviewers but, as *Combat* suggests, maybe the questioning Silent Majority ought to give a little more attention to this branch of television.

Incidentally, one should be tolerant of the views expressed by theatrical people who appear on such shows. People in show business are traditionally and actually kind and generous, with soft hearts that bleed easily. But sometimes they have heads to match, and this often causes them to espouse questionable causes.

If you want to ascertain the liberal or liberal-left position on almost any issue, you can quickly find out from a certain type of run-of-the-mill comedian, the fellow who deals in so-called topical humor. Usually an ardent liberal, he is likely to provide a clue as to why, in his routine. This usually deals with his poor but objectionable relatives, his early life in the slums and so on. After savagely disposing of his relatives, this comic attacks the big issues and goes to work on people he dislikes. The targets of such comedians are changed to tie in with the headlines, but for months Spiro Agnew has been a favorite butt.

A reason for the barrage against the Vice President was advanced by TV critic Jack Gould, in the *New York Times* of January 11, 1970. According to Gould, the funny people were implicitly given a green light by the networks to take out after the Vice President.

"On the other hand," he wrote, "if the Vice President succeeded in persuading some individual stations to adopt a more neutral position in covering the controversy over the Vietnamese war, he and President Nixon are learning that, in many instances, the networks are leaning over backward to see that they are not immune to a sustained assault by comedians and their guests. Vice President Agnew is now a running gag on many segments of TV and the President himself is coming in for barbs as pointed as those which were directed against former President Johnson."

It is interesting to recall that President Johnson was treated respectfully when he first assumed the Presidency. He was, after all, liberal in many respects. But when it became apparent that this liberalism did not include the surrender of Vietnam to the Communists, as the liberal community demanded, the President was cruelly treated. Some of the funny ladies and gentlemen of show business proved to be sadists in the way they lampooned LBJ.

In a *TV Guide* interview with Edith Efron, Howard K. Smith said that the same treatment is in store for President Nixon: "The negative attitude which destroyed Lyndon Johnson is now waiting to be applied to Richard Nixon. Johnson was politically assassinated. And some are trying to assassinate Nixon politically. They hate Richard Nixon irrationally."

Howard K. Smith was talking specifically about newscasters, but the news people are not the only political assassins awaiting their cue in the wings.

One might think that a memo from the heads of the networks would put a quick stop to this sort of thing, but it is not that simple. Such a move would bring strident cries of "censorship" from liberal opinion makers and thought controllers. And as everyone knows, the only word that is more intimidating is "McCarthyism." The cry of censorship rolled across the country like thunder when the Smothers Brothers were eased off the CBS network, and the boys have since made this a standard part of their routine. However, there are some who do not take their martyr role too seriously.

In a newspaper column that told of the cancellation of the *Smothers Brothers* show, Joseph N. Bell quoted Dan Rowan, of the *Laugh-In* show, as follows:

> I told Tom that the CBS brass didn't buy a couple of political polemicists for an hour of social comment when they signed the Smothers Brothers. They bought two fine comedians who did funny music together. That's what you sold them, and if you are going to turn it around and do something else, your boss is perfectly within his rights to say get out of here.

Obviously the Smothers boys were unable to see it that way. They sulked publicly and found many to commiserate with them. However, they got a respite in the form of steady work on ABC when they were signed to do a summer series on that network.

A charge of censorship can be most embarrassing to the networks. Not only does it tarnish their treasured liberal image, but it usually inspires liberal columnists and editorial writers to take pen in hand to demand full freedom of expression for all those who think the same way they do.

As TV viewers are well aware, Messrs. Nixon and Agnew are not the only targets of television's funny folk. Others who are currently unpopular are Governor Reagan, Mayor Daley, FBI and CIA agents, policemen, Southerners and those silly people they call flag-wavers. Such people, in the nature of things, must be depicted as nitwits, lacking the culture that is so obvious in their betters (who dispense the humor).

Military people are also prime targets of the comedians, and there seems to be a standing rule that the higher the rank the more stupid and ridiculous the officer must be made to appear. Thus the fellow with four or five stars gets the dirtiest stuff the comedian can dish out. But of course that is only fair because, as every leftist-liberal knows, that's the fellow whose hand itches to push the button that will start the ICBMs on their way to Moscow and Peking.

Still, even the generals and admirals do not rate the special venom reserved for puritans—those pious people who are always squawking their disapproval of all those hilarious jokes and routines dealing with sex, homosexuals, unwed mothers, pregnancy, pot and the Pill. People like these can cause contracts to be terminated, so self-preservation demands that they be silenced or destroyed through ridicule.

Although Hugh Downs is not a comedian, technically speaking, he expressed a widely held opinion concerning critics, especially organized complainers, in his book *Truly Yours:*

"It gets down to this," he wrote. "Be careful of any group with a slate of officers and a letterhead—The American Legion, The American Medical Society, The American Dental Society, The Spam Marching and Chowder Society of Retired Officers. A sponsor is very aware of all these groups that write letters, and is very intimidated by them."

Implicit in Mr. Downs' warning is the liberal credo: "Don't criticize us; we'll criticize you."

Now surely it is permissible and indeed healthy to poke fun at silly, pretentious people, particularly nincompoops who take themselves too seriously. Comedians have often done a magnificent job of cutting charlatans and tyrants down to size. Who can forget the way people were made to laugh at Hitler and Mussolini, to their diminution? And the way in which bombastic, shoe-pounding Khrushchev was lampooned? But today one wonders about the targets.

On February 12, 1970, the Metromedia station in New York carried a one-hour special based on the musical comedy *Red, White, and Maddox.* It mercilessly ridiculed the governor of Georgia but went beyond that. In the course of poking fun at Maddox it reached out—far out—to ridicule Southerners generally, military people and anti-Communists. On the other hand, extreme enthusiasm was expressed for well-known liberal symbols.

Sophisticated liberals are inclined to guffaw at the kind of flagwaving George M. Cohan employed in the theater of his day. Old Glory would be unfurled to a ruffle of drums and a trumpet fanfare and the show would be a hit. In the Maddox production there was no Old Glory, of course. But the audience was subjected to the same technique when screen-filling pictures of Rev. Martin Luther King, John F. Kennedy and Robert F. Kennedy were presented to evoke wild enthusiasm. Love interest was provided by a pair of star-crossed lovers who apparently made a career out of demonstrating on a cross-country basis. In working for a brave new world, these youthful rioters made it as far as Muncie, Indiana, where they were shown being cut down by gunfire in the midst of a riot. Police brutality. What else?

A person such as Lester Maddox is considered fair game by liberals, with some reason. But why does show business, including television, consistently ignore other well known people who could provide the basis for a lot of much-needed comedy? Why not have some fun with such personalities as J. William Fulbright, William Kunstler, William O. Douglas, Dr. Spock, John V. Lindsay, W. Averell Harriman, Teddy Kennedy and certain university presidents, to name just a few? The list of liberal VIP's who have made themselves eligible for comic treatment could be extended indefinitely, but you are not likely to see any of these people being treated with anything less than reverence. India is not the only place where they maintain large herds of sacred cows.

In all fairness, it should be pointed out that quite often it is not the comedians who are primarily responsible for programs that sometimes outrage viewers. The fault frequently lies with anonymous people in the background who prepare and select the comedian's material for him. These people sometimes use the comedian as their Charlie McCarthy, to give voice to ideas they fancy, or they may be ignorant or uncaring about the reaction that some of their contributions can evoke.

The way in which a star's career can be jeopardized by those who provide him with material, advise him or speak for him was explained by Edward G. Robinson in an article he wrote for *The American Legion Magazine* of October 1952. Mr. Robinson frankly admitted that he had been played for a sucker and the result was that he became *persona non grata* in Hollywood during a period when the movie industry was trying to rid itself of Red influence. Explaining how he had come to contribute to various Communist causes and even join in them, he said he had done so on the advice of a publicity man.

Subsequently the publicity man was identified in sworn testimony before the House Committee on Un-American Activities as a member of the Communist Party. The actor then offered some advice that might well be pondered by many of today's liberals:

> Yet the Communists were very successful in making "herd thinkers" out of a substantial section of Americans who wanted to be liberals. Given an idea that sounded sympathetic or tolerant, we were prone to accept it blindly. I did so and so did many others. We allowed ourselves to be carried along by the emotions and stresses of historic times. We were, therefore, ready to support whatever appealed to our emotions. . . . Furthermore I have already shown that I supported this and that *because other people did.* That isn't real liberalism, it's "follow the leader." . . . We liberal Americans owe ourselves a forthright declaration of independence—to again start thinking for ourselves and to stop drinking from just one well of information and opinion.

Mr. Robinson's unhappy experience is being repeated by many gullible Americans today, who are whooping it up for various liberal causes. Some day they are likely to find that some of these causes were not quite so noble as they were made out to be.

Two decades ago when Hollywood was under attack for its permissiveness toward Communists and pro-Communists who had become well entrenched in the industry, it had a stock reply to critics who questioned the content of films: "How many movies can you name which are openly pro-Communist or pro-Soviet?" Actually there were very few which could have been so classified, but the Communists would have been stupid to make films that moviegoers would immediately spot as propaganda. Instead, "progressive writers" insinuated certain concepts into their scenarios. They stressed this country's corruption, injustice, bigotry and discrimination, and they downgraded patriotism, religion and similar values.

Roy M. Brewer, a union leader who fought the Communist infiltration of the movie industry, has explained how strongly organized writers under the leadership of John Howard Lawson forced a significant change in motion-picture content. Lawson, it might be mentioned, was an identified Communist who was looked upon as "the Cultural Commissar of Hollywood." Films had been considered entertainment, and controversial subjects had been avoided. But this concept was discarded and Hollywood's radicals won acceptance of the idea that movies should deal with "the realities of life" and present messages of social significance.

"Out of this," said Brewer, "came a tendency toward stories dealing with violence, sex, divorce, prostitution and miscegenation. Pictures began to make heroes and sympathetic characters out of persons who were outside the pale of social acceptability. The underlying theme of all these motion pictures was that America was a nation of 'decadent bourgeoisie.' "

Many of these films can still be seen on television, on various late shows, but there is no need to wait up for such messages. They are being presented constantly, at all hours of the day and night, sometimes in the form of news and sometimes as entertainment.

Fortunately, there is mounting evidence that while Americans are seeing more of this sort of thing, they are believing it less.

Speaking before a Public Relations and Media Symposium at the Waldorf-Astoria in New York in September 1968, George Gallup said: "Never in my time has journalism of all types—book publishing, television, radio, newspapers, magazines, movies—been held in such low esteem."

Such esteem the media have fairly earned.

CHAPTER THREE

Ministry of Truth, American Style

IN the world of *1984,* as envisioned by George Orwell, the citizens of Oceania were fed a steady diet of acceptable ideas by the Ministry of Truth. Through its newspapers, films, plays, novels, textbooks and "telescreen programs," the Ministry exercised a rigid thought control in behalf of Big Brother. While it dabbled in the past, its main job was to make sure that the people of Oceania understood the present as Big Brother wanted them to. Heresy was severely punished.

Many people have the uncomfortable feeling that they are now living in a world that has certain aspects of Orwell's *1984.* Certainly there is a remarkable uniformity of thought in the output of the major communications media, but this is not because of government control. On the contrary, by 1969 the situation had become so obvious, and disturbing, that Vice President Agnew publicly protested against the kind of thought control that was being practiced by the media.

New York City is headquarters for this country's unofficial Ministry of Truth, and there the nation's thought patterns are designed and mass-produced in much the same way that the nation's automobiles are designed and mass-produced in Detroit, with a facility that turns out millions of cars that most people cannot tell apart.

The extent to which midtown Manhattan has become the nation's idea center and the reasons for it are not generally understood.

However, an interesting comment on this subject was made by Theodore H. White, the author, in the course of an appearance on William F. Buckley's *Firing Line* telecast. Since Mr. White is a bona fide liberal, his contribution cannot be dismissed as conservative argumentation:

"What worries me most about the cultural pattern in the U.S.A. today," said Mr. White, "is its increasing concentration . . . especially in the media. You can take a compass with a one-mile radius and put it down at the corner of Fifth Avenue and 51st Street, and you have control of 95 percent of the entire opinion and influence making in the U.S.A."

Describing the way in which television networks, news magazines and other influential media are based in New York, White then talked about the men and women who worked for them and their manner of operation: "These people drink together, talk together, read the same esoteric and mad reviews. . . ." Then he made a serious charge. Although the men and women of the media profess to scorn conformity, he said that they "control the cultural heights . . . and one who does not agree with them has enormous difficulty in breaking through."

That intolerance unquestionably is a major reason why we find a noticeable bias in news and other things. Media people often exhibit the same fanaticism that is shown by student dissenters who drown out with hoots and jeers the expressions of anyone who happens to dissent from them.

Mr. White made an interesting, though tongue-in-cheek, recommendation—that the headquarters of the three television networks be dispersed. One, he said, could remain in New York, but the second would have to move to Chicago, and the third to Los Angeles. The result, he said, would be better perspective and balance in the news.

Some idea of the concentration of the nation's media—thought controllers, if you will—in Manhattan can be gained from a quick look at the familiar Yellow Pages of the Manhattan Classified Directory. You will find approximately four hundred newspapers listed, from the *New York Times* and the *Daily News* to small neighborhood weeklies and foreign-language papers, together with local representatives of newspapers published elsewhere. There are two and a half *pages* of book publishers and four and a half *pages* of periodical publishers, with approximately four hundred to a page. There are two columns of radio stations, one column of television stations, two columns of television producers, and five columns of music publishers—with approximately one hundred names to a column. In addition there are 38 newspaper feature syndicates listed, and 82 literary agents, representing authors from everywhere.

An important, and possibly the most important, reason for this concentration of the mass media in Manhattan appears in another category—more than four *pages* of advertising agencies, approximately fifteen hundred of them, which in the aggregate have billions of dollars to spend in newspapers, magazines, radio and television. So, quite logically, the media come to where the money is, as well as the action.

Similarly, but for other reasons, the motion-picture industry long ago concentrated in Hollywood. An interesting comment about this appears in *A History of the Movies* by Benjamin B. Hampton. The author quoted a movie mogul of three decades ago as saying: "The trouble with picture-making is that it is located in Hollywood. The Hollywood colony is small, and the principal studio people are so clannish and so divided into little cliques that they never see beyond the boundaries of the tiny world they've built around themselves. They've simply 'gone Hollywood,' as some white men in Oriental countries 'go native,' and in 'going Hollywood' they have lost touch with the public. . . ."

Which proves once again the truth of the saying, "The more things change the more they remain the same."

Theodore White's comment concerning the way in which a liberal clique controls the cultural heights and shows little tolerance for those who refuse to conform to its way of thinking was illustrated in a story published in *Variety,* January 14, 1970. This told of a "crisis" that had developed on WNEW-TV, the Metromedia station in New York. This station has a one-hour news show at 10 p.m., with Bill Jorgensen as anchorman.

Variety reported that the show was "in a state of critical upheaval" because the news staff objected to having a conservative commentator in its midst. The unfortunate conservative, Dr. Martin Abend, was so unpopular with his liberal colleagues that 19 out of 20 of them signed a petition that he be fired. The liberals probably would have gotten a clean sweep in their petition but, as *Variety* put it, "the lone non-signer was in a contractual snarl at the time." Abend was not dismissed but his comments were restricted to half-hour shows on weekends.

Thus, liberal news people who have been known to wax indignant about any threat to freedom of expression struck a powerful blow to protect television viewers from dangerous ideas of a conservative nature.

A more extreme example of vindictiveness came to light in mid-April 1970 when a Washington television editor was fired from his job because his wife went to work for Mrs. John N. Mitchell, wife of the U.S. Attorney General. Mrs. Mitchell is a forthright person who forcefully expresses her conservative opinions. One of her transgressions was to take out publicly after the renowned liberal from Arkansas, J. William Fulbright. Such expressions cannot be condoned, naturally, and so educational station WETA-TV fired William Woestendiek, editor of its Newsroom program. Mr. Woestendiek had nothing whatever to do with Mrs. Mitchell, but there are occasions when the doctrine of guilt by association is considered entirely valid by liberals, even to the second or third degree. And so Mr. Woestendiek was thrown out of work because his wife went to work for a woman whose ideas the station detested.

According to the *New York Times* account of the incident, quoting "television industry sources," pressure to fire William Woestendiek "could only have come from Fred W. Friendly and Max Kampelman." The *Times* went on to explain, "Mr. Friendly, former Columbia Broadcasting System producer for Edward R. Murrow, is now with the Ford Foundation which gives financial support to the Newsroom show and many other enterprises in educational television." Mr. Friendly also heads the television department at Columbia University's School of Journalism. Max Kampelman, chairman of the board of WETA-TV, was described as a close associate of Hubert H. Humphrey. Friendly denied the charge that he had exerted pressure while Kampelman could not be reached for comment. Some unconscious humor was injected into the matter by a station spokesman who is quoted as having said, "We did what we thought was right, and there were no political overtones to it."

To give credit where credit is due, three contributing editors on the Newsroom program resigned because of the high-handed action. These were Hugh Sidey and Bonnie Angelo, both of *Time,* and Tom Wicker of the *New York Times.*

Unfortunately, this is an old story. Tolerance for a conflicting viewpoint is not one of the characteristics of some who like to think they are liberals. Passionate likes and dislikes, not to mention prejudices, are often displayed by supposedly objective members of the press. One of the most famous demonstrations of this was the historic appearance of Whittaker Chambers on *Meet the Press,* August 27, 1948.

Chambers describes this in his book *Witness,* telling how he was badgered by Tom Reynolds of the *Chicago Sun,* James Reston of the *New York Times* and Edward T. Folliard, who worked for the *Washington Post,* virtually a house organ for the Hissites. The program, as Chambers puts it, "was enlivened by an unprecedented personal venom . . . a savage verbal assault and battery on the guest, without pause, and with little restraint or decency." Later, as he drove home, his young son asked, "Papa, why did those men hate you so?" He explained, "It is a kind of war. They are on one side, and I am on the other side."

It would be ridiculous to say that Messrs. Folliard, Reston and Reynolds were Communists or pro-Communists. But to call them objective, at least on that occasion, would be equally nonsensical. Which is why many Americans, having seen such prejudice on their television screens and having sensed so much prejudice in print, are increasingly dubious about much of what they find in the mass communications media.

While liberals in the communications media go in for a form of *de facto* segregation, aimed at discouraging conservatives and the conservative point of view, it would appear that there are no great mobs of conservatives breaking down the doors of television, demanding employment. This interesting point was made by Frank Shakespeare, who said:

> I'll tell you the reason that I think there is an imbalance in television. Television is an art form much more than the press is. You have scenic designers, you have cameramen, you have floormen, you have producers, you have directors, you have broadcasters who have a certain aspect of being a performer in addition to being a journalist, and so the elements of being an art form are ever-present in television. Now the thing that God puts in a man that makes him a creative person makes him very sensitive to social nuances and that sort of thing. And overwhelmingly—not by a simple majority, but overwhelmingly—people with those tendencies tend to be on the liberal side of the political spectrum. People on the conservative side of the political spectrum end up as vice presidents at General Motors. For the same reason, that that's the thing they're interested in and that they do.
>
> Now what happens as a result of that? The overwhelming number, the preponderant number of people in Hollywood are on the liberal side, the people in the New York theater are on the liberal side. If you go out and put together a television news department, and you hire people purely on the basis of their ability with no regard whatever for their ideology (and that's the American system and it's very commendable) and you put together 200 men you are quite likely to end up with 175 men who would be quite proud privately to call themselves liberal, and 15 who don't care, and 10 conservatives who will soon quit! Now you have a very serious psychological problem. Because can 10 liberals in a room over an extended period of time, by trying hard, be fair to the conservative position? In my judgment, no —any more than 10 conservatives over an extended period of time can be fair to the liberal position. In my view, fairness comes in the mix, in the clash of ideas in the marketplace. That's where the real fairness is, in the give-and-take of ideas.

An extreme form of unfairness was described in *National Review,* December 2, 1969, which told how a group of radical journalists announced their intention of exploiting the media that employ them:

The revolutionary Left also moved into the struggle over the media, organizing the New York Media Project, composed of "professionals in the communications industry" who are determined to oppose the war not, as in the past, outside their jobs, but in their professional capacity. Members have been recruited from *Time, Newsweek, Fortune, Look, Esquire, Sports Illustrated,* the Associated Press, United Press International, the *Wall Street Journal,* the *New York Times,* ABC, CBS, Random House, McGraw-Hill, Doubleday, Harper & Row, and elsewhere.

The story told that these extremist types, with access to many of the nation's most influential media, are not only intent on stopping the war in Vietnam; they have other goals as well. This is their manifesto:

There must be an end to the conspiracy of silence and all methods that have blacked out and distorted the rebellion and protests of blacks, workers, women, GIs, students and all Third World Liberation movements. . . . We must apply pressure by whatever means we can to open up space in the mass media in which [Black] Panthers can publicly defend themselves, and explain their progress in their own words. Media brass will resist our pressure but we are going to have to be clear among ourselves who and what we're working for, besides our paychecks.

One might ask why the people who sign the paychecks for these people do not simply fire them. There would appear to be cause. They are not objective reporters and writers of news, but admitted propagandists, special pleaders, who as insiders have direct access to the nation's most influential communications media. Firing these people would do much to curtail the left-wing propaganda that floods the nation, but it is not easy to fire people in the communications media.

A personal case may give some indication of this. Almost two decades ago the magazine I then edited published an article that was critical of the left-wing bias in book reviewing, and it singled out the *New York Times* and the *Herald Tribune* for special attention. The *Times* sent letters to those who wrote about the article asking if it were true. The paper said the charges were false—that there were no Communists employed by the *Times*. This was interesting because the article had made no such allegation.

The response from the *Herald Tribune* was different. The magazine was visited by a long-time employee of the paper who said he was doing so at the request of Mrs. Ruth Reid, the publisher, because she knew he had friends on the magazine staff. The caller said that Mrs. Reid wished to get some answers to several questions, the most important of which was, "Were there to be other articles of this nature?" Told that this was up to the *Times* and the *Trib* and whether they continued their slanted book reviews, our caller was apparently satisfied and volunteered some information.

Explaining that he worked in one of the mechanical departments, he said, "From where I sit I can see men who, to my personal knowledge, are members of the Communist Party. In the editorial department, to my knowledge, there are others, and everybody knows it's the same thing over at the *Times*. But there isn't a thing Mrs. Reid can do about it. If she tried, the place would be closed down with a strike, and that's something the paper can't afford."

This is not to imply that the leftward pitch of the news media in New York is the work of Communist Party members, though subsequent hearings by the Senate Internal Security Subcommittee did turn up a few comrades in the editorial departments of certain New York newspapers. The point actually is not too important. With a lot of crusading leftist liberals in the media, who needs Communists?

As an amusing footnote to this, I was occasionally visited by an old friend who worked at the city desk of the *Times*. Bill was a staunch conservative who looked with misgivings at the way in which the liberal element operated there. His customary introduction to the girl at our reception desk indicated this:

"Tell the editor there's a man here from the American cell of the *New York Times*."

There are in fact "American cells" throughout the communications media, patriotic men and women who are well aware of what their leftist colleagues are up to and, wherever possible, they try to thwart them. You might call these people a Silent Majority of journalists, and their number includes many authentic liberals. Quite often there is a continuing struggle between right and left to see whose policies will prevail and which viewpoint will get through to the public.

There was an example of this conflict at the time the Matthews articles glorifying Castro were published in the *New York Times*. Other members of the staff objected—Hanson Baldwin, James Reston and Arthur Krock. Another objector was Ruby Hart Phillips, now retired from the *Times* but then the paper's resident correspondent in Havana and a bona fide Latin American expert. This disagreement was referred to by Seymour Freidin and George Bailey in their book *The Experts:*

"To Matthews and his newspaper, Fidel Castro was the best phenomenon in Latin America in many generations. This led, in time, to some bitter conflict on the *Times* Olympian board. . . ."

Matthews has lauded his newspaper as "the most powerful journalistic instrument that has ever been forged in the free world." He also said, "Those who work for it use arms that, metaphorically speaking, are the equivalent of nuclear bombs."

Regrettably, the *Times* is not nearly as conscientious as the Pentagon is in keeping its journalistic Dr. Strangeloves from messing with all that fissionable material and occasionally using it with disastrous results.

The uniformity of thinking that marks those who have attained New York's cultural heights was amusingly described as Babbittry by Theodore H. White in his interview in the *Columbia Journalism Review*. "There was the Babbittry of the 1920s," he said, "and there's the Babbittry of Greenwich Village, which is just as much a conformist group of people as is Sauk Center, Minn. Greenwich Village is probably more conformist than Sauk Center."

The results, however, are not amusing. The thinking of the avant-garde babbitts of Manhattan and that of most other Americans is so different that it has created not only a political crisis in this country but a cultural crisis as well.

"With this growing split in culture," White continued, "has come another development, which is the near-total concentration of the control of the national media in Manhattan. Basically that's a function of technology, a function of electronics, a function of the high-speed printing press and distribution mechanisms. But this concentration of thinking in the New York–Washington–Boston area puts it in the hands of villagers who, I think, have never been more remote from the broad basin beyond the Alleghenies."

A similar premise was set forth by the estimable William S. White in his newspaper column of December 26, 1969, which discussed what he called the "galloping process of Balkanization that is dividing region from region in this country." Using Gallup Poll figures, William White showed how President Nixon's war policy was approved by 60 percent of college students in the South, by 52 percent in the Midwest, and by 50 percent in the Far West. However, in the East, the figures were turned around, with only 36 percent approving the President's war course.

"All these data," said Mr. White, "no matter how you slice it, offers the most positive of testimony that the East is out of step with the remainder of the nation to an extraordinary and indeed to an unexampled degree."

This, he said, was the result of "a long campaign—led, most predictably, by Eastern professors and publishers and an Eastern-based television monolith—to suggest that whatever is 'Eastern' is necessarily superior to what is not. . . .

"Moreover, all this rubbish has both fed and fed upon a violently far-liberal political movement which in effect argues that, even though it is greatly and demonstrably in the minority, it nevertheless must be conceded the right to national leadership."

The Democrats, he continued, have been playing up to this "coyly immature and fraternity house-like attitude," having convinced themselves that there really is such a thing as an Eastern elite. Agnew's "hot anti-snob rhetoric" puncturing the bubble of Eastern pretensions, he said, is "paying off for the Republicans simply because very large parts of this country are fed up with an Eastern superiority complex that is so plainly and even embarrassingly absurd."

Spiro Agnew recognized this in his speech on television news bias. Talking about the men who produce and direct network news, Agnew pointed out that, to a man, they live and work in Washington and New York. The latter city, he said, was "the most unrepresentative community in this United States," but this caustic comment he attributed to James Reston. Both Washington and New York, he continued, "bask in their own provincialism. We can deduce that these men read the same newspapers. They draw their political and social views from the same sources. Worse, they talk constantly to one another, thereby providing artificial reinforcement to their shared viewpoints. . . .

"The views of the majority of this fraternity do not—and I repeat not—represent the views of America."

There was a dramatic example of that during the first week of May 1970 when the President announced that he intended to break up Communist sanctuaries in Cambodia which had long been used as bases for attacks into South Vietnam. The nation was thereupon provided with an example of news distortion on a mammoth scale. To read the *Washington Post* or the *New York Times* or to watch television or listen to radio news reports, one would have thought that virtually no one in the United States backed the President. Indeed it appeared as though no one in the world approved of his action, except of course the U.S. military. Understandably every nation behind the Iron Curtain was reported as being infuriated by the move. The predictable U Thant came on strong in this vein, speaking for that "last great hope of the human race," the United Nations. And one got the impression from the media that the people of the United States were as angry as such Communist leaders as Mao Tse-tung and the various Red negotiators in Paris.

Various senators, notably Church, Kennedy and Fulbright, loudly deplored the President's action and were extensively quoted to that effect. Dr. Spock shuffled off to Washington where he was photographed and interviewed extensively with a motley group in front of the White House, the vanguard of another New Mobe invasion. Many others managed to get into the act, but the drama was provided by college students in approximately 300 colleges and universities who went on a rampage.

With much of the action taking place in Washington it was highly educational to observe the coverage of the ultra-liberal *Washington Post*. The newspaper was of course strongly and obviously on the side of the anti-war, anti-Nixon demonstrators and its sympathies were reflected in its news coverage, editorials, syndicated columns and letters to the editor. Herblock contributed a rather artless cartoon that showed a figure representing the United States bogged down to his ears in quicksand labeled "Indochina Quagmire." Looking down, laughing at him, was a Russian officer labeled "Russian Pilots in Egypt."

The *Post*-owned television station and its radio stations kept up a similar drumfire, which left the impression that an irresistible ground swell was under way, and this would doom the President's war policy. More than implied was the thought that this signified the beginning of the end for Mr. Nixon and his administration.

Curiously, in the midst of this, on May 7, the *Washington Post* featured a lengthy story that contained more than a touch of irony. Datelined San Francisco and written by a *Post* staff man, it told that "a vast communications empire is being challenged here in a case involving allegations of managed news, conflict of interest and spying on witnesses."

The challenge was aimed at the Chronicle Publishing Company, publisher of the *San Francisco Chronicle,* that city's only morning newspaper. It also owns KRON-TV, one of San Francisco's four VHF stations and the local NBC outlet, an FM radio station and a number of cable TV franchises. Among the issues being explored at an FCC meeting was whether this represented "an undue concentration on control of the media of mass communications in the Bay Area." Plus the question of alleged "managed news."

When the FCC finishes with the Chronicle Publishing Company, it might look into the situation in Washington where there are some interesting parallels. The Washington Post Company owns the *Washington Post,* the capital's only morning newspaper. It also owns WTOP-TV, a VHF station which is a CBS outlet. It owns an AM station and an FM station as well, the former presenting a constant outpouring of news. It also owns the influential news magazine *Newsweek.* This would certainly seem to raise a question concerning "undue concentration on control of the media of mass communications." And in view of the way various *Post* properties operate, the FCC might also look into the matter of "managed news." It is not pleasant to think of the news being managed in an area where news can have a profound effect on both foreign and domestic policy.

The kind of thought control that is exerted on the nation's think-ing and actions by and through Eastern-based media sometimes evokes the kind of angry resentment that Barry Goldwater once expressed, "Sometimes I think this country would be better off if we could just saw off the Eastern seaboard and let it float out to sea."

Certainly tremendous leverage can be applied by Washington-based media since that is where the political decisions are made. However, the most strategic center is New York City, which has long been the nation's largest fabricator and distributor of ready-to-wear ideas. New Yorkers take great pride in this but people from the hinterland are becoming increasingly skeptical of the merchandise. They become annoyed when New Yorkers, through their influential media, presume to tell the rest of the nation how to conduct its affairs. Since New Yorkers seem to be utterly incapable of running their own city and have permitted it to become a crime-ridden, tax-wracked jungle where it is no longer safe to visit, let alone live, non-New Yorkers are beginning to look upon their city cousins as not as all-fired smart as they pretend to be. Why then take seriously all those city slickers who pontificate on television and on the printed page?

Some of those pontificators say they are not city slickers at all, just country boys who came to the big city to make good. This argument was used by Walter Cronkite in a broadcast aimed at rebutting Spiro Agnew's charges. He pointed out that many of his colleagues, like himself, were just small-town boys and he implied that you couldn't take the country flavor out of them any more than you could take it out of Salem cigarettes. However, Mr. White expressed an opinion on that too: "I think we are a self-selected group. We came here, or we were chosen to come here, because somehow we were ahead of the common thinking or at least were thought to be ahead of the common thinking. My point is, right now are we too far ahead?"

Maybe that is the question that some of the erstwhile country boys should ask themselves.

To use a well-worn cliché, many of them are "not communicating" and have created a formidable credibility gap between themselves and their audiences. This is indicated by the way in which so many

Americans seconded the Vice President's remarks about the bias that is all too apparent not only in television but in other media as well. This strong reaction should not have been surprising. A Louis Harris survey conducted in December 1968 indicated that 70 percent of American adults considered themselves either conservative or middle-of-the-road, while only 17 percent looked upon themselves as liberals. In view of the way in which television venerates statistics in the form of ratings and market surveys, it is surprising that it chooses to ignore this essential bit of intelligence about its audience.

Television has been called a vast wasteland because of its preoccupation with the great majority. When criticized for the low cultural level of the stuff that is dispensed on television, the stock reply is that the medium is only giving the people what they want. However, an exception is made when it comes to anything of a conservative nature. Even though statistics strongly indicate that the American people are inherently conservative, liberalism is what they get.

The liberal viewpoint is presented not just in the news but in other types of programming as well. Sometimes the huckstering is obvious and at other times it is subtle. Always it is offered on a take-it-or-leave-it basis. If listeners complain they may be told that if they don't like it they can always turn off their sets. But this overlooks completely the fact that the station owners do not own the airwaves, which are the property of the audience, the public. If enough people became aroused they could force station owners to turn off *their* sets, and make the edict stick. For those fantastically lucrative TV franchises are supposed to be valid only so long as the holders serve the public as they should.

The Federal Communications Commission has promulgated a "fairness doctrine," which can be found in the appendix of this book. This sets forth certain guidelines "applicable in any case where broadcast facilities are used for the discussion of a controversial issue of public importance." Complaints have been brought under this doctrine against stations presenting only one side of an issue, and decisions have been handed down on the principle that the public has a right to be informed of "conflicting views of issues of public importance."

It could be argued that Spiro Agnew was not trying to intimidate the networks when he charged them with bias but was merely calling for a little fairness under the fairness doctrine. However, the bellicose reaction was significant. It has been pointed out, correctly, that restraints against the enormous power of the communications media are inadequate and becoming more so.

Despite some of the hysterical response, the Vice President was merely calling for greater objectivity. That is all anyone expects and certainly the American people have a right to that. Some television people concede this and are trying to provide greater diversity and a broader range of political and economic thought in what goes on the air.

One of the leaders in this crusade is Thomas B. Petry, former president and general manager of WCNY-TV, an educational television station serving central New York from Syracuse. Irked at the constant flow of material from New York City with a left-wing bias, he organized support from more than a fourth of the nation's educational television stations in a move to provide viewers with unbiased programs. (See Appendix D.)

"This should, however, not be interpreted as a clarion call to radical reaction," Petry stated.

> On the major issues facing the American people, liberalism and conservatism are far closer together than either are to the left and right wing forces of revolutionary radicalism or reaction—nevertheless, *their differences are significant.* Nothing is served by ignoring a major and perfectly respectable political philosophy and code of practice, nor by revealing it only in its most distorted and exaggerated forms: the caricatures of radical reaction; the black magic of fascism. The cause of liberalism is also ill served by spicing up its image; by lending undue respectability to the anarchists, new leftists and revolutionary radicals of any hue or misguided persuasion.

This seems to be a reasonable "fairness doctrine," which, if adopted, could have a tremendous influence for good.

CHAPTER FOUR

The TV Establishment

THE three major networks operate in a way that is reminiscent of the three tailors of Tooley Street. Those three Londoners, it will be recalled, once addressed a petition of grievances to the House of Commons, beginning, "We, the people of England."

But while the networks assuredly do not speak *for* the people of the United States, any more than Standard Oil or U.S. Steel does, there is no denying that they have the facilities to speak *to* all America, and Americans pay close attention to what their television sets bring them. Today an estimated 98.5 percent of all the homes in the United States have a TV set, often more than one, and Nielsen reports that the average set is kept running more than six hours a day. In most American homes it is the primary source of news, and it has been estimated that by the time a child reaches the age of 16, he has spent more time in front of a television set than he has in school.

Network officials may be forgiven if they look upon themselves as highly influential people, for the fact is they are. They can facilitate the spread of ideas, good and bad. Almost overnight they can turn a nobody into a Very Important Person, and conversely they can topple someone from the heights. Following the 1968 Presidential campaign, Hubert Humphrey charged that it was television's portrayal of the Chicago riots that kept him from the Presidency.

Despite the power they wield, the men who run the networks are not "the voice of the people" reflecting "public opinion," even though they seem to give that impression. Quite often the only public opinion they reflect is that which they themselves wish to create. Actually, more than anything, television is a vast entertainment medium. It may be likened in this respect to Hollywood as it was in the old days, but the movie industry never had access to almost every home in America, on an open-door basis, as television has.

Commercial television is necessarily an entertainment business. It has to be. You do not keep millions of eyes glued to the TV tube hour after hour by presenting the news or explaining the big issues. Nor do you gather vast audiences with educational programs. There would be little profit in such presentations and commercial television pays considerable attention to the balance sheet.

What television does provide, primarily, is funfare, such diversions as *Laugh-In, Gunsmoke, Bonanza* and sports of various kinds in massive doses. Not to mention those dramatic offerings in which soap and tears are fluffed together in a sad, sudsy solution. These are the things that draw the big audiences, and these are the things that attract sponsors willing to pay fabulous prices for the opportunity to peddle their wares.

By astute management, capitalizing on anything and everything to build and maintain large audiences, network and station owners have created a fantastically valuable property. Through so-called ratings, notably the Nielsen surveys, they can prove to advertisers that they are capable of delivering tens of millions of viewers as prospective customers. Even though viewers are very expensive when sold in such tremendous lots to the advertising agencies, the investment usually pays off handsomely. And the money flows in.

In *Survey of Broadcast Journalism,* reporting the results of a study made by Alfred I. du Pont–Columbia University, the following statement is made:

> Of all those Americans who are trying to get more out of life than they have put into it and who are laying waste to their country in the attempt, none in recent years has appeared more successful as a group than the broadcasters. In what other business can a moderately astute operator hope to realize 100 percent a year on tangible assets, or pay

out $150 for a franchise that in a few years' time he can peddle for $50 million—should he be so foolish as to want to sell? The most fantastic rewards associated with broadcasting in many instances grow from enterprises that do as little for their fellow countryman as they legally can.

FCC Commissioner Nicholas Johnson said almost the same thing when he declared:

The average return on depreciated tangible capital investment [in broadcasting] runs about 100 percent a year. Over 340 stations last year grossed in excess of $1 million per station. There is an active market for stations . . . capital gains providing an even more lucrative source of private profit . . . than the exorbitant revenues.

Television thus is Big Business. During 1967, according to the FCC, the three networks and their 15 owned and operated stations, and 604 other stations reported revenues of $2.3 billion. During that period profits were $414,600,000 before federal taxes. Time sales during that period amounted to $1,847,000,000, with networks and their owned and operated stations getting the lion's share, $1,216,-600,000, and pre-tax profits of $160,100,000.

That the situation was rosier in 1969, from the standpoint of at least one network, is indicated by a financial statement published on February 12, 1970:

The Columbia Broadcasting System, Inc., achieved a 24 percent increase in earnings last year on a 17 percent gain in revenues, which topped $1 billion for the first time, William S. Paley and Frank Stanton, president, reported today.

Like the other networks, CBS is engaged in many other businesses, and the earnings statement pointed out that all of its major enterprises had greater revenues than ever before. Still, "the high profits were attributed mainly to the substantial increases shown by the broadcasting and locally owned stations and to the CBS Records division."

Thus most of the prosperity is the end result of an unceasing and increasing volume of commercials. According to *TV Guide,* prime-time messages have increased 33 percent in the past four years, and it quoted Edward H. Meyer, of the Grey Advertising Agency, about the reasons for this: The price of time was raised even though there was no appreciable increase in TV homes. This meant that advertisers had to pay more per thousand viewers. To offset this, advertisers experimented with 30-second commercials instead of 60-second ones and found they were effective. Viewers then began to see more commercials. Broadcasting economics resulted in even more advertisements when advertisers, unable to afford the sponsorship of entire shows, participated in many different ones through brief spot commercials. Complaints from viewers about too many interruptions brought another development. The TV code was changed to permit the clustering of commercials. Now when a station interrupts a program, a person can do more than hurry to the refrigerator for a snack. He can almost drive to a restaurant and eat a seven-course dinner.

Most generous of those who contribute commercials to the American viewing public is Procter & Gamble, whose 1968 expenditure was $100,979,300. Runner-up in the great TV spending sweepstakes during that year was Bristol-Myers, with $46,660,300. R. J. Reynolds Tobacco was third with $46,288,400 and Colgate-Palmolive fourth with $46,266,400.

Quite possibly such spending has peaked. Tobacco advertising has been banned, and with many large advertisers cutting their budgets, the financial picture is becoming cloudy. If earnings drop, we will probably find the economics reflected in the kind of programs offered.

Money flowing into the networks in such amounts becomes the lifeblood of impressive corporate structures consisting of much more than television properties. Actually the three major networks do not themselves own many TV stations, only 15 in all. But most of the nation's 600-plus stations are affiliated with them and are largely dependent on the people based in New York for the news and entertainment they relay to local viewers.

Some of the areas into which the networks have expanded are closely related to broadcasting, others are remote. The National

Broadcasting Company, for example, is a subsidiary of the RCA Corporation, which concerns itself primarily with the manufacture of electronic products, appliances, phonograph records and so on. But NBC has an interesting corporate cousin in Random House, an important book-publishing concern, and Random House in turn controls Pantheon and Modern Library, among others. Another corporate relative of NBC is the Hertz Corporation, the nation's number-one car rental agency, as you doubtless know from frequent TV commercials.

American Broadcasting Companies, Inc., was incorporated in 1949 as United Paramount Theatres, Inc., to take over domestic theater and other properties of Paramount Pictures. In 1953 the name was changed to American Broadcasting–Paramount Theatres, Inc., when there was a consolidation with American Broadcasting, Inc., and the present name was adopted in 1965. Today its list of subsidiaries reflects the corporation's interest in all aspects of television broadcasting—stations, news services, music, records, etc. In addition to television stations, ABC owns and operates several hundred motion-picture theaters, and other subsidiaries include farm publications and tourist attractions in Florida and California.

The Columbia Broadcasting System, Inc., has an even more diversified setup. In addition to TV and radio broadcasting, CBS does an extensive business in phonograph records, tapes, radios and speaker systems. But that is only the beginning. If you want to start a musical combo, and perhaps some day perform before CBS cameras, you can buy guitars and drums from CBS subsidiaries. Young children can play with toys made by another CBS subsidiary, while grownups can divert themselves with another CBS property, the New York Yankees. CBS made millions out of the musical comedy *My Fair Lady,* which it backed, and it's also in the book- and magazine-publishing business in a big way. One of its subsidiaries is Holt, Rinehart & Winston, and it owns W. B. Saunders, a Philadelphia publisher of medical and other textbooks. It also owns magazines, *Field & Stream* among others.

Not all of these network-affiliated enterprises are located in New York City, but if you are looking for important decisions concerning any of them, a logical starting place would be close to the center of that one-mile radius in midtown Manhattan mentioned by Theodore H. White. There you would be almost at the door of the RCA Building housing NBC. To get to the CBS Building at 51 West 52nd Street, you would have to walk only a short distance, and the American Broadcasting Company, at 1130 Avenue of the Americas, would be around the corner and two blocks north.

With such empires as their responsibility, network officials follow shrewd business practices to insure continuing prosperity. And those practices explain much of what millions of Americans see on their television sets.

One thing that must always be kept in mind is that the competition among the networks is intense, particularly between NBC and CBS, with ABC making strenuous efforts to catch up to the two leaders. One might think that this would make for variety, as networks competed to attract viewers with fresh and original programs. But as everyone who watches television knows, the last thing you are likely to find is something new. Originality represents a gamble, and the networks prefer to play it safe with the kind of material likely to keep the ratings high to attract the advertising dollars.

Cynthia Lowery, who covers television for the Associated Press, put the matter statistically when she recently wrote, "The odds against pushing an idea into a sponsored prime time series work out as something like 2,000 to one."

When this long-shot event takes place and a show with an unusual idea proves popular, there is usually a rush of imitators, with the copycats trying to outdo the other in some way. When *Laugh-In* became popular on NBC, ABC came up with a show called *Turn-On*. However, following customary TV practice, *Turn-On* tried to top *Laugh-In*'s occasional off-color humor and the public outcry knocked the show off the air.

Probably the most flagrant example of television's tendency to play follow-the-leader was the succession of quiz shows in the 1950s. Radio originated an intriguing idea in the *$64 Question* program, and television characteristically turned this into something that offered a lot more loot, the *$64,000 Question*. This was in turn topped by *The Big Surprise*, which had $100,000 to play with, and another show called *Twenty-One*. Viewers watched in fascination as a succession of walking encyclopedias made themselves wealthy by demonstrating superhuman mental powers. But in 1958 this particular TV bubble burst when a grand jury and a congressional committee investigated the quiz shows. Wholesale cheating was disclosed and ten persons pleaded guilty to perjury before a grand jury. This unfortunate episode, indicative of the strange and flexible morality of show business, did much to damage the image of television and people associated with the medium.

Today the terrific competition between networks for viewers and the advertising revenue they represent results in programming that has been called "a vast wasteland." However, network officials have a point when they say they only give the public what it wants. If a network were to devote a Saturday afternoon to presenting *Tristan and Isolde* live from Lincoln Center, it would represent a great cultural achievement, but it would probably prove calamitous to the network's ratings. Further, it would bring thousands of complaints from irate viewers asking why they were being deprived of the Green Bay Packers or the New York Jets.

This can be a serious consideration. Testifying before a Senate subcommittee, the head of a regional television network, Richard D. Dudley, of Wausau, Wisconsin, told of a call from a lady at the time of the Apollo moon landing. The lady asked why the station was not carrying a certain soap opera she liked and was told, "This is an important news event in the history of the country, probably something you can't imagine the equal of."

The lady replied, "Well, I hope they crash."

Certainly there are many people in this country who would prefer Wagner and Verdi, even to one of the superbowl games, but this sort of minority represents television's underprivileged, disadvantaged— and out of luck. But for the great majority, television goes all out to present fun and games. And who makes up this majority? An answer was provided by E. William Henry, former chairman of the FCC, quoted in an interview in *U.S. News & World Report,* July 4, 1964:

"Get a broadcaster into a down-to-earth conversation, he will tell you that the image he has to keep uppermost in mind is the fellow in his undershirt with a can of beer." This fellow could be the son of radio listeners of some years back, those "average listeners" that some broadcasters looked upon as having 12-year-old mentalities.

This concept usually brings indignant denials from network officials, who prefer to depict their average viewer, to time buyers at least, as a discriminating person with a lot of money to spend on the merchandise set before him in TV commercials. And obviously, TV viewers do spend money, and not just on six-packs of beer and cartons of cigarettes. They obviously buy expensive cars, plane travel, costly cosmetics and other luxury items.

Unfortunately, the programs offered on television's prime time do not always give the impression that they are directed at an audience of cultured, discerning viewers. One is likely to get the impression from many commercials and programs that more than a few people in advertising agencies and television broadcasting look upon TV viewers either as morons or as juveniles, lacking either the energy or the good sense to get up and turn off their sets.

What is the usual fare offered in prime time?

There are of course the movies, which consume a great deal of TV time. Here the medium is largely limited by what Hollywood did when it was the film capital of the world. Frequently Hollywood turned out excellent motion pictures and many of them are now appearing on television—sometimes again and again and again. But Hollywood's usual output was the sort of stuff that caused thousands of theaters to go out of business, and TV viewers are getting those films too. That indeed is what they usually get, and such movies look no better after the third, fourth or fifth showing.

Along with the old Hollywood product, viewers are now seeing more motion pictures made especially for television. Occasionally such films are pretty good and probably would have rated as B pictures in Hollywood terminology. Most are not even that good. However, television has been forced into such production because so many current films are pornographic. To their credit, the networks are making some effort to keep such smut out of the home, for the time being at least.

Another large segment of prime time is given over to variety shows, usually presided over by a personality-projecting male or female star. These stars come on with a retinue of other stars, a veritable galaxy of "big names" that, it is hoped, will top the "big names" on other networks. But after awhile the viewer gets the impression that he is seeing the same things over and over again. There is the same format—the same flowery introductions, and essentially similar dance routines. Then there is the procession of stars, which is likely to include Sammy Davis, Jr., the Gabor girls, the Smothers boys, Phyllis Diller, Tiny Tim, Peter Lawford, various members of the Sinatra family and a few other gregarious souls. After a time the jokes begin to sound alike, too, possibly because the comedians listen to each other or patronize the same used-joke dealers. And enlivening the festivities are the inevitable guitar-smiting troubadours, who keen about unrequited love, downtrodden people, the wickedness of war and other miseries that preoccupy the "in people."

Still another sizeable chunk of prime time is given over to situation comedies. Here is where you will meet the lovable lady witches, the widowed professor with the sharp kids, the dedicated schoolteacher working with the disadvantaged, the man from Mars, the prison-camp GIs who make monkeys out of their German captors week after week and the U.S. enlisted men who week after week make monkeys out of their stupid officers.

For the most part this is pretty bland stuff. Watching it one gets the feeling that he is turning the pages of the Sunday funny papers. The characters remind one of Dondi, Beetle Bailey, Mandrake the Magician, citizens of Dogpatch and other products of the drawing board. Still, one must admit that Americans dote on comic strips, and often read them before they look at the front page of their newspaper or even turn to the sports page. Conceivably this realization has entered into network thinking, plus the fact that most such shows are usually without the sex and violence that have brought so much criticism to the networks.

There has been a drop in the number of prime-time network shows dealing largely with violence, but viewers who like to see people beaten to a pulp, pumped full of lead or strangled or knifed to death have little reason to complain. Such entertainment is still available without stint. The gunslingers of the Old West are still putting people they dislike in Boot Hill, and the secret agents and private eyes who protect our nation and its citizens are still slugging it out with enemy agents, with members of the Mafia and with lone wolf–type hoods. Such shows are always embellished with sexy females, it being axiomatic that sex and violence are a combination that cannot possibly lose.

Television's preoccupation with violence over the years has been the subject of extended official investigations. Educators, psychologists, clergymen, police officials and others have testified that violence on television contributes to crime, notably to juvenile delinquency, but network officials refuse to be convinced. For years they have insisted that not only has no definite link been proved between TV violence and crime in the streets, but TV violence is actually an influence for good. People who watch violence on the tube, they say, work off their aggressions passively.

In the course of extended hearings conducted by Senator Thomas J. Dodd in the early 1960s, a procession of witnesses told how violence was ordered into television programs, virtually as a priceless ingredient to insure the highest possible ratings. Writers and producers sometimes disagreed with this emphasis but the networks were in control. If writers and producers did not conform, there were others available to give the networks what they wanted. Incidentally, in the course of the Dodd hearings the extent of network control of programs was revealed in surprising terms. If a network did not own a certain program, it often took steps to acquire "financial participation." Here is how it was put by Maurice Unger, executive vice president in charge of productions for Ziv-United Artists, Inc., testifying before the Senate subcommittee on July 28, 1961:

> Under today's conditions, the network assumes the following position with film producers:
>
> You make a program and we'll make a program, and then we, the network, will decide which one goes on the air.
>
> Now if you want to make us a financial partner in your program, you may have a much better chance of getting on the air. We won't promise—but you may have a chance.
>
> Also, if we're going to be a partner, we must have absolute control over your program.

Mr. Unger then made a remark strikingly similar to Vice President Agnew's comment about the power held by a few men in television:

> If you people come to the conclusion that there is excessive violence on television, and that it is detrimental to the best interests of the public, you can stop it instantly. Simply convince seven men on the FCC to reduce the excessive power held by three men.
>
> The three men to whom I refer are, of course, the heads of the three networks—three men who have virtually complete control of the public's airwaves—more power than the Constitution gives to the Congress or the President of the United States.

The FCC for the most part takes a tolerant view of television. Ralph Nader, best known for his interest in cars that he considers unsafe at any speed, commented on this in an article that appeared in *Time*. He stated that 75 percent of the former commissioners of the FCC are employed or retained by the communications industry, and this, he charged, amounted to a "deferred bribe." To prevent this, he recommended that agency officials who resign their jobs should be barred from accepting immediate employment in the industry they had been policing.

In network operations, as was mentioned earlier, the general idea is to try to top the competition. For years the various networks competed in their presentations of violence, one trying to outdo another. The reason was simply because TV slaughter seemed to result in higher ratings. However, violence is gradually being toned down. Those ratings are as important as ever but TV violence has brought so much criticism, official and other, that the networks are becoming more circumspect.

This does not mean that television officials relish the kind of criticism their programs and policies often evoke. A schoolteacher friend of mine encountered what might be called a characteristic reaction on the local level when she recently phoned a nearby station to complain about the violence that monopolized that station's afternoon schedule, day after day. These programs, she found, were having an adverse effect on a class she taught—emotionally disturbed children. Through some happenstance her call was put through to the owner of the station, one located in northeastern Pennsylvania. This individual cut her off with the arrogant remark:

"Lady, what we put on the air is none of your business!"

When the Vice President of the United States made his famous complaint, he got a somewhat similar reaction from a higher echelon of TV officialdom.

Criticism of any business, profession or organization is almost certain to be resented, particularly if the criticism comes from an outsider. If the actions of a shyster-type lawyer move you to utter or pen some unflattering comments about the legal profession, you are likely to find yourself the target of many barristers and solicitors, many of whom would not touch their shady colleague with a ten-foot pole. Get up in a PTA meeting and wonder out loud about Johnny's inability to read or ask why it is necessary to spend millions on an elaborate new school and you will find yourself denounced as "an enemy of education." Criticize theater owners who show smutty films in your community and you may be surprised to find out how many liberal-minded people there are in your community who will label you a dirty-minded prude for not appreciating such cinema art as *I Am Curious-Yellow.*

After all, where do you, a non-expert, come off? What gives you the right to question your betters and tell them how they ought to do things?

This is not to say that criticism is not welcome. However, it should always be "constructive" and couched in respectful terms. This particularly applies to television broadcasting, which of course you as a non-pro cannot possibly understand. If in criticizing the medium you forget your place, you may be told that if you don't like all that wonderful stuff you get for nothing, you should turn off your set or give it to the Salvation Army.

Walter Cronkite repeated the familiar suggestion that TV viewers can always turn off their sets, in a program that attempted to refute the Agnew criticism of the medium. However, this totally ignored the fact that viewers, as well as broadcasters, have rights, and this point was tellingly made by Herbert Hoover years ago. Discussing radio, Mr. Hoover said:

We hear a great deal about freedom of the air; but there are two parties to freedom of the air and to freedom of speech, for that matter. There is the speechmaker and the listeners. Certainly in radio I believe in freedom of speech for the listener. He has much less option upon what he can reject, for the other fellow is occupying his receiver. *The listener's only option is to abandon his right to use his receiver.* [Emphasis added.]

Like other professional groups, the people who run broadcasting have an organization devoted to looking after their interests, a very efficient outfit which swings considerable weight. It corresponds roughly to the American Medical Association, the National Education Association, the American Bar Association, the Association of American Railroads and so on. Here is how the *Survey of Broadcast Journalism*, previously mentioned, describes it:

To insure fullest Congressional sympathy, the networks and the National Association of Broadcasters maintain one of the most elaborate lobbying operations in the capital. The NAB, with a staff of over eighty, moved into a beautiful new $2.6 million building in the spring of 1969. Many of the network and more important broadcasting and multimedia owners employ representatives to see that their interests get favorable attention by the lawmakers.

But that is not all. The Survey pointed out that broadcasters can also count on the services of lobbyists employed by the corporations that have broadcasting properties. And not to be overlooked are "more than five hundred communications specialists in Washington law firms" that represent individual stations and broadcast groups. Not to mention "some two dozen Congressmen and Senators" who have significant family holdings in broadcasting.

The Survey then went on to tell about a highly important bill (s. 2004) that was introduced by Senator John Pastore of Rhode Island in 1969. As the law now stands, each station holds its license for three years, after which it must be renewed for another three years. Rarely if ever has a station lost its license, but the holder can be challenged. If it can be shown that he has disregarded the public interest, he is at least put on the defensive. In short, the three-year term imposes some control, possibly the only meaningful control, over those who have been given television franchises.

However, the senator felt that this was unfair. So he introduced legislation that would have had the effect of giving station owners their licenses in perpetuity. No one else could ever apply for a station's license unless the present holder lost it. Joining Pastore in this move were twenty other senators who signed the bill as co-sponsors. Shortly after it was introduced, eighty bills, almost identical, were offered by members of the House.

The move was defeated.

Senator Pastore's solicitude for station owners is more than passing strange because he has headed a committee that has been highly critical of the medium's role in juvenile delinquency. But then the senator is a temperate man. He may disagree with some of the things that television officials do but he bears no personal animus. This is indicated by his remarks at the opening of hearings on March 12, 1969:

> Now I know you gentlemen, I admire, I respect, and I have affection for you all. You are decent men, you are concerned with the public interest; you are in a sensitive business, a lucrative business. I know you to be men of good will.

These men of good will were later put to a test of sorts when Senator Pastore took the lead in trying to get them to make a drastic cut in the cost of television time for political campaigns. He set forth the problem as this: "Television is an indispensable means of political campaigning but its cost is appalling. A candidate may have to spend $2 million on television to win a Senate seat paying $42,500 a year." Other politicians feel the same way, with reason.

Unquestionably, television and other influential media have politicians in a box, and the high cost of campaigning in the media is just one part of the problem. In an article in *Life* for November 28, 1969, Spiro Agnew presented a more disturbing facet:

> One of the great dangers of the media is the constant temptation of elected officials to use them to their political advantage. It does not

take great perception to know that if an elected official advocates certain policies and eschews others, he will not only get news space but editorial plaudits as well. If all an elected official wants is a good press, he has only to recite certain accepted precepts . . . and most of the media will respond with a conditioned accolade to the ringing phrase. Couching it in negative terms, if an elected official wants to avoid a bad press, all he has to do is fuzz the controversial issues or work his way around them.

It is hardly necessary to point out that the author of these words is not one to "fuzz the controversial issues," and so his "press"—or that representing the influential segment of the media—is usually not very favorable.

The reason for television's prosperity and its rapid growth as an advertising medium is obvious—its proved ability to influence viewers. People may wonder about the mentality that produces many of the commercials they see, but there can be no question about one thing: All those hundreds of millions of dollars are not being spent on television for altruistic purposes. Commercials, which may cost more than $60,000 a minute, sell mountains of soap chips, rivers of mouthwash and trainloads of candy, cars and cola drinks. If you don't believe it, the networks will prove it to you, with persuasive promotion pieces.

Yet whenever television is charged with influencing human behavior by offering violence, sexual promiscuity and civil disobedience, the medium assumes an air of injured innocence. It maintains that it doesn't have *that* kind of influence at all. Anyway, they say, no one has been able to prove it.

Charges that television bears at least some responsibility for the upsurge in crime and violence have been made since 1954, and possibly before. In 1954 Senator Estes Kefauver's famous subcommittee investigated complaints from parents and educators who felt that the emphasis on crime, brutality, sadism and sex on television was contributing to juvenile delinquency. Based on testimony, a report was issued indicating that TV violence could be potentially harmful to young viewers. However, little was done about it.

A report issued late in 1969 by the Surgeon General's Scientific

Advisory Committee on Television and Social Behavior brings the matter up to date:

> Representatives of television networks acknowledge the large amount of televised violence and promised to change the content [following the Kefauver hearings], but subsequent surveys by the Senate Subcommittee, in 1961 and 1964, revealed that the degree of violence in prime time had substantially increased. After this third survey in 1964 the overriding conclusion of the Subcommittee was that "the extent to which violence and related activities are depicted on television today has not changed substantially from what it was in 1961 and remains greater than it was a decade ago. Further, violence and other antisocial behavior are, to an overwhelming degree, televised during time periods in which the children's audience is a large one."

There was a notable reason for the latter charge. Testimony showed that programs which had originally been prepared for showing late at night, when small children are presumably in bed, were subsequently peddled by the networks to individual stations that could and did schedule them at times when children were bound to see them. There was no attempt at control. If one wonders about the kind of thinking that sees nothing wrong in this, there may be an answer of sorts in the experience of a woman's group called "Action for Children's Television," which called on NBC, CBS and ABC to refrain from running commercials on children's programs. All parents are familiar with the insidious form of huckstering that brings children to parents demanding that they buy this or that item presented on television: "Mama, I want a Dumdum Doll. The man says it's only $49.95 and it walks and carries a picket sign. And the man says you can get a nice mink coat for it for only $29.95. Mama, buy me one . . ."

The complaining ladies quickly learned the facts of life. NBC "thanked them for their interest." ABC ignored them. CBS talked to them but that was the extent of it.

"Nobody questioned that children were special," said one of the ladies, "but they kept coming back to the fact that we are asking them to give up revenue."

Of course, one must be realistic about this. It stands to reason that if CBS gives up revenue in this way it may not top the billion-dollar figure it attained in 1969.

Few people realize the many problems that beset television executives in their efforts to make their networks bigger, more influential and more profitable, year after year. Certainly *Variety* was not giving these men their due when, in its December 10, 1969, issue, it expressed the following opinion:

> Making money in broadcasting is not that hard to do. By playing safe, continually appealing to the broadest possible taste, and jacking the rates at a healthy clip, profits have to result unless those responsible are totally incompetent. But is that all there is to broadcasting? Is that all there is to an industry that sells better than $3,500,000,000 worth of time and service a year?

By implying that network officials need not do much more than sit back and watch the money roll in, *Variety* does them a grave injustice. Television did not become the second largest communications medium in only a few years, topped only by newspapers in advertising revenue, because of the medium's inherent power alone. To get ahead, TV officials have fought a hard fight, with other media and with each other. And that fight is likely to become even more cutthroat. Business will not have quite so many millions to spend in the months ahead, and before long cigarette advertising will probably go off the air, meaning a nine-figure loss to the networks.

Television's fight with other media has left casualties, such as the *Saturday Evening Post,* and some of them will be missed by many people. However, that is always the price of progress. If someone invents a better mousetrap, the manufacturer of the Old Faithful Brand trap may end up on relief. If television can deliver millions of prospective customers to an ad agency cheaper than *Life, Look* or *McCall's,* then something has to give—or go.

This hard fact of economic life was set forth in the January 12, 1970, issue of *New York* magazine, in an article which told that *Life* was in financial trouble, having lost $10 million in 1969, and that other major magazines had reason to worry. This was not because of any loss of readership but because advertising money was going to television in increasing amounts, and today's publishing economics require vast amount of advertising revenue.

"A single full-page, four-color ad in *Life,*" The article explained,

> which may be seen by some 48 million people, costs $62,400 today. For the same money, a national advertiser can buy a minute on NBC's *Laugh-In* and reach 50 million people. Thus, television has punished the mass magazines, not by turning readers into viewers, but by offering good value—in "cost per thousand," as they say—to national advertisers.

Television viewers find this reflected in a seemingly endless parade of commercials. The magazine reader suddenly realizes that general magazines which used to be bulky with advertising and editorial material are becoming anemic, the way *Collier's* was in 1957 and the way *Saturday Evening Post* was just before it expired a couple of years ago.

Certainly the networks do not set out to kill those big magazines, but that's the way it goes and business is business.

The same thing goes for competitors in other networks. NBC, CBS and ABC will form a united front against a common enemy but among themselves there is unceasing warfare. Or, if you will, a constant seeking for advantage. And this is understandable. The stakes now run into the billions and the network that is unable to keep up or move ahead is likely to suffer the same kind of financial troubles that now beset *Life.* If things got very bad, the network could go the way of the *Saturday Evening Post, Collier's* or *Liberty.*

The criterion is the ratings, those unending surveys which advertisers and their agencies accept as proof that they are getting their messages across on programs that give them the millions of viewers they pay for. Here is where the networks compete on a no-holds-barred basis. You can see this competition at work as the networks set up their schedules in ways that attempt to weaken or topple popular shows on other networks. One aspect of it is evident in the way one network will have a popular show overlap the half-hour time break or run past the hour, hoping to discourage viewers from switching to a competing network.

In this competition, shows that are unable to make the grade in the ratings are killed off ruthlessly, and stars with long ties to a network are sometimes given short shrift. One of the most striking examples of this was CBS's cancellation of the Red Skelton hour after 16 years on the network. In this case the reported reason is interesting. The Skelton show is one of the most popular of all network shows, a fact proved by the ratings. However, CBS officials felt that its appeal was largely to older viewers and they are said to be anxious to build an audience in the 18–49 age group, as that is where the big spenders are concentrated. So, Skelton had to go. However, NBC apparently does not mind if senior citizens look at its shows, so Skelton was invited to that network.

Jockeying for top position in the television ratings reaches a climax each year as the TV season comes to a close prior to the summer doldrums. Each network makes intricate moves, usually accompanied by publicity fanfare, in hopes that it will outpace the competition. The 1970 sweepstakes, as reported by AP television-radio writer Jerry Buck, had this result: "Last year's rating race ended in a bitter feud between NBC and CBS. CBS said it had won for the 14th straight year. Lost in the crossfire was the fact that the difference was within the margin of error." He reported that NBC unilaterally declared the 1970 season over as of March 22, and announced it had won with a Nielsen figure of 20.2. As might have been expected, CBS refused to concede either that the season was over as of that date or that it had lost. As far as CBS was concerned, it was competition as usual and even more so.

This is a strange world indeed. In it "the ratings" take the place of the Golden Rule, the Ten Commandments and the Code of Hammurabi. If a person keeps that in mind, almost everything that he views on television and everything he reads and hears about the TV establishment is understandable.

CHAPTER FIVE

The War Away From Home

THE feelings of many Americans concerning the Vietnam War were expressed by a member of the British Parliament, Philip Goodhart, in a letter he wrote to the U.S. ambassador in Saigon. Mr. Goodhart, who had made frequent trips to Vietnam, wrote:

"The Viet Cong cannot beat you, but I think the Columbia Broadcasting System and the *New York Times* can."

He also expressed his belief that our will to win in Vietnam had been broken by the manner in which the war was shown on the television screen.

And the impact is not only at home, as shown by *National Review* in its July 28, 1970 issue:

Vice President Spiro Agnew recently raised the issue of domestic dissent at a GOP fund-raising dinner in Cleveland. "It is not President Nixon blocking the road to peace; it is Hanoi—and Hanoi's most effective, even if unintentional, apologists today are not in Paris," Agnew told his Republican audience. "They are in the United States, and their prescription for ending the war amounts to surrender."

A recent private survey of foreign broadcast transcripts for the month of May and the first two weeks of June shows substantial media coverage in the Soviet Union, Communist China and North Vietnam of domestic American criticism of President Nixon's decision to attack the Vietcong and North Vietnamese sanctuaries in Cambodia. Democratic senators topped the list of those quoted, and many of the quotes were pungent phrases that had a very anti-American slant.

A quick rundown on the media and those quoted:

North Vietnam: Senator Fulbright, eleven times; Senator Mansfield four; Senators Cranston and Gore, two each; Senators Kennedy, Muskie, Church, Proxmire and Symington, one each.

Soviet Union: Senator Kennedy, four times; Senator McGovern and Lawrence O'Brien, twice each; Senators McIntyre (D., N.H.) and Fulbright, two each; former Ambassador Averell Harriman and former Attorney General Ramsey Clark, two each; Senators Eugene McCarthy, Gore, Church, Proxmire, Symington and former Defense Secretary Clifford, one each.

Communist China: The Chinese media devoted significantly more coverage to student protests against the move into Cambodia than to criticism by individual members of Congress, probably in keeping with the Maoist doctrine of continuing revolution.

Typical of the damaging quotations used by the media is an excerpt from a May 30 Radio Hanoi broadcast in Vietnamese to South Vietnam:

"On May 17 Senator Fulbright, Chairman of the United States Senate's Foreign Relations Committee, stressed that Nixon's decision to send U.S. troops into Cambodia was a tragedy of America. Fulbright pointed out that the U.S. armed aggression against Cambodia proves the complete failure of the Vietnamization policy."

As the Vice President implies, the question of whether domestic dissent is useful to the enemy has already been answered. The only question now is whether or not those doing the dissenting care.

A much different situation existed at the time of the two world wars. In a foreword to George Creel's book, *How We Advertised America,* which described the propaganda of both sides in World War I, Secretary of War Newton D. Baker wrote: "So, it was of the greatest importance that America in this war should be presented not merely as a strong man fully armed, but as a strong man fully armed and believing in the cause for which he was fighting."

In his book, George Creel explained how important it was to reach the people through their minds rather than through their emotions so they would understand why we were at war. He praised both the newspapers and the academic community for their patriotism in this effort.

Today there is reason to question the attitudes and actions of Big Media and the academic community, but at the time of World War I and World War II they threw themselves into the war effort. There was no commercial television at the time of World War II but radio contributed $100,000,000 in time and talent to explain the war to the American people, to arouse patriotism and win support. The National Association of Broadcasters even coined a slogan to boast of the part they were playing: THIS IS AN ARMY HITLER FORGOT!

The situation today is much different. Although we have had more than a half-million American men fighting in our behalf in Vietnam, and although more than 40,000 of them have died there, we have not been called on by Big Media to give them even our moral support. Public-service announcements on TV urge us to give to medical research, stop smoking, support education, contribute to charities, help the underprivileged, etc. However, it would appear that our fighting men in Vietnam are outside the pale, participants in a disgraceful business and certainly not worthy of public backing. When our GIs get back from Vietnam, let us hope that they will at least not be discriminated against by our intellectual elite for having fought in what these people refer to as "an immoral and illegal war"

The ambivalence of liberals is incomprehensible. One of the bitterest critics of American intervention in Vietnam is John V. Lindsay. Time after time the mayor of New York has called for an immediate end to the U.S. presence in Vietnam. Yet, speaking before a group of Jewish leaders at Miami Beach on February 28, 1970, he showed hawkish sentiments concerning the Middle East. Doffing his customary pacifist role, he declared that the United States could not be a "benevolent neutral" in the conflict between Arabs and Israelis. Such a role, he said, would be an "abdication of our moral responsibility." He went on to say: "Our policy must be to preserve peace in the Middle East. Yet today that goal can only be achieved by insuring that Israel is immune to attack."

That such insurance could mean an escalation of that war directly involving this country, as in Vietnam, did not seem to trouble the erstwhile dove. Lindsay did, however, attempt to justify his inconsistency on moral grounds. We should not be helping Vietnam, he declared, because that country is "a military dictatorship, jailing its opponents and shutting down the press."

In addition to being obvious, John V. Lindsay is remarkably un-original. That same argument was used by left-liberals and Communists who persuaded this country to stop supporting Chiang Kai-shek when the Communists started their drive to seize China. Chiang, we were told, ran a military dictatorship and jailed his opponents. A decade or so later the same types were arguing that we should throw our support to Fidel Castro because Batista was running Cuba as a military dictatorship and jailing his opponents. Similar arguments have been used to topple anti-Communist governments in other countries.

It is often said that Americans never learn, but it would be more accurate to say that they quickly forget such things and Big Media fails to remind them of past mistakes even when they are about to repeat them.

Television has been harshly condemned for its coverage of the news and its usual reply is that it does not make the news, it only reports it. Why should it be blamed if the news from Indochina and college campuses is so disheartening? People who think like that, say apologists for television, are as benighted as the kings of old who beheaded messengers who brought them disturbing news.

The analogy does not hold. King Arthur would have been a wicked and sinful man indeed if he had sent to the headsman a messenger who brought him a truthful dispatch telling him that his Knights of the Round Table were in imminent danger of being torn apart by dragons. On the other hand, Arthur would have been justified in his wrath if he learned that the messenger for some reason had fabricated the news and Sir Lancelot and his combat team were actually making mincemeat out of the fearsome beasts.

The American people have proved time and again that they can take bad news. Certainly they did not denounce the media that brought them news of Pearl Harbor, the greatest military disaster that ever struck this country. But what the American people refuse to accept is news that they suspect has been doctored to sell them a bill of goods, and this is what they have often been getting.

To get to the bottom of the many charges of television's bias in its coverage of the war in Vietnam would require an in-depth congressional investigation. But such an investigation is unlikely to take place.

There is no denying that TV reporters and cameramen who cover the action in Vietnam operate under conditions that are difficult and dangerous. Nor can it be denied that many of these men have done a superb job under conditions which make it hard to provide a balanced picture of the war. The greatest obstacle to this is the obvious fact that, since these men cannot go behind the enemy lines to show Communist terror tactics and atrocities, viewers are shown a war in which it appears that our side commits all the acts that make war hateful.

A composite filmed report of the war in Vietnam, as TV presents it, would show American bombers dropping their lethal loads, helicopters firing into the jungle and patrols of GIs inching along through jungle or swamp, occasionally firing at unseen targets. That is the standard fare, with commentary provided by a reporter holding the inevitable mike. But occasionally there is something more dramatic.

As viewers of television vicariously accompany American soldiers or marines into a Vietnamese village, they witness many unpleasant things. Our troops burn the village and viewers are shown clusters of old men, women and children who stare or weep as their homes go up in flames. In the foreground, for dramatic effect, a burly grim-faced soldier stands with rifle at the ready. In the middle distance, our tanks crunch along, providing booming sound effects as their guns blast at buildings and rip great holes in them. Then the camera rests on bodies strewn through the wreckage. We hope they are enemy dead but our side has suffered too, and we see a group of wounded GIs, waiting to be evacuated, together with some blanket-covered figures, Americans who failed to make it.

Now and then we are shown something special, such as the famous shot of a Vietnamese police official firing his pistol point-blank at a Viet Cong. Unfortunately there is no way of knowing what the fellow did or whether he did anything to warrant such punishment. Or we may listen to a lot of interviews with people discussing the massacre of Mylai. There is considerable confusion as to the facts, but the discussions usually leave viewers with an impression that is distinctly unfavorable to the military. Then, away from the fighting, we are shown the gay life of Saigon, and told how a lot of rich Vietnamese are getting richer out of the war and exploiting our men in the process.

Frank Shakespeare, a former CBS executive who now heads the USIA, told of an incident he had witnessed in Vietnam and how the same incident had been presented to viewers back home. He came upon five soldiers who had been out in the field fighting for two days. They were "dead tired, exhausted and scared to death," and a new second lieutenant ordered them to go out again and they refused to go. It was actually a minor incident, but it was magnified out of all proportion by television. On his return to the United States, he said,

> "I saw two television programs on major network news programs in the United States and both of these programs indicated that perhaps the American Army was refusing to fight. Now I submit—and it's a personal judgment—that could not have been further from the truth and it was totally misleading the American public.

At the time U.S. troops were sent into Cambodia on April 30, 1970, there was a tremendous outcry from radicals and liberals operating in a united front against the President's move to destroy Communist sanctuaries in that country. This bitterness was apparent in one television program after another. One program so aroused Senator Bob Dole of Kansas that he said the CBS reporter responsible "has come perilously close to attempting to incite mutiny by playing on the emotions of soldiers just before they were to go into battle."

The program in question was a newscast by Gary Sheppard, who interviewed a number of GIs as they were about to strike into Cambodia. One of the exchanges that aroused the senator's ire was this:

Q: How many of the men here do you think really want to go in there today?

A: Very few. But there's not very many of them willing to stand up for what we know is right but . . . a lot of them will probably go on in anyway.

Q: So you say the morale is pretty low in Alpha Company?

A: Definitely. Very low.

Q: Why?

A: Well, we've been getting pushed around, we don't get supplies like we're supposed to, they don't tell us what's going on or what we are going to do or anything, so it's very definitely very low . . .

Senator Dole commented: "It appears to me that, in some cases, a concentrated effort is being made to destroy our national will and character by playing first on the emotions of our battlefield soldiers and then, by feeding the results back home, to play on the emotions of the American people."

The emotions of the American people were given a thorough going-over by the media during this period, and CBS was not the only network that participated. One of NBC's contributions was a special report on the Huntley-Brinkley show, which report portrayed the way in which draftees in the San Francisco-Oakland area were malingering. Half of the men called failed to show up, and of those who did, many refused induction. The other side of this coin showed how a callous and ungrateful government behaved toward men who had served in Vietnam and had been wounded there. This report showed deplorable conditions in VA hospitals, an idea that may have been suggested in a *Life* magazine feature of the same nature.

Because of its war coverage, NBC ran afoul not of Spiro Agnew but of a majority of its affiliated stations. *Variety,* for May 27, 1970, reported that in a closed meeting of NBC affiliates held May 21 in New York, 60 percent of the stations by a hand vote declared the network news coverage was biased. "Specifically," said *Variety,* "the 60% majority was accusing the network news division of being slanted against the war in Vietnam."

It was not just the news that was slanted. Following the invasion of Cambodia, anti-war propaganda of all kinds was broadcast, and it grew in volume with virtuoso performances by solo voices, by groups and, it sometimes seemed, by massed choirs. A procession of doves, senators and others, cooed its opposition. The gabfesters provided forums for Joan Baez, college students and other experts in foreign policy. An interesting exercise in propaganda was offered by ABC, in a pathetic special which told how the death of a young GI in Vietnam affected relatives, neighbors, teachers and friends in his home town. It was understandably sad, and there was general agreement on the part of those interviewed that the war was utterly senseless. There were also some World War II movies. These were not the type that had been used to build morale when Hitler had to be defeated, but post-war films expressing disillusionment. Soldiers were shown being blown apart by mines and cut down messily by small-arms fire.

Because of these and other things that blossomed on the television screen, all in a short period of time, a skeptical viewer might have gotten the impression that someone was trying to sell him a bill of goods. He might also have felt that it was remarkably like that peddled so assiduously by New Left leaders who commute to Havana, Hanoi and other cultural centers. However, in view of the action taken by NBC's affiliates, not all the skeptics were TV viewers.

Congressional investigators could ask a lot of questions about the way in which the Vietnam War was being covered, with the constant accent on the negative, but it would probably be impossible to get satisfactory answers, especially as to motivation. In an earlier phase of the war, when liberals organized their *putsch* to get rid of Diem, the motivation for that infamous act was discussed by the late Marguerite Higgins, a truly great reporter. Writing in *America* for January 4, 1964, she said: "There is no doubt that the overwhelming majority of the American press corps thought—out of the most idealistic and patriotic motives—that they were serving a good cause in arousing world opinion against Diem."

As a lamentable end result of this misguided idealism, President Ngo Dinh Diem and his brother Ngo Dinh Nhu were assassinated by conniving Vietnamese officers encouraged by top American officials in Saigon and Washington. The country was thrown into chaos and the Communists were the major beneficiaries as they exploited the situation.

It would appear that some of our present-day press corps serving in Vietnam believe—no doubt with the most idealistic and patriotic motives—that they too have a mission. That is, to bring about a situation in Vietnam in line with that which is advocated by such eminent foreign-policy experts as David Dellinger, Joan Baez, Joseph Kraft, I. F. Stone, Paul Newman, Dr. Spock, Rennie Davis and Mayor John V. Lindsay.

But how does one prove such a thing and say flatly that certain correspondents are angling their comment and pictures to make certain points? The distortions we see may be explained otherwise. For instance, a study of *all* the film that comes to the networks from Vietnam might show a well-rounded picture of the war. The apparent bias might have crept in during the editing process, for as Edwin Newman once said, "We do not censor the news, we edit." Editing is often done to enhance entertainment value, to provide the kind of "good theater" necessary to keep the ratings high.

That is the way apologists for television explain it, and there is probably some truth to this assertion. But it is not the whole truth. There is ample reason for questioning the actions of some TV people in Vietnam who are obviously not objective. Their prejudices are openly displayed in the way they present "facts," in the way they conduct interviews and in a kind moralizing that is out of place in such coverage.

Some of them make little effort to conceal their disenchantment with American foreign policy and with those who make and implement it. This annoying pomposity is explained by Seymour Freidin and George Bailey in their book *The Experts:* "There is a predilection among the up-and-coming TV journalists to become young stuffed shirts. They see, alas, many of their veteran colleagues go places in their business by sounding sententious. It also leads to a competitive know-nothingness. . . ."

One may be reasonably sure that if some of these people were permitted to prescribe military strategy for Vietnam it would not

have as its objective the winning of the war. The concept of "uncon-
ditional surrender" was thrown overboard when the Nazis and Fas-
cists were smashed in 1945, and the concept that "there is no
substitute for victory" was jettisoned when President Truman fired
General MacArthur. Now the idea is to get peace through negotiations. You give the Communists enough of whatever they want to
keep them satisfied for a time, and hope that some day they will give
up their goal of world conquest.

Aware that they cannot possibly win a military victory in Vietnam
against American troops, the Communists now rest their hopes on
generating sufficient anti-war pressure in the United States to gain
victory there. There is no denying how effective this strategy has
been. Soon after our troops moved to destroy the enemy potential in
Cambodia, a move that badly hurt the Communists there, hundreds
of campuses in this country exploded in violence as students demanded that we pull back and stop the war then and there. With vast
self-approval, these people looked upon themselves as idealistic crusaders for peace. Unfortunately, an equal number of the Viet Cong
operating in the United States could not have done more damage to
the American cause. Thanks to student disruptions, duly noted by
Communist strategists, the peace we eventually get will bear a higher
price tag.

Opportunistic politicians provided a running sound track for the
"theater" that was being staged by demonstrating students, and by
the road shows of the New Mobe. Impressed by the mobs screaming
"Peace!" various politicos decided this was a good vote-getting issue.
It also meant headlines and TV exposure, all of a sympathetic nature.

Unfortunately there was another aspect to this, as indicated by the
following excerpt from an item in *Inform,* a newsletter.

> Soviet newsmen in the United States keep an eye on Congress, they
> comb all our newspapers and periodicals, and monitor most TV and
> radio circuits . . . . Roughly, in the order named, the following U.S.
> Senators are used most in Soviet broadcasts reporting "rising opposi-
> tion" in the United States on various government policies: Fulbright,

McGovern, Kennedy, Young of Ohio, McCarthy, Goodell, Hatfield, Javits, Gore, Pell, Aiken, Hartke, and Moss.

Thanks in no small measure to television, we will get the kind of peace demanded by these and other politicians, students and those who look upon themselves as the intellectual community. However, it will be a fragile thing, like that in Korea, which has to be maintained with large contingents of troops. We may even have to continue indefinitely in Paris or elsewhere the same kind of farce that we have been forced to endure with Communist negotiators at Panmunjom. This is all part and parcel of Communism's strategy, which looks upon a negotiating table as a battlefield that can often give Communists victories impossible through military measures—meanwhile making the enemy, meaning us, look ridiculous.

All this is probably too complicated to be grasped by thousands of university students, the kind who seem capable only of thinking in terms of slogans—the slogans supplied by resident or traveling agitators or relayed via television.

Since higher education has produced so much evidence of failure, maybe television should be given the opportunity to work its magic. In view of what the medium has been able to promote, and because of its proven ability to sell anything in massive quantities, I believe it could cause an abrupt change in public opinion concerning Vietnam even at this late date. By presenting the war in a different perspective, and explaining it to the American people as World Wars I and II were explained, or sold, to them, I believe the war in Indochina could be turned into a veritable crusade. With the power of TV behind it, such a crusade would fill our streets with paraders, bring out bands, cause American flags to blossom in front of every home and persuade young Americans to form long lines in front of recruiting offices. I even believe it could get the facts through to the now-radicalized collegians and cause them to join those lines, possibly carrying placards reading, "We Won't Come Back Till It's Over Over There."

But as the saying goes, "that will be the day!"

Those who recall World War II have probably noted a strange

discrepancy in the Vietnam War. At that time there was a vast outpouring of motion pictures that portrayed the iniquities of Hitler, Mussolini and the Japanese. Their atrocities were repeatedly emphasized, as were the heroic qualities of Americans fighting against them in the Army, Navy, Air Force, Marine Corps and Coast Guard. But this you doubtless know, since the same films are shown almost on a nightly basis, even though the war has been over for two and a half decades.

Do you recall ever having seen a motion picture of this type on television, portraying the brutalities of the Communist North Vietnamese and the Viet Cong, and glorifying the hundreds of thousands of Americans engaged in fighting these aggressors? Hollywood has not seen fit to turn out such pictures, and those who order full-length original movies for TV apparently find the subject as distasteful as Hollywood does.

When John Wayne tried to produce *The Green Berets* he was discouraged on every hand by the major studios, who obviously wanted no part of it. He finally did the film pretty much on his own, and then liberal film critics tried to kill it by general condemnation. The Communist press called on Red goon squads to disrupt showings and this was done. But despite all this, *The Green Berets* was an outstanding success. The American people flocked to see it. Usually when a movie is a hit there is a series of films of the same nature, but *The Green Berets* proved to be an exception. Which fact would indicate that to some movie people, there are some things more important than money.

The Green Berets is not likely to be seen on television for a long time but one movie about the Vietnam War has been shown. This, incidentally, may be the only other movie ever made on the subject. Titled *A Yank in Viet-Nam,* it was made in that country, and although it cannot be described as a great film, it is far superior to most of the movies shown on television. Further, it sets forth an important and timely message by presenting some reasons why we are fighting in Vietnam. Unfortunately, NBC, which showed this film over WNBC-TV, Channel 4, New York, on April 21, 1970, did not see fit to schedule it till 1:45 am.

A query to the network asking whether the film had ever been shown before, possibly at an earlier hour, brought a curious reply. A publicity representative denied that NBC had shown the film and said it must have been seen on an affiliated station. Possibly the very idea of presenting such a film was incredible to the NBC representative, but shown it was.

From the beginning of large-scale U.S. involvement in Vietnam, the war there has been presented in a single dimension, as a military confrontation with Communism. This, more than biased news, explains why the American people have so little understanding of what the war is all about. Actually we are in a struggle in which military action is just one part of the conflict. Our enemy, which happens to be international Communism and not merely one of its small subsidiaries called North Vietnam, is employing a strategy against us that utilizes diplomatic, psychological and political tactics—in addition to military pressures—to gain its objectives. Sometimes in grand strategy, as this is called, the military aspects are not the most important, and they can be the least important.

Marx and Engels in their writings showed their awareness of grand strategy, and they frequently quoted Clausewitz, who had earlier written extensively about it. Followers of Marx and Engels show their familiarity with the subject. They use such strategy against us with devastating effect and we are utterly mystified as we suffer one setback after another. Propaganda is of course a key element in all this.

One of its precepts is that victories can be attained by pressures exerted far from the scene of battle. The Communist victory over the French in Indochina was not won because of any lack of bravery on the part of the French fighting man. We know that it was the home front that failed. The French people lost their will to win and they surrendered ignominiously to the Communists in Indochina in 1954. In terms of grand strategy, France was subjected to economic, political and psychological pressures at the time it was trying to hold onto Indochina with its military forces. In combination they forced France to get out of Southeast Asia.

There were military reverses, of course, notably that at Dien Bien

Phu, which contributed to psychological pressures in the form of propaganda calling for withdrawal. This was keyed in with political pressures that were not resisted by a government that was moving to end French colonialism. And there were economic pressures, since the war was costing France dearly in men and money. Communists, anxious to remove French influence from Southeast Asia so that Communism could continue its course of empire there, skillfully exploited all these pressures.

Certain parallels with U. S. experience will be noted, with two exceptions. Although we have suffered many casualties, we have had no serious military reverses of a sort that would jeopardize our position in Vietnam. Militarily we have been winning, and our major setbacks have been suffered on the home front, the result of other pressures, generated from within and without.

The other exception is that, unlike the French, we are not fighting a war in Southeast Asia to sustain colonialism. The argument, often advanced by liberals and radicals, that we are fighting to extend imperialism is sheer nonsense. We have been spending at the rate of $30 billion a year to preserve a small part of Southeast Asia from being overrun by Communists. Profits from U.S. investments in *all* East Asia, Japan included, come to less than a quarter-billion dollars a year. This is hardly the kind of economics that Wall Street believes in.

It was France's failure in Indochina that led to our presence in that country. Ho Chi Minh moved into Hanoi and started the customary Communist purges in which tens of thousands of Vietnamese were murdered. To escape Ho's butchery, a million North Vietnamese fled south, pursued by Ho's troops.

Because of this unprovoked aggression and Ho's terror tactics, the United States became involved. South Vietnam called on us for help, and under the terms of the SEATO Treaty we provided help, even though other signatory nations not only provided no help but were often a hindrance. The greatest help indeed came from a nation that was not a signer of the SEATO Treaty, South Korea. That valiant little nation helped us for two reasons. It knew at firsthand the harsh facts about Communist aggression, and it wanted to show its gratitude to the nation that had saved it from being seized by Red "liberators" two decades ago.

At first our involvement in Vietnam was minor, of an advisory nature, but when Ho Chi Minh started putting more pressure on South Vietnam, President Kennedy responded with U.S. ground troops. At the time of his assassination there were approximately 16,000 GIs in Vietnam, a number which President Johnson rapidly increased in the hope of getting a quick victory. This has been criticized as a serious error of judgment. Although a favorite liberal stereotype portrays a general officer as one who has a pathological desire to lead vast armies into battle, some of our foremost military leaders have expressed strong opposition to committing American men to a land war in Asia. General MacArthur and General Wedemeyer repeatedly advised political leaders in Washington to avoid such involvement.

With hundreds of thousands of American men in South Vietnam, our military operations were then hamstrung by political decisions. Military leaders were not permitted to bomb strategic centers. The harbor of Haiphong, where arms from the Soviet Union were delivered in massive quantities, could have been embargoed, but that idea was vetoed. Communist forces engaged in hit-and-run tactics, striking at our men and then withdrawing into sanctuaries, and our men were not allowed to pursue them until May 1970 when Communist havens in Cambodia were broken up by President Nixon's move.

Today few Americans are aware of even these sketchy details concerning the way we became involved in Vietnam and the restrictions under which our men have been forced to fight there. Certainly our involvement was anything but dishonorable, yet that is the way it is often presented by leftists and liberals who appear with frequency on our television screens.

The fact that the propaganda they dispense is widely accepted as the truth shows how far we have traveled along the same road that France followed. However, we cannot be accused of one thing that made France vulnerable to powerful attacks of psychological warfare. We are fighting not to take advantage of the Vietnamese but to prevent their enslavement.

While paying close attention to the war against Communism that we are waging in Southeast Asia, television and other communications media have neglected to relate that war to the one that is being waged against the American people here at home, a subject that will be treated in detail in the next chapter.

Many people have the impression that the most harmful propaganda concerning the Vietnam War has been disseminated through news programs. Much has been, of course, but other facets of television have been more explicit in promoting the line that we are fighting an immoral and illegal war there and should get out at once. It has been a favorite theme on programs which discuss "the big issues," and such doves as Senators Church, Goodell, Javits, Fulbright, Kennedy, Mansfield, McGovern and McCarthy have done considerable cooing before the TV cameras.

The wickedness of war—or rather *that* war—also comes up for discussion by the erudite people who keep dropping in on the gab shows. However, in one case at least the mountain went to Mohammed when David Susskind journeyed to Montreal to provide eleven deserters from the U.S. Army with a two-hour television forum. This marathon of sophomoric gabble started at 11:30 p.m. on April 19, 1970, and spilled over into the 20th. The big event was advertised, but some additional publicity was provided on the 19th when Susskind was mentioned in an article published in the *New York Times Magazine.* The article dealt with William J. Kunstler, and at one point it told how at one time the lawyer had been associated in broadcasting with David Susskind.

"David and I," Kunstler is quoted as saying, "both got our start on the Barry Gray show. We both used to take over the program when Barry was on vacation." Had Kunstler conducted the April 19th show with the deserters, it probably would have come over much as it did, because Susskind showed a touching sympathy for the boys and their abhorrence of war.

Most of his guests affected the trappings and general untidiness of dissident students. One was an effeminate type who even talked with a swish, while another was a bewhiskered dese-dose-and-dem guy who had difficulty in expressing himself but never stopped trying.

One, whose I.Q. seemed to be a few points above the general level, confided that he was writing a book—between trips to the States to take part in demonstrations. Another, who was obviously no genius, contributed some unconscious humor when he said he had to leave the army because his fellow GIs were stupid. Then there was a doctor, utterly enthralled with the sound of his babbling voice.

Susskind was not dealing with mental giants, but even so he came off second best as the deserters turned it into their show. They viciously attacked the army, the U.S. government and the President, with no rebuke from Susskind. At one point they called on him to apologize for calling them cowards, and apologize he did. At another juncture, he offered the talkative doctor some strange advice, telling him that if he had stayed in the army, he could have gotten others out by saying they were medically unfit.

To assure them that his heart was in the right place, he told them he felt the same way they did about the war. Only he felt that they should not have deserted but stayed in, to change the system from within.

If there had been a scoreboard in the studio, it would have shown zero for the American side. The score for "them" would have included a propaganda home run when Susskind, after a shrug, permitted the deserters to explain how other servicemen could join them in Canada, what organizations to contact, employment possibilities, etc. Potential deserters were told that Canada is a great and hospitable country but it would be wise to bring money—at least till they could get jobs with organizations set up to encourage desertions from the U.S. Army, in which organizations most if not all these people were employed.

What Susskind thought he was doing by giving these fellows a forum is hard to understand. It did the United States no good and it certainly did not add to Susskind's stature.

Even programs that are supposed to be entertainment are by no means free of such propaganda. Comedians are likely to come up with some profound thoughts on the subject. As everyone by now knows, the irrepressible Smothers Brothers feel deeply about the war, while many folk singers have a phobia concerning it. Take Pete Seeger, for instance. On one of his many guest appearances on networks, this one on NBC, the bearded thrush intoned the following:

> If you love your Uncle Sam, bring 'em home
>   Bring 'em home—bring 'em home.
> Support our boys in Vietnam, bring 'em home
>   Bring 'em home—bring 'em home.
> It'll make our generals sad, I know,
>   Bring 'em home, bring 'em home.
> They want to tangle with the poll,
>   Bring 'em home, bring 'em home.

There was more, and all reminiscent of a time when Seeger was anxious to keep America neutral in another war. This was at the time of the Hitler-Stalin Pact, when the two dictators wanted no one butting in while they were greedily dividing Poland between them. There was a New Mobe then, called American Peace Mobilization, which demonstrated for peace in front of the White House. Pete Seeger was popular with this outfit and sang for them at a gathering in Washington. One of his ditties of that period had the line, "Franklin, oh Franklin, we don't want to go to war." Another was, "I hate war and so does Eleanor, but we won't be safe until everybody's dead." Seeger at that time was a member of the Almanac Singers, cited as a Communist front, but he had other connections. In its annual report for 1961, the House Committee on Un-American Activities said: "Seeger . . . has been identified as a member of the Communist Party and today, as for many years past, is an inveterate promoter of party fronts and the party line."

Even so, Seeger keeps popping up on network shows, ready to express opinions, often with guitar or banjo accompaniment. On March 4, 1970, he was on the Johnny Cash show on ABC. He was given little opportunity to provide some of his usual soapbox oratory, but even so, in a few words he managed to slip in a snide remark about the need to oppose "74-year-old judges in their black robes." It so happens that Judge Hoffman, who made himself anathema in left-wing circles because he cracked down on Kunstler & Company, is 74 years old.

In a different manner, the anti-war theme and other liberal concepts are insinuated into the so-called news specials. A good example was provided by CBS's *60 Minutes* on March 3, 1970. There a large segment of the entire show, one whose time costs would have been too expensive for many big advertisers, was turned into a sustained plug for a song, an anti-war ditty, telling of a soldier killed in Vietnam.

The backers of this project said they hoped to make a million dollars on a recording of the song, which seems to put them in the same class with other cynical people who don't mind making a fast buck out of the misery of war. Those charged with plugging the record—who had already done exceedingly well by getting all that valuable CBS time for nothing—said they hoped to get additional free time on the Johnny Carson and Dick Cavett shows. They also said they had high hopes of getting the record into all the nation's half-million jukeboxes. Here, if they are successful, the song's lugubrious message about death in Vietnam should make a profound impression on boys and girls who buy their culture at such stands. It may even induce some kids to run off to Canada, to join David Susskind's friends there.

The composer, a balding little man with a moustache, who looked more like a grocery clerk than a troubadour, sang a few bars of his masterpiece. He too said he hoped to make a killing with his product, but it is difficult to understand why.

This was followed by considerable footage in which the Pentagon took a few lumps—a highly critical look at procurement policies. Speakers, prodded by Mike Wallace, told how carelessness and incompetence in the military-industrial establishment had hiked the cost of a submarine torpedo to almost three billion dollars. This was followed by an extended interview with Golda Meir, who told of Israeli determination in the face of all pressures.

The way in which television has presented the war in Vietnam is said to account for most of the critical mail and caustic comment directed at the networks. Significantly, one segment of the population is not complaining. Demonstrators, who are inclined to be highly critical and emotional when anyone or anything opposes them, apparently approve of the way TV does things.

None of the bearded ones has shaped up in front of NBC, CBS or ABC to express his revolutionary annoyance at this branch of the establishment. No representatives of the academic elite have put in an appearance to shout obscenities, toss rocks or wreck the offices of network officials. No full-page ads have blossomed in the *New York Times* denouncing television, bought and paid for by concerned clergymen, educators, lawyers or others. Dr. Spock has not marched arm in arm with Jane Fonda, Staughton Lynd, David Dellinger, Shirley MacLaine, Jerry Rubin and other liberals in a show of solidarity opposing network coverage of the Vietnam War. Senator Fulbright has uttered no sententious statements expressing his usual deep concern, and the New Mobe has not summoned its road companies to perform in the Radio City area.

Considering these things, an old advertising slogan comes to mind: "Such popularity must be deserved."

CHAPTER SIX

The War at Home

UNTIL recently, despite campus disruptions and riots in the streets, there were still many Americans who remained unperturbed. They believed that "the long hot summers" that had erupted in the cities would eventually moderate, and so would the tumult that had caused chaos at colleges and universities.

Many indeed looked upon the campus turmoil, as little more alarming than collegiate roistering of the past which had expressed itself in panty raids on girls' dormitories and other nonsense. In time, these optimists believed, the high-spirited kids of today would get some sense, settle down to good jobs and raise families.

Then came the May 1970 riots on hundreds of American campuses, climaxed by the shooting of four Kent State students. There was no element of college humor in any of this and the American people started to have second thoughts about the nation's colleges and universities and what was happening there.

Those who remembered Hitler's rise to power noticed some disturbing parallels. Like Hitler and his brown-shirted hoodlums, today's youth leaders deliver apocalyptic statements and threatening manifestoes. Like Nazis of old, they act the part of an elite class, a master race with a mission to rule those they consider their inferiors.

There is another frightening parallel between those who established Hitler in power and our own New Left. Professing idealism, our campus revolutionaries use brutality and hatred to attain their goals. The vicious attacks of these apostles of peace against those who oppose them, and their wanton destruction of property—even of their own universities—are strictly in the Nazi tradition. Proclaiming peace, they conduct a war against their fellow countrymen. Preaching non-violence, they deliberately provoke violence and then enact the role of martyrs.

While their tactics resemble those of Hitler's storm troopers, these people certainly bear little physical resemblance to the Fuehrer's jackbooted, close-cropped hoodlums. Many of them are freakish characters, and allied with them are debutante types, pretty and promiscuous, whose wealthy families sent them to prestigious colleges where they learned a pathological hatred of their native land. There are strutting black militants who bombastically make demands and threaten to bomb, burn and kill if their demands are not met. And not too far in the background can be seen trained conspirators pulling the strings that activate their sinister puppets. The puppets may not have a clear idea of where their course leads but the puppeteers certainly have. Lenin said it back in 1919: "No Socialist revolution is possible without civil war."

What has television to do with all this?

There are many answers to this, testimonials provided by the revolutionaries themselves, and statements made by those who have to cope with the revolutionaries. Television is not solely to blame for what has been happening, but because of its widespread influence and tremendous impact, it bears a great responsibility for what the revolutionaries have been able to accomplish to date.

Abbie Hoffman, one of the flamboyant Chicago Seven who has become a TV star of sorts, paid a great tribute to the medium when he said, "We get on that tube . . . we get information out and our information is heavy and it sticks, it's exciting, it's alive." He described the goal that television is helping him and his radical colleagues attain:

"There's no doubt about it. We're going to wreck this——society. If we don't this society is going to wreck itself anyway, so we might as well have some fun doin' it."

Testifying before the House Committee on Un-American Activities on December 2, 1968, notorious New Leftist Tom Hayden explained another kind of help provided by the media. Asked about the source of his income, Hayden replied, "Speaking, based on the notoriety that people like you and the mass media have given me." He went on to say that he also made money from writing: "Well, as I said, I was at work on the contractual basis with Random House on a new book on Vietnam."

North Vietnam's leaders are duly appreciative of the help they get from many Americans, notably those who have access to the media. In a November 8, 1966, broadcast Radio Hanoi said: "The Vietnamese people highly value the protest movement of the American people. We praise the American peace champions who courageously turned the courts which were trying them into forums to condemn the war. We praise the American journalists and writers who, in defiance of repression and threats, valiantly exposed the crimes of the Johnson clique in Vietnam."

There is one obvious fallacy in this propaganda—the idea that those who plead Hanoi's cause to the American people are repressed and threatened. What the Communists want, as their major objective, is immediate withdrawal of all American troops from South Vietnam. What many of our most influential opinion makers want is precisely the same thing and there is little indication that they are inhibited in expressing their opinions.

The storm troopers of the New Left take more drastic steps by shouting down or threatening those who appear in public to advocate a course denying victory to the Communists. Frequently these "dissidents," having silenced their opponents, are then permitted to set forth their arguments.

This sort of thing has produced an inevitable reaction on the part of the Silent Majority and this has gone beyond resentment of the dissidents themselves. Anthony LaCamera, television critic of the *Boston Record American,* reported that "strong and widespread anti-television feeling" was being expressed by viewers because of its treatment of the radical element. He described viewers as "angry, frustrated, fed up and seemingly ready to explode" because of television's increasing permissiveness in allowing itself to be used as a public platform by the weirdest and most extreme elements in our society . . . To them the home screen sometimes looks like the relentless dispenser of one long assault on everything they hold dear. Crackpots, neurotics, misfits and exhibitionists seem to have little trouble finding TV time on which to spew their personal venom and emotional violence—even in the pious names of love and peace. La Camera continued,

> There are so many talk shows, and so much intense competition among them for attention and audience, that they are jumping at almost every opportunity to capitalize on the guesting availability of the turbulence-makers, some of whom refuse or are unqualified to engage in rational dialog. It is not enough, apparently, that such characters are duly covered in hard newscasts; they also keep turning up in feature segments of newscasts and as celebrity interviewees on one talk show after another, there to pour forth pent-up hatreds, far beyond the norm for reasonable coverage. . . .

These hate-mongers, whose hatred is directed at their own country, like television because it can get things done. Indeed, the medium should feel flattered at the faith the revolutionaries have in its power to persuade. It probably surpasses even that held by Madison Avenue and the great American industries that spend billions advertising on television. Strangely, those advertisers do not seem to mind the fact that militants get millions of dollars worth of TV time for nothing. For that matter, complacent businessmen often sponsor at fabulous cost programs in which their mortal enemies are glorified and their own downfall predicted.

However, if leaders of American industry and their advertising people don't mind the buildup given to people who intend to "liberate" the United States from its capitalist exploiters, police officials take a dim view of it. But that is because the police are aware of the seriousness of the problem.

Policemen understand what is behind much of the violence on campus, and why it usually aims at such strategic targets as the Indochina war, ROTC, the draft and research. Students who are rallied to oppose real or fancied campus wrongs find their dissent channeled into actions designed to cripple this nation's military strength and potential. A prime target has been ROTC, whose units have been damaged and destroyed from one end of the country to the other. Army, Navy and Air Force records show more than 400 such incidents, and this harassment has had a serious result. ROTC enrollment dropped from 212,416 in 1968–69 to 157,830. And even further in 1969–70.

What happened at Kent State is an excellent example of what the revolutionaries are after. The *New York Times,* whose early reporting of the uprising there gave the utterly false impression that the university was a pastoral place previously untouched by violence, described the revolutionary drive in an article in its magazine for June 21, 1970:

> The radicals, favoring "direct action," broke up a dance on campus, then swept the crowd off to the R.O.T.C. building, where windows were broken and torches were thrown to start the fire. . . .The firemen were being pelted by rocks there, and their hoses were being cut by students wielding axes and machetes. The guardsmen threw a ring around the building and did the same for the other campus buildings thought to be "torch targets."

One of the buildings that the radicals wanted to destroy housed a research project, of special interest from a military standpoint. This was the Liquid Crystal Institute, one of two such projects in the United States, and one in which the Soviet Union had evinced considerable interest. Heat-sensitive crystals developed there have a vast scientific potential, and among their military applications is their ability to sense the presence of troops and installations.

So strategic was Kent State in radical planning that one of the top SDS activists, Terry Robbins, was given much of the responsibility for radicalizing the campus. As part of his activity he co-authored a revolutionary tract titled "The War Is on at Kent State," and he was the author of "Organizer's Manual for the Spring Offensive." The offensive was of course aimed at Kent State. What happened later was pretty much as Robbins planned it:

During the course of the struggle, it will probably be necessary and
helpful to carry out a series of "mini" actions to help build conscious-
ness and dramatize the issue. Beginning with guerrilla theater actions
in dorms we can escalate to disrupting classes, street marches, quick
assaults on buildings, etc., before moving to the major confrontation
of the struggle.

According to Bernardine Dohrn, now a fugitive from justice, Robbins was one of the three persons blown up in the Greenwich Village
bomb factory.

However, in covering the Kent State shootings the media advanced other reasons for the tragic event. Television viewers were
told by various pundits and politicians that the four students were
victims of President Nixon's move into Cambodia and student anger
over "Agnew rhetoric." Long afterwards the truth started to emerge,
but millions probably still believe the version that was first peddled
by the media.

On the face of it our would-be Lenins and Che Guevaras are well
versed in the fine art of agitprop, or agitation-propaganda, and it is
unfortunate that the media so often fall for their tricks. The fact
remains though that many media people feel the same way as the
New Left does about President Nixon, Vice President Agnew and
other members of the administration.

This was evident when our home-grown radicals demonstrated
their understanding of grand strategy at the time the President ordered U.S. troops to destroy Communist bases in Cambodia that had
long claimed a toll of American and South Vietnamese lives. Our GIs
met little resistance there, but a powerful counterattack came from
within our own borders.

As though on signal, demonstrations erupted on hundreds of campuses across the country. Demonstrations became increasingly violent, climaxing in the Kent State shootings. Naturally all this
received considerable television exposure, most of which was highly
sympathetic to the rioting students and critical of the President's
action that had "triggered" the rioting.

In time, the way in which all this happened will probably come under official investigation, as similar riots have been investigated in the past. Meanwhile, the following statement made some time ago by J. Edgar Hoover to law enforcement officials is still valid:

> There can be no quarrel with the all-important role of keeping the public informed as quickly and as completely as possible. No one rightfully expects riots to be played down or salient facts withheld.
>
> On the other hand, militant agitators, hate-mongers and publicity-seeking rabble-rousers who incite riots have no fear of overexposure. They know that television, radio and front page news stories are the best and quickest means of getting their stories before the public. Thus, they seek attention from the news media.

And usually manage to get it, without stint.

Dr. S. I. Hayakawa, San Francisco State College president, flatly accused the news media of building up militants, saying, "in the process, the media themselves are setting the stage for serious disturbances in the future." Vice President Agnew said much the same thing: "It is time to stop dignifying the immature actions of arrogant, reckless, inexperienced elements within our society. The reason is compelling. It is simply that their tantrums are insidiously destroying the fabric of American democracy."

Such actions are also causing us to lose a war, with international Communism the beneficiary. Still, even though some of our well-publicized black and white revolutionaries maintain liaison with Communist functionaries at home and abroad, this does not necessarily prove that they themselves are Communists—even when they refer to themselves as communists with a small *c*. Relatively few are Party members. This is a fact that the American people should clearly understand, for nothing is more helpful to the Communist cause than a charge that a certain person or group belongs to the Party when such is not the case. In refuting such a charge, Communists give the impression that *all* charges against Communists and Communist causes are false and malicious lines—in short, "McCarthyism."

Today's New Left, which spearheads the revolutionary action in this country, includes a bewildering array of Marxist-Leninists, Trotskyists and Peking-oriented Communists who look to Mao and Che for their inspiration rather than to the Kremlin. But along with these various Reds, and forming a united front with them against the United States, are fanatical nihilists and anarchists, with an insane compulsion to tear down our government.

The diversity was dramatized at Chicago where the New Left militants proudly carried the banners of the Viet Cong and North Vietnam together with the red flag of Communism and the black flag of anarchism. On the other hand, these people obviously held the flag of the United States in low regard. One of the most disgraceful episodes at Chicago occurred at a huge rally at the Amphitheatre, when the flag of our country was pulled down from a flagpole to be replaced by a red banner. Infuriated policemen, some of whom had fought for Old Glory, charged the crowd at this point. This of course constituted "police brutality," but a certain amount of "New Left brutality" is indicated by the fact that 30 policemen were injured in the melee.

Thus while few of the revolutionaries are, technically, members of the Communist Party U.S.A., it would certainly not be accurate to say that no Communists are involved. Testifying before the National Commission on the Causes and Prevention of Violence, the so-called Eisenhower hearings, J. Edgar Hoover, on September 18, 1968, stated:

> Communists are in the forefront of civil rights, anti-war and student demonstrations, many of which ultimately become disorderly and erupt into violence. As an example, Bettina Aptheker Kurzweil, twenty-four year old member of the CPUSA's National Committee, was a leading organizer of the "free speech" demonstrations on the campus of the University of California in the Fall of 1964.
>
> These protests, culminating in the arrest of more than 800 demonstrators during a campus sit-in, on December 3, 1964, were the forerunners of the current campus upheaval.
>
> In a press conference on July 4, 1968, the opening day of the CPUSA's special national convention, Gus Hall, the Party's General Secretary, stated that there were Communists on most of the major

campuses in the country and they had been involved in the student protests.

It might be mentioned that Bettina Aptheker Kurzweil comes naturally by her talents. Her father, Herbert Aptheker, has long been known as the Communist Party's leading "theoretician" in this country. In addition, he teaches at Bryn Mawr College, but this academic chore obviously gives him time for other activities. Testifying before the House Committee on Un-American Activities on December 2, 1968, Tom Hayden provided some unconscious humor with the following: "Yes, I traveled—I was a fellow traveler to Hanoi with Herbert Aptheker in 1965. . . ."

Mr. Hoover, in an article published in *The Prosecutor* for May-June 1969, gave details of the way in which Communist influence operates in the New Left:

> Marxist influence is growing within the New Left. The Old Left (the Communist Party U.S.A., pro-Moscow; Progressive Labor Party [PLP], pro-Red China; Socialist Workers Party [Troskyite]) has always had considerable inroads in the New Left, even though many New Leftists detest its bureaucracy, discipline and ideological dogmatism. . . .

He explained that it was the PLP faction, which is pro-Red China, that split Students for a Democratic Society and caused the emergence of the Weatherman faction, which specializes in bombings and other violence. "Yet even the non-PLP forces in SDS," Mr. Hoover went on,

> find the attraction of Marxism almost irresistible. After all, it was Marx who laid down the so-called "scientific" rules for conducting a revolution. How can you circumvent Marx's influence if you are planning a revolution? Here is the dilemma of the New Left. Is it possible to have a revolution without Marx? The answer: it would be most difficult. No wonder large segments of SDS and the New Left are drifting more and more to the Marxist principles of the Old Left,

whether they be Communist Party U.S.A., or Progressive Labor Party.

The dreary answer is that the New Left, starting with great promise and idealism, has been so compromised, maneuvered and betrayed by Marxist and extremist elements that it has degenerated into a fanatic rabble of divisive voices hostile to the beliefs of a free people. It is marching forward to chaos!

Television's contribution to the New Left's march to chaos was described by Mr. Hoover in a statement made on September 18, 1968:

> Far too much emphasis is also being paid on television to the antics of a publicity-seeking extremist minority. Impressionable youths and immature individuals can easily conclude from television news coverage that everyone is protesting, demonstrating, marching and burning draft cards when, in some cases, the reporters, cameramen and assorted technicians appear to outnumber the demonstrators. Usually rational explanations or refutations are not supplied.

Television's heavy responsibility for instigating and encouraging rioters is apparent. Certainly the instigators of the "free speech" movement at Berkeley had no reason to complain that television ignored them. TV camera crews have been prominent wherever black and white militants have engaged in violence. Probably the most publicized of the "happenings" was that which took place at the time of the 1968 Democratic National Convention in Chicago. As the report to the National Commission on the Causes and Prevention of Violence says about those riots:

> Camera crews on at least two occasions did stage violence and fake injuries. Demonstrators did step up their activities for the benefit of TV cameras. Newsmen and photographers' blinding lights did get in the way of police clearing streets, sweeping the park and dispersing demonstrators. Newsmen did, on occasion, disobey legitimate police orders to "move" or "clear the streets." News reporting of events did seem to the police to be anti-Chicago and anti-police.

The report tells, too, how the protesters "played to the cameras," and says that "they often did it very effectively," having learned from other demonstrations.

One of the incidents was reported by Senator and Mrs. Gale McGee, who told of seeing a newsreel crew in Grant Park arrange to have a girl demonstrator with a bandage across her head walk up to a line of National Guardsmen and start shouting, "Don't hit me!" upon which signal the newsreel crew started shooting. The U.S. District Attorney for the Northern District of Illinois, Mr. Foran, reported seeing an individual near the Logan Statue in Grant Park who was holding a bandage to his head and talking to a three-man camera crew, one of whom had a CBS trademark on his jacket. After a brief conversation, the camera crew began filming the individual as he held the bandage alongside his head. When Mr. Foran approached, the camera crew quickly walked away and the man with the bandage cursed him and left the area. All three networks denied knowledge of the incident.

During the filming of the riots it was charged that television lights not only encouraged violence but were usually turned toward the police, making them targets for missiles. When the lights were turned on, the hoodlums started throwing things and the policemen were placed at a disadvantage by the blinding lights. Once the lights were turned off, the throwing stopped. Police orders to turn off the lights were disregarded.

Hugh Downs, NBC's liberal luminary, provided a fitting finale for the Chicago riots on his *Today Show* when he asked TV viewers if there was any word that better described Chicago policemen than "Pigs!" This brought a strong rejoinder from Frank Sullivan, the press officer for the Chicago police. He described the leaders of the riots as Communist revolutionaries, but said, "They are a pitiful handful. They have almost no support. But, by golly, they get the cooperation of the news media. They are built into something big. . . ."

As an aftermath of this, when several of the ringleaders were tried and convicted for their part in the riots, television persisted in its wayward ways. Writing in the *New York Times* of March 22, 1970, Jack Gould said, "At the moment, the Chicago Seven and their attorneys are all over the TV dial giving their version of the trial. . . ." TV exposure continued to such an extent that viewers became bored at the sight of them and more than fed up with their gibberish and their menacing manifestoes.

Probably the most obnoxious performer was foul-mouthed Abbie Hoffman. This fellow was invited to appear as a guest on the Merv Griffin show, to project himself and his views over the CBS network, and he turned up wearing a shirt made of the American flag. Instead of being escorted out of the studio, he was taken before the cameras where he went into his routine. Many viewers, angered at the desecration of the flag, protested. CBS then made an incredible move. The program had been taped for another showing two days later, but becuase of the complaints network officials ruled that the show could go on but that Hoffman's offending shirt would have to be blocked out electronically. This time leftists complained, saying that their boy should be seen as well as heard. Thus Hoffman became a martyr.

Meanwhile, another celebrated rabble-rouser started making guest shots on television—Stokeley Carmichael. For many months he had been sojourning abroad with his bride, an African performer, and with Kwame Nkrumah, the self-styled redeemer, whose long-suffering and impious subjects had finally kicked him out of Ghana after years of corruption and Marxist misrule. Among Carmichael's television performances was one with David Frost, which gave him the Metromedia audience. A guest appearance on the Dick Cavett show then gave him the ABC audience for his revolutionary pitch.

On the Frost show Carmichael peddled his dialectric like a vacuum cleaner salesman demonstrating his Little Dandy Model, and like a slick salesman, he permitted no interruptions. Frost usually handles his guests in a competent manner, but on that occasion he failed to cover himself with glory. The high spot of the show was Carmichael's comment that he considered Adolf Hitler the greatest white man, "a genius."

A similar exhibition of ineptness was the before-discussed occasion when David Susskind traveled to Canada to interview deserters from the U.S. Army. Susskind was either unable or reluctant to answer the most outrageous slanders the deserters uttered against the United States. His performance on that occasion makes one wonder about a statement made during an appearance on a Bill Buckley telecast. He blandly assured Buckley that liberals predominate on television because TV requires intelligence and intelligent people are just naturally liberals.

Such things underscore the point made in the report issued by the city of Chicago, that the news media were guilty of "surprising naiveté." Nor would it appear that the media have acquired any more sophistication since the time of the Democratic National Convention. That report also expressed concern about "the lack of public awareness" of what the radical left was up to, but that is not likely to change until the media look upon these people differently. As for TV, it must stop plugging revolution as though it were a television spectacular with a star-studded cast of performers.

It is the show-biz mentality rather than any desire to foment disturbances that is back of so much of the exposure that is so freely given to the New Left and to black militants. Such people as Rubin, Hoffman and Carmichael are looked upon as stars, capable of bringing a good Nielsen rating. They can be counted on to provide a rousing, controversial performance, they often get publicity for the networks, and best of all they usually perform free or for a small honorarium, and even provide their own costumes.

Dr. Hayakawa, a thorough realist, has told how he used a New Left tactic to get more television attention. He merely bought a colorful tam-o-shanter and perched it on his head—as millions of TV viewers have seen. Because of that touch of showmanship, the media showed more interest in what he said and did.

While much of the revolutionary oratory and violence presented on television can be attributed to showmanship and "theater," there is another reason. The liberals who dominate the medium are likely to have an emotional kinship with people on the left, even when they are so far left that they cannot be categorized. This peculiar tolerance was demonstrated by Herbert Matthews, who insisted that Fidel Castro was no Communist even after Castro himself proclaimed he was one and would remain one till he died. On that occasion, Matthews presented this remarkable apologia: "Today Castro may believe he is a Communist but tomorrow he may believe something else." This was too much even for the *Times,* which did not print it. The statement appeared in the *Herald Tribune.*

It would appear that common sense would dictate that people who deal in treason and revolution should be dealt with summarily, but common sense does not always govern. Many leaders of rioting mobs are turned loose through legal loopholes and immediately start generating more chaos. However, it is becoming quite obvious that the patience of the American people is running out, and our revolutionary element is likely to learn that the polarizing process it employs is a two-way thing. For example, in the course of his triumphal tour of campuses following the trial of the Chicago Seven, William J. Kunstler turned up at Notre Dame University. According to an article in the *New York Times Magazine,* in his speech he made some derogatory remarks concerning President Nixon's Vietnam policy and cried, "WHO THE HELL DOES HE THINK HE IS?" (The capital letters appeared in the *Times* story.) Then, according to the article, he gave the clenched-fist salute and received "a thunderous ovation" from thousands of students.

Such histrionics can have a backlash. Millions of Americans hearing or reading about the left-wing lawyer's insulting reference to a President of the United States are likely to react with, WHO THE HELL DOES KUNSTLER THINK HE IS? Certainly public patience is wearing thin with universities that give rabble-rousers a forum packed with enthusiastic students. This is reflected in the way many Americans are refusing to contribute to colleges and universities, and in growing opposition to the use of public funds for higher education.

Almost as much of a New Left cliché as *polarize* is the word *radicalize.* In the course of radicalizing students, the revolutionaries first polarize them, and this mystical transformation is accomplished by getting people involved in situations where they have to take sides. For example, in a demonstration the trained revolutionaries will provoke the police into swinging their clubs and firing tear gas. Then they will get out of range and let others take the rap, suffer injuries, or even die. Resentful victims of rough—and sometimes needlessly rough—police action can often be persuaded by radicals to join their ranks.

Television serves to "polarize" people far removed from the scene of a confrontation. When TV viewers see on their screens a wild melee, with police wading into crowds of pathetic-looking hippies, male and female, beating them with clubs and roughly tossing some of them into paddy wagons, they are likely to side with the forlorn victims. For all too often television does not show what led up to that "police brutality." Those same hairy cretins and their lady friends may have been laying down a deadly barrage of rocks and bottles, screaming obscenities and insults, and overturning and burning automobiles, that being customary procedure when ideologues are trying to make a point.

The ultimate objective of course is the radicalizing of everyone who can be sold a bill of goods. This is an important job and some of our most illustrious revolutionaries served their apprenticeship in the specialized task of winning friends and turning them into radicals like themselves. Among them was Theodore Gold, who perished along with another radicalizer, Terry Robbins of Kent State fame, in the bomb-factory explosion in Greenwich Village. Gold had served as deputy to another noted rabble-rouser, Mark Rudd, who became a television celebrity in the course of his efforts at crippling his alma mater, Columbia University—efforts that unfortunately succeeded. To television viewers, the team of Gold 'n' Rudd was for a time as famous as the Smothers Brothers, as G & R did their thing on the Morningside campus. Incidentally, Rudd also performed on campus at Kent State prior to the happening there.

After Gold 'n' Rudd and their storm troopers disrupted Columbia, the late bomb-maker apparently felt he had earned a trip to Cuba. After all, his pal Rudd had made the pilgrimage just prior to turning his attention to his university. As his companions, Gold had two females, Kathy Boudin and Cathlyn Wilkerson. The father of the Wilkerson woman owned the quarter-million-dollar town house that served as the bomb factory, while the father of the Boudin woman is a lawyer who busies himself with left-wing litigation. His firm has served as Castro's official representative in the United States, and he had defended Dr. Spock when he was tried for counseling draft dodgers.

Surely one cannot consider Mark Rudd, Theodore Gold, Bettina Aptheker Kurzweil and others of that stripe bona fide students.

What we are up against are professional *un*-students, who travel from campus to campus arousing the *lumpenproletariat* to wreck its universities, man the barricades, and eventually do battle with the police and the National Guard. When violence erupts, the instigators are usually somewhere else, safely watching their silly stooges encountering "police brutality."

The elite members of the radical world may indeed be on their way to Havana, Hanoi, Paris, Bratislava, Prague and other points since their work often calls for consultation with experts overseas. The Cuban junket of Mr. Gold and Misses Wilkerson and Boudin has been mentioned. William Herman (Che) Payne and Ralph E. Featherstone, who were snatched to Abraham's bosom when their bomb blew up their car, had recently visited Cuba. Other gadabouts who have made pilgrimages to Cuba, North Vietnam and other places where America's future is considered are H. Rap Brown, David Dellinger, Eldridge Cleaver, Tom Hayden, Rennie Davis, Stokeley Carmichael, Robert Williams and Jerry Rubin—all of whom need no introduction to television fans.

Their number is being augmented through a project known as the Venceremos Brigade, made up of an estimated 1,000 impressionable, left-leaning American students who traveled to Cuba to help harvest sugar cane. Many of these are now helping Castro in other ways, though some are said to have been disillusioned by what they saw while there.

However, Castroism does have some highly idealistic concepts. Everybody knows what happens when an idealistic American decides to dodge the draft. He is occasionally put to some inconvenience and a few, but very few, draft dodgers have even been put in jail. By way of contrast, if a Cuban refuses to serve in Castro's army, he is not forced to do so. Instead, he is called on to give a copious blood donation to the Cuban Red Cross. After this generous gesture there is only one further technicality, after which he need no longer worry about military service. He is taken to the wall and shot. This is a compelling reason why Cubans, unlike so many American college students, do not try to shirk their duty to Castro and fatherland. Dr. Spock and Rev. William Sloane Coffin, Jr., would probably get little attention if they traveled to Cuba to counsel the people there on how to duck military service. It is indeed conceivable that they would become involuntary blood donors, too, if they were so foolhardy as to try.

When Americans travel to Communist Cuba or Communist North Vietnam and return to engage in some activity that somehow promotes a Communist cause, the question may be asked, "Are these people Communists?" Actually the question and whatever answer it gets are purely academic. Under Supreme Court and other rulings, it would probably be impossible to prove that Brezhev and Kosygin are bona fide Party members. But, as the old saying goes, when something looks like a duck, acts like a duck, and makes noises like a duck, meanwhile associating with other ducks, it may very well be a duck.

Television viewers who see such "ducks" being interviewed by respectful newscasters and gabfesters should keep another picture in mind. However, it is one they will have to visualize for themselves because it has never been presented on the tube, nor is it likely to be. And that is unfortunate because it would make an exciting and highly educational TV spectacular.

Latin American Report, a newsletter based largely on intelligence supplied by anti-Castro, anti-Communist agents in Latin America, told of an important international conference that was held in Havana, January 3–15, 1966. Called the Tricontinental Conference, it was attended by hundreds of accredited Communists from countries in Asia, Africa and Latin America. From this conference developed what is known as the Tricontinental Organization (OSPAAAL). The Soviet Union gave it overt sponsorship and sent 40 official delegates, including Sharaf Rashidov, a candidate member of the Supreme Soviet; Red China was represented by 36 delegates. These two powers emerged as leaders of a Havana-based central strategy that is now directing "wars of national liberation" throughout Asia, Africa and Latin America.

Vietnam was taken as a test case, with these goals:

> All progressive forces are to join in a mass movement to demand the immediate cessation of the war of aggression in Vietnam; the immediate, final and unconditional cessation of air raids against North Vietnam; the withdrawal of all North American troops as well

as the troops of satellite countries from South Vietnam; and the
dismantling and removal of the North American military bases in
South Vietnam.

How were these goals to be achieved?

To develop in every way—through demonstrations, rallies of protest, boycotts against the loading and transportation of arms and war
material and North American troops, celebration of days and weeks
of solidarity (Moratorium) against the war. . .

Who was to help attain those goals?

We congratulate the youth of the United States who refuse to
become accomplices to the crime of genocide perpetrated by Johnson's government against the Vietnamese people, who destroy their
draft cards in order not to participate in the slaughter . . . refuse to
permit the recruiting of mercenaries on American campuses . . .

As the *Report* points out, OSPAAAL did more than congratulate
American youth for acting as traitors. It gave instructions to "launch
a wave of sabotage against Yankee interests throughout the world,"
and to stage "demonstrations, death marches, protest meetings and
denunciations of Yankee policy." It appears that certain dissidents,
who so detest conformity that they will destroy a university that
attempts to impose it, have conformed amazingly to OSPAAAL
dictates.

In August 1967 Stokeley Carmichael took part in an OSPAAAL
conference at Havana. David Dellinger, aging youth leader and one
of the Chicago Seven, also made a pilgrimage to talk things over with
his peace-loving friends in Havana. George Murray, who played a
key role in disrupting San Francisco State College, likewise made the
trip, as did Mark Rudd, the Columbia flash. Rudd returned to Columbia early in 1968, to lead the revolting element there. Another
distinguished revolutionary and bestselling author, Eldridge Cleaver,
at last report was sojourning in Algeria after a stay in Havana.

According to *Latin American Report*, the telephone is often used
to maintain liaison between Havana and its stooges in this country.

Among the users it reported were H. Rap Brown, Bobby Seale and Floyd McKissick.

When David Dellinger testified before the House Committee on Un-American Activities on December 4, 1968, the following was part of the record:

Mr. Conley: . . . Havana radio summarized another telephone interview it said it had with you, and this is not a literal translation, as I understand it, of your words. It is a summary by Havana radio, which they broadcast, which we picked up and which has been translated again, and if I may read this to you and then ask you if it substantially states what you said at that time:

"U.S. Pacifist Leader David Dellinger declared in Chicago that the Heroic fight of the Cuban people today serves as an inspiration to those who fight in the United States to put an end to the criminal hand of the Government of Washington. Dellinger granted Radio Habana a telephonic interview in connection with the demonstrations in Chicago that aim at halting the U.S. aggression in Vietnam.

"He added that the demonstrators had been brutally treated by tens of thousands of policemen and soldiers mobilized in Chicago. The U.S. leader also said that millions of his fellow-citizens had lost their faith in the so-called U.S. democratic system and that they have decided to fight to end the war and to do away with poverty, exploitation, and racism in their home country.

"Dellinger who is president of the National Committee of Mobilization against the War in Vietnam and publisher of the Magazine *Liberation* said that the official position of the Yankee Government in the Paris talks is false and hypocritical. You cannot ask the victim and the aggressor to reduce their military operations at the same time, said David Dellinger, and he added: the one side is fighting for the home country and for its liberation and the other side is trying to curb the aspirations of that people.

"After pointing out that people in the United States are becoming aware of what is really happening in Cuba, the prominent U.S. pacifist stated: If one appreciates both the heroism and the dynamism of the peoples of Vietnam and Cuba, one draws from two sources of enormous capacity.

"David Dellinger concluded his statements made by phone to Radio Habana Cuba with these words: "We, Americans, are determined to liberate our country in the same way; may we also assure you of our solidarity."

Dellinger admitted he had been interviewed by Radio Havana, but said that some of the phrases were not his phrases and that he "was not suggesting that we should go into the Grand Canyon or the Rockies and organize a guerrilla force which would attempt to overthrow the United States."

But why should Dellinger or anyone else do such a thing when it is so much easier to work in the groves of academe, convenient to TV stations whose crews are ready to move on a moment's notice to cover "wars of liberation"?

When on May 7, 1970, the New Mobe brought hordes of demonstrators to Washington in an attempt to intimidate the administration after the Cambodian move, its leaders produced a mixed bag. With the many sincere Americans were a few whose sincerity could well be questioned—people obviously dedicated "to destroy the imperialist monster from within," to quote H. Rap Brown. Their message, repeating the goals set by the Tricontinental Conference held in Havana "to demand an immediate cessation of the war in Vietnam," got a nationwide hearing. And why not, when the festivities were graced by such world-renowned leaders as Jerry Rubin, David Dellinger, Jane Fonda, Senator Javits, Shirley MacLaine, Senator Goodell, Ben Spock, Abbie Hoffman and Coretta King?

But with all the ballyhoo and despite all the tumult on campuses during the preceding week, something went wrong. The American people obviously failed to get the message being beamed at them by Big Media and Big Men on Campus—that *all* America had swung violently against President Nixon for sending troops into Cambodia. The same issue of the *Washington Post* that described in depth the big confrontation staged by the New Mobe carried on page two a story datelined Princeton, New Jersey. It started: "A majority of Americans, 57 percent, gave President Nixon a vote of confidence for his handling of the Presidency in a survey conducted following his occasion to send U. S. troops into Cambodia." This Gallop poll report showed that the President's popularity had been climbing since a low of 53 percent had been reported late in March.

CHAPTER SEVEN

The In-Things

A common charge made against American society is that it is sick. This is part of the present-day liberal credo, and it is carried to extremes by revolutionaries who insist that the sickness is terminal.

This nation is obviously suffering certain aches and pains but it is far from being *in extremis,* even though there are some who like to think so. Like greedy heirs waiting to seize control of a vast estate, these vulturous nephews and nieces of Uncle Sam listen eagerly for his death rattle, and do everything in their power to induce it.

Actually they are the ones who are sick, and much that is wrong with the American body politic can be attributed to these people who attack it like cancerous cells. Indeed, if America were as sick as many of these, we would indeed have reason to worry.

Television provides a constant procession of these unfortunates, for a reason advanced by Edwin Newman of NBC. Addressing the Board of Governors of the National Conference of Christians and Jews, he said: "When we show students demonstrating on campus, people ask us why we don't show the students who are not demonstrating. That is like saying that when we show a flood we need to balance it by showing areas where they are having pretty weather."

Unfortunately, all that emphasis on stormy weather and floods is bound to have a bad effect. A half-century ago there was a fad that developed from a formula devised by a French psychotherapist,

Émile Coué. Millions of people went around saying to themselves, "Day by day, in every way, I am getting better and better." Many were convinced that this self-hypnosis worked, and maybe it did.

Today we are being given the Coué treatment in reverse. We are told that we are getting worse day by day, but this is not self-hypnosis. It is being induced by those "floods" mentioned by Newman, unrelieved by any pleasant weather, and it shapes up in the following:

A fantastically rising crime rate, particularly for such crimes of violence as murder, rape, armed robbery and assault.

A growing use of narcotics, mind-warping drugs and marijuana.

Cities that are unsafe by day or night.

Mobs that threaten violence at the least provocation.

Sexual promiscuity and a growing tolerance of sexual perversion.

Aimless mobs with the time and money to travel, by tens of thousands, to rock festivals, love-ins, anti-war demonstrations and other happenings from coast to coast.

Open warfare waged against those charged with maintaining law and order, and with our courts.

Actions designed to outrage—insults to the flag, use of the foulest obscenities, public sexual acts, defecation, etc.

Widespread circulation of hard-core pornography in the form of books, periodicals, motion pictures and stage productions.

Subversion of the young by radical teachers who substitute indoctrination for education.

Abject cowardice, portrayed as idealism, as young men flee to Canada, Sweden and elsewhere to escape military service.

The establishment of ghettoes of permissiveness such as Haight-Ashbury and Greenwich Village where young people become the prey of degenerates, dope pushers, thieves, etc.

Reckless disregard of the rights of others as teachers, trainmen, postal employees, policemen and firemen walk off their jobs.

Politicians who set poor examples by greedy salary grabs.

Organized crime growing bigger and more formidable as profits from crime permit it to gain control of legitimate business and venal public officials.

A tendency to sneer at things that were once considered admirable—love of country, devotion to God, honesty, morality, loyalty, integrity, responsibility, ambition, thrift, sobriety and respect for duly constituted authority.

Many reasons have been advanced for the rapid upsurge of these developments, which threaten to tear apart the very fabric of our civilization. Basic to them all is one provided by Alberta Engvall Siegel, of Stanford University. In a paper published in *Mass Media and Violence,* a staff report to the National Commission on the Causes and Prevention of Violence, Dr. Siegel made the point that "every civilization is only twenty years from barbarism." That is how much time we have to civilize the babies born into our culture, and in two short decades those new arrivals on earth must be taught many things, not the least of which are morality, decency, respect for the rights of others, customs and traditional values. Over the centuries these things were taught by the elders—parents, teachers, clergymen and others, but today new methods are gaining the ascendancy, and the most powerful of these is television.

Unfortunately, the tremendous teaching potential of television has been sadly perverted, possibly because those who control it have ideas and ethics different from those who used to teach the young. An amusing example of the results of the new teaching was cited by Dr. Siegel. A few years ago, she said, college students played a question-and-answer game called Trivia. Contestants were quizzed on things they had learned from radio, television, comic books and popular songs while growing up. The students showed they had learned a very great deal indeed, but most of it was rubbish. The winner of an intercollegiate Trivia contest staged at Columbia University credited his achievement to his "garbage-filled mind."

With some reason Dr. Siegel asked, "Is it fanciful to imagine that there may be a relation between the Trivia game at Columbia in 1967 and the violence at Columbia in 1968? Where did the students learn the attitudes and the aggressive behaviors that they vented against the police? Where did they learn the implicit values that seemed to justify their expressing what may be entirely legitimate grievances in such profoundly anti-social ways?"

Other questions could be asked. Somewhere along the way had there not been a shocking failure to impart some ideas of morality, decency, respect for the rights of others and for traditional values? In previous times such concepts seemed to be transmitted more effectively from generation to generation. Possibly that communications gap we keep hearing about is actually a result of improper use of the communications media.

Dr. S. I. Hayakawa, of San Francisco State College, who is probably the nation's foremost expert on barbarians who never grew up, used a fairy tale to describe television's role in the making of youthful minds. He likened it to a powerful sorcerer who took children away from their parents for several hours a day. The magician amused them by conjuring up a fascinating dream world in which the children lived happily and without problems for several years. Sometimes parents tried to break the spell, but they were no match for the sorcerer. He had the children completely in his power.

"Is it any wonder," asked Dr. Hayakawa, "that some of the children, as they grew to adolescence, turned out to be strangers in their own homes?"

In this connection, studies show that the spell cast by the "sorcerer" is strongest among children of the poor. In the Progress Report of the National Commission on the Causes and Prevention of Violence to President Johnson, dated January 9, 1969, this statement appears:

"The media habits of teenagers show that they are even heavier users of television than their parents. Moreover, recent studies have indicated that 40 percent of the poor black children and 30 percent of the poor white children (compared with 15 percent of the middle-class white children) believe that what they see on television is an accurate portrayal of what life in America is all about."

This has special significance when considered in connection with a statement issued by the Surgeon General's Scientific Advisory

Committee on Television and Social Behavior on September 23, 1969. This concluded that "violence on television encourages real violence, especially among the children of poor, disorganized families."

The timing of the rise of crime in this country is interesting when considered in relation to the growth of television. By 1953 there were almost 20 million television sets in American homes, a number which represented a fantastic growth in the short period of five or six years since the late 1940s, when television sets became commercially available. Many of the children who grew up with those and later TV sets are now in college. They might be called the first television generation. The great majority of these young people are of course decent and responsible, but all too many have been conditioned by influences and indoctrination that have produced results that bode no good for the future of the country. If not sick, these young people appear to be highly susceptible to sickness.

Obviously not all the germs of that sickness swarmed out of the Pandora's box we call television. Two other powerful influences come to mind, and sociologists may think of others. Curiously, our age of permissiveness in child-rearing coincided with the publication of a book by the ubiquitous Dr. Benjamin Spock. This book, *Common Sense Book of Baby and Child Care,* counseled parents to refrain from disciplining their offspring. Originally issued in 1946, the Spock baby book has long been a bestseller, with 16,000,000 copies sold as of 1965. Many are convinced that it helped produce a generation of "spoiled brats." As everyone who watches television is aware, the baby doctor is now making a career out of advocating another form of permissiveness. A loquacious if not eloquent opponent of the war in Vietnam, the erstwhile pediatrician can be found all over the television dial and all over the country, holding forth on the wickedness of the war being waged against the Communists.

Jerry Rubin, the Yippie leader who has been described as "bushy-haired, unkempt, obscene, drug-sodden, many times arrested, few times jailed," is a product of the kind of permissiveness that has been widely advocated during the past two decades. In an article in *Esquire* ("The Making of a Yippie," by J. Anthony Lucas, November

1969), Rubin tells of the loving care that was lavished on him by his doting parents:

> They had total dedication to me. . . . I knew that if I cried I'd get my way; if I insisted I'd get my way; if I screamed I'd get my way. It was really total toleration, total permissiveness. . . . It's a kind of key as to why I could become so rebellious. Many of the tactics I now use I learned at home. I learned how to play one parent off against another, because my mother didn't really approve of some of my father's methods. . . . I'm really convinced that the whole of my recent activity in the Movement has been a playing out on a massive political scale of the things I learned in the family.

One may well wonder how many of the obnoxious "youth leaders" who arrogantly make "non-negotiable" demands of universities and the government are essentially spoiled brats. Having gotten everything they wanted by throwing tantrums at home, they think they can continue to get their way from the world at large by shouting, sulking, screaming, making threats and stamping their feet in anger. Instead of putting such people in jail—although they seldom end up in jail, thanks to slick lawyers—it might be more realistic to view them as cases of arrested development. As such, they should be put back in nursery school, to start their education all over again, without the customary permissiveness.

The church, which once exercised considerable influence in the training of the young, has also become permissive. Addressing a gathering at Fort Lauderdale, Florida, early in May, Vice President Agnew told how today's children "of affluent, permissive, upper-middle-class parents" are "dropped off by their parents at Sunday school to hear the 'modern' gospel from a 'progressive' preacher more interested in fighting pollution than fighting evil—one of those pleasant clergymen who lifts his weekly sermons out of old newsletters from a National Council of Churches that has cast morality and theology aside as 'not relevant' and set as its goal on earth the recognition of Red China and the preservation of the Florida alligator."

In the classroom a general aura of permissiveness is likely to prevail. Teachers are required to treat their young charges with the utmost delicacy and restraint. Any attempt at discipline, even when obviously called for, is likely to bring a violent reaction from Spock-minded parents and threats of legal action from liberal crusaders of the American Civil Liberties Union, who will fight for permissiveness right up to the U.S. Supreme Court.

Most of the discipine that used to be considered part of the educational process has been eliminated through another kind of influence that has had a profound effect on today's youth. This is the product of various left-wing disciples of Dr. John Dewey, the highly touted educational innovator who held forth at Teacher's College, Columbia University. Dewey is looked upon as the father of "progressive education," but educationists who once loudly proclaimed the wonders of this fad are now inclined to be reticent about it. Indeed, Dr. Dewey shortly before he died at the age of 92 expressed dismay at the way in which his principles had been distorted by some of his enthusiastic disciples into a notion of unlimited freedom from discipline for students. In his obituary the following anecdote appears:

"Never was he so shocked, Dr. Dewey said, as when he entered a nursery school in which his son was enrolled and found another child on top of the boy in a fight. When he asked the teacher why she permitted it she replied:

" 'Why that's progressive education. Your son isn't going to meet gentlemen all his life.' "

It was not only permissiveness that Dewey's left-wing followers insinuated into our educational system. As VIPs in the educational hierarchy based at Teachers' College, they had easy access to the nation's public schools, which they hoped to use to promote what they called "a new social order." Their basic premises are similar in many ways to the revolutionary concepts of today's New Left, though they used different tactics. A manifesto under the title "A Call to the Teachers of the Nation by the Committee of the Progressive Education Association on Social and Economic Problems," issued in July 1933, called on teachers "keenly aware of the injustice and misery wrought by the existing economic system" to do something about it, and to work for "a better social order" in which democracy must be "rephrased in terms of the collectivist reality."

It would be an exaggeration to say that the Progressive Education Association spoke for the teachers of the nation, any more than it would be correct to say that SDS speaks for the nation's college students today. Most teachers had little sympathy for the radical ideas of this vociferous group of educationists who wanted to use the schools to effect a social revolution. However, it would be equally erroneous to say that the PEA exercised no influence. Its adherents held strategic positions which they used to further their concepts. In time these concepts became evident in ways other than that exemplified by the nursery school brawl witnessed by Dr. Dewey, and a common sight today.

The kind of competition that produces leaders in a democracy was de-emphasized. In some schools, report cards were abolished or so changed that they were little more than terse notes from teacher to parent, giving only a general idea of the child's progress or lack of it. Children found out they could get by without exerting themselves, and in some places the system was so lax that students barely able to read or write were graduated from high school.

Significant omissions became evident in the kind of education being promoted by the frontier thinkers, as they called themselves. America's glorious past and the reasons for its greatness were glossed over or sketchily covered in an academic mishmash called social studies, which instead laid considerable emphasis on such liberal fetishes as the United Nations. Today few colleges require American history credits for admission.

Little wonder that when many of our young people get to college they are poorly prepared for the academic hucksters they often find there. In fact, the academic woods are full of them. As just one indication of this, the annual meeting of the American Historical Association, held in Washington, D.C., December 28–30, 1969, was disrupted when a caucus of radical historians walked out. This group, headed by Staughton Lynd, an ultra-leftist who has come under attack for his dealings with Hanoi, went to the Justice Department to protest the war in Vietnam and moves being made against the Black Panthers.

Subsequently, Lynd's radical comrades put him up for president of this important academic organization; he received approximately 400 votes and his opponent approximately 1,000. Lynd's followers represent a minority, certainly, but it is a formidable minority, and you can figure out the kind of education in history that this group is providing. You may be reasonably sure that the students subjected to such historians will never turn out to be superpatriots or flagwavers.

All of which may help to explain some of the peculiar aspects of higher education that puzzle so many parents with children in college, and others who watch student dissenters on television.

While acknowledging the contributions of such doctors as Lynd, Spock and Dewey to our present predicament, we must give television the credit it has earned in its three turbulent decades. J. Edgar Hoover, who has to cope with a rising tide of lawlessness and who, presumably, has some understanding of the reasons for the growing crime wave, said this:

> Entertainment and communications media exert a strong influence upon our national tastes, standards, and even our pattern of conduct. Television, which reaches into the nursery and playroom as well, has been a powerful force in the lives of our youth.
>
> Although the television industry has control over the programs it presents, the extent of violence depicted in many shows is unbelievable. Viewers are constantly bombarded with a steady stream of sex, sadism, and criminal acts that, through repetition, might appear to some as normal behavior.

To put it another way, to those who regularly watch television, including millions of children, the in-things are violence, sex, the use of narcotics and alcohol, and anything else that will provide personal gratification and pleasure. Lessons in hedonism pour forth constantly from the boob tube, steadily eroding the nation's spiritual fiber and stirring a growing tide of lawlessness.

When Newton Minow, chairman of the FCC during the Kennedy administration, made his famous May 9, 1961, speech in which he referred to television as "a vast wasteland," he said something else which is not as widely quoted as that phrase: "When television is good, nothing—not the theater, not the magazines or newspaper—nothing is better. But when television is bad, nothing is worse."

He invited people to study TV closely for themselves, then said:

> You will see a procession of game shows, violence, audience participation shows, formula comedies about totally unbelievable families, blood and thunder, mayhem, violence, sadism, murder, Western bad men, Western good men, private eyes, gangsters, more violence and cartoons. And, endlessly, commercials—many screaming, cajoling and offending. And most of all, boredom. True, you will see a few things you will enjoy. But they will be very, very few. And if you think I exaggerate, try it.

The Minow statement aroused almost as much anger among television officials as Spiro Agnew's more recent comments did about the medium. But after almost a decade, the cultural wasteland Minow described has changed little, if at all.

Not long after that appraisal was made, there was another, this by Judge Frank J. Kronenberg, president of the New York County Judges Association. The judge addressed himself to television's effect on the young, telling how it made children indifferent to death, suffering and sadism.

"Day after day," he said, "our children are exposed to, injected, and fed with principles completely repugnant to a successful posterity. Hour after hour, simply by the flick of a switch, a child can see a swiftly flowing panorama of human misery, despair, homicide and thievery. Exposing children to such violence can be compared to taking children to public tortures and hangings in medieval times."

Judge Kronenberg concluded his remarks with this: "In the opinion of many, America's worst menace is not Communism, but is the threatened destruction of American youth by the mass media of television, spewing crime and violence to such an extent that the virtues of peace, love and honesty are ignored."

Granted, the judge was talking about a situation that existed a decade ago, but recent studies show the same pattern. Senator Pastore's committee which investigated television programming presented testimony, in the form of a *Saturday Review* article written by Richard L. Tobin, "as evidence that television shows today are dosing the public . . . with a flood of unrelieved one-dimensional, dehumanized violence which lacks commentary and proportion."

The article stated:

> A few weeks ago we took the time to monitor TV programs on the three major networks and the local independent stations and we found scarcely a show in which the most blatant cruelty and obscene sadism were not *an integral part of plot and production.* [Emphasis added.] In the course of an 8-hour exposure to ABC, CBS and NBC, as well as half a dozen local outlets, we marked down 93 specific incidents involving sadistic brutality, murder, cold-blooded killing, sexual cruelty, and related sadism so much in the vogue of mass media nowadays. . . . In the course of this 8-hour vista . . . we encountered seven different kinds of pistols and revolvers, three varieties of rifle, three distinct brands of shotgun, half a dozen daggers and stilettos, two types of machete, one butcher's cleaver, a broadax, rapiers galore, an ancient broadsword, a posse of sabers, an electric prodder and a guillotine. Men—and women and even children—were shot by gunpowder, burned at the stake, tortured over live coals, trussed and beaten in relays, dropped into molten sugar, cut to ribbons in color, repeatedly kneed in the groin, beaten while being held defenseless by other hoodlums, forcibly drowned, whipped with a leather belt, and dealt with in many other ways before our very eyes—and the eyes of hundreds of thousands of children who must have been watching some part of what we saw.

It would be erroneous to say that the industry is not concerned about such criticism, which keeps occurring. For one thing, it is bad public relations and the sort of agitation that often results in official investigations that in turn tarnish corporate images still more. But though network officials express concern, they argue that there is no real, scientific proof that the all-pervasive violence and general lawlessness portrayed on television are reflected in real life. It is quite possible that they believe this, too.

Experts on psychology and social scientists have been arguing about this matter for years. Committees have been appointed, extensive studies conducted, tests made, and books and articles written based on the findings. However, the most that can be said with absolute certainty is that there are two schools of thought on the subject. Some experts hold that viewers, particularly susceptible types, respond to violence on the screen with violence on their part —a case of "monkey see, monkey do." On the other hand, some experts maintain that television produces a catharsis effect, that viewers work off their aggressive drives through exposure to aggressive TV content. Television people are inclined to favor the catharsis hypothesis, understandably, even though in doing so they show an obvious inconsistency.

This inconsistency was noted in a statement by Dr. Peter J. Lejins, professor of sociology at the University of Maryland, published in the interim report of Senator Dodd's Subcommittee to Investigate Juvenile Delinquency:

> The assertions that crime, violence, and horror movies and TV shows do not have any or only an extremely small delinquency-inducing effect on children usually cite the failure of all efforts by the social scientists to prove any such effect. One is invited to believe that in spite of the tremendous number of exposures to such programs, the children emerge hardly affected by this specific content. It is paradoxical that the moment one leaves the discussion of these particular programs and turns to audiovisual communications of other contents and purposes, one is faced with an avalanche of claims of how tremendously effective these media are in teaching subject matter, changing attitudes, modifying people's values, and so forth.

Not to mention the claims made for television as an effective advertising medium. Indeed, if television has so little influence on what children do, it is hard to understand why it does not give in to the ladies of Action for Children's Television (ACT) who want commercials banned from children's programs. If the medium cannot persuade the kiddies to buy certain cereals, soda, candy, toys and other desirable things, why should it take money for commercials pushing such items?

After extensive hearings, the Kefauver Subcommittee to Investigate Juvenile Delinquency held that television did contribute to juvenile delinquency, and issued a report indicating that it felt television violence could be potentially harmful to young viewers. In 1964 the hearings held by Senator Thomas Dodd reported finding more violence on television and said a relationship had been established between televised crime and violence on the one hand, and anti-social attitudes and behavior among juvenile viewers on the other. While praising television's achievements in some areas, the report declared, "yet it seems clear that television has been functioning as what an informed critic has termed 'a school for violence.'" The report by Senator Pastore's Subcommittee on Communications, which conducted hearings in 1969, has not yet been issued, but an equivocal statement issued by the senator provides a clue that nothing much will result from his efforts. He recommends that the Surgeon General appoint a committee, to be made up of the usual "distinguished men and women," and the matter is likely to rest there for the foreseeable future.

In the course of various hearings, interesting cases were cited to show cause and effect. During the Pastore hearings, Senator Hartke declared: "You may recall, I don't know if you do, but a few years ago there was an intention to portray terror on the tracks, which dealt with a subway murder, in which the transit authority of New York City requested that it not be put on and objected to it. They had not had any murders on the transit up to that time. Do you recall that? The next morning after that was presented they had their first murder. Does this just happen to be coincidental?"

Another example of cause and effect, which obviously was not coincidental, developed from an NBC-filmed drama called *The Doomsday Flight,* presented on December 13, 1966. This told the story of a deranged man, a mad genius, who placed a bomb on a plane. Tragedy was averted when the plane landed at an altitude different from that which would have triggered an explosion.

Learning of the scheduled broadcast, and being more skeptical of human nature than benign TV officials, the Air Line Pilots Association urged NBC to keep it off the air. The network refused. While the program was still being aired, one airline received a bomb threat, and within twenty-four hours there were four similar threats. Within a week, eight bomb calls were received by U.S. airlines, including TWA, Eastern, Pan-Am and Northwest.

At the time of the Dodd hearings, Rev. Joseph E. Schieder, director of the Catholic Youth Organization, made an impassioned plea to stop televising violence. He said,

> In our regular dealings with great numbers of youth, the vast majority of whom would be labeled as "outstanding" or "good," we find in the year 1961 young people possessed of an almost appalling sophistication. They are accustomed to the idea of vice, of violence, of the element of the brutal in life to a degree that stuns. Now we are far from applauding the vague and naive young person; nevertheless, it is a serious matter when one encounters in fairly virtuous young people a tolerance of evil induced by nothing more nor less than the diet of terror fed them by the mass communications media—and more forcefully by television.

Monsignor Schieder then told of a brutal murder, that of a 16-year-old girl. She had gone out with some teenage friends and they returned at 9:15 p.m., leaving her near her home. However, she never made it to her house. The next morning her horribly raped and beaten body was found. Three days later, Msgr. Schieder said, the sheriff called him to say the mystery had been solved. The priest talked to the young man who had murdered her. He explained how and why he did it. His reason—he felt the girl had questioned his manhood and he had to prove himself.

"I said, 'Son, I had the misfortune of viewing that body.' I said, 'What in the name of God could have possessed you, inspired you, prompted you to do something like that?'

"He said, 'A television program.'

"It is awfully hard to listen to something like that."

In the course of the various hearings there were a few lighter moments. When Newton Minow, then chairman of the FCC, testified before the Dodd committee, he told of a letter he had received from a mother of six children. She reported that when she told her 4-year-old his grandfather had died, the youngster asked, "Who shot him?" The Pastore hearings were enlivened by testimony concerning the public-service announcement that asks viewers, "Do you know where your son is tonight?" One woman wrote to the station, answering the question:

"I know precisely where my boy is tonight. He is looking at a dirty movie on your station."

In addition to suggesting felonious ideas to impressionable people —a group which may include all those who respond to TV commercials—the medium sometimes provides helpful hints of a kind that can prove helpful to criminally minded viewers. One such case is mentioned by Theodore White in his book telling of the 1968 Presidential campaign. In Los Angeles one station did some enterprising reporting of the Watts riots by using a helicopter that carried cameras right to the center of the disturbance. Viewers could see exactly where the action was and what was going on down below. They could also see looters making off with some highly desirable merchandise—appliances, furniture, television sets, etc. Commenting on this, Mr. White asked, "When does reporting go beyond reporting and become a disturbance factor itself?"

However, television bears another responsibility in the way it provides a powerful incentive for criminal acts—justification. TV productions go by a code of sorts, and although this has no relation to reality or legality, it is taken seriously by the simpleminded viewer who confuses the real with the unreal. Such viewers know that violence is justified as long as it is employed in a good cause, such as righting a wrong. The pioneer in a TV drama who draws a bead on a renegade Indian, or on a cattle rustler, or on a blackhearted scoundrel who poisons the water hole, is entirely within his rights. The private eye stalking someone who must be bad because he looks evil does no wrong when he breaks into that man's house to find incriminating evidence. Nor is there anything wrong with beating the aforesaid suspect to a pulp if he intrudes on the shamus while he is doing his job. The end justifies the means.

The Task Force on Media and Violence, mentioned earlier in this chapter, found another disquieting factor in the dramatic programs it studied. These offerings not only placed great emphasis on violence but even rewarded it:

> One of the clearest content analysis findings is that the violent characters in television portrayals are often rewarded for their behavior. Reward comes most directly to "good guys" who often achieve success through violence. In addition, the use of violence is not often punished in the television world. Thus, if viewers infer from their exposure that violence not only goes largely unpunished but is rewarded, they may be more likely to transfer this inference into an expectation that they might be rewarded or go unpunished for using violence.

In the report of the hearings of the Dodd committee, a statement by Dr. Isidore Ziferstein, a psychiatrist, bears this out:

> The values presented are often not the kind that the child can identify positively. The interpersonal relations of the characters are often destructive. Life is presented as all conflict, strife, war. Science is shown as destructive, with the stereotype of the "mad scientist" who is busy inventing ever more destructive gadgets. There is rarely an attempt to show the constructive, beneficial aspects of science. The heroes usually operate outside the law. They use extralegal, violence tactics—to attain worthy ends, of course. Thus is inculcated the cult of the omnipotent, infallible "strong man," the "fuehrer." These values do not help our children develop confidence in the possibilities of cooperation, of friendly relations among men, of a peaceful world. They tend to add to the burden of neurotic anxiety by giving the child the feeling of general insecurity, because they shake his confidence in the reliability of his parents, his friends, and the society in which he lives.
>
> Once we recognize television's great power, that it is potent medicine, we may be more willing to make the necessary efforts to see to it that our children get the good medicine and not the bad.

What is some of that bad medicine so liberally dispensed by TV? It is often condemned merely as "violence," which is an oversimplification. That word conjures up a picture of a fictional portrayal of some criminal act that is soon imitated by an impressionable youngster. Actually there is much more to it than that, and it is not only fictional fare that causes trouble.

Because of the premium it places on the sensational, television has given the impression that many abnormal things are actually the norm, and it has displayed a marked reluctance to point out that some of these things are morally wrong. Television's code of ethics seems to be that the only time something is wrong is when it can be physically harmful or cause a severe financial loss. Thus, mainlining heroin is a bad thing because it obviously destroys the body. On the other hand, the smoking of marijuana rates only mild censure, if that, because there is some doubt about the extent of the physical harm it causes.

There was an excellent example of this kind of thinking in an NBC production that dealt with venereal disease. This was portrayed as a great and prevalent evil because of the fact that it exacts a fearsome toll in physical suffering and can lead to death. However, the promiscuity that is the major cause of the growing rate of venereal disease was viewed with the utmost equanimity. The impression given was that everyone must understand how to cope with syphilis and gonorrhea because it can interfere with the pursuit of happiness, much like an unwanted pregnancy.

However, a person who is critical of this point of view is usually dismissed as an anachronism suffering from "the Puritan ethic." To liberal opinion makers, such a person is the modern-day version of the Biblical leper, crying "unclean" because he has a dirty mind.

Obviously television cannot ignore such phenomena as the mammoth gatherings of aimless, self-indulgent and affluent young people at such places as Woodstock and Fort Lauderdale. Nor can it ignore the disgraceful ghettoes of permissiveness that have come to flourish in Haight-Ashbury, Greenwich Village and elsewhere. But in its presentation of these things, TV has given them a halo that they certainly do not deserve. This of course makes them in-things for countless other young people. It would be interesting to know how many more Woodstocks we will see as promoter types see how well publicized the original was by an overly impressed media. It would be interesting to know how many impressionable youngsters have drifted to Haight-Ashbury and Greenwich Village, to be corrupted there, because what went on there was glamorously presented as the in-thing.

It would be refreshing, for a change, if television were to show something different. Instead of depicting American youth at rock festivals, driving dune buggies, surfing, entertaining lovely companions in expensive sports cars and otherwise enjoying *la dolce vita,* TV might consider showing something more realistic. This would call for some talent, and maybe television does not have that kind of talent, but it could perform a tremendous service if it portrayed American kids as they really are. They are the ones who should be held up as examples, not the ones we keep seeing on television.

Edwin Newman notwithstanding, many Americans would like to see some "pretty weather" for a change, instead of the oft-contrived claptrap that floods from television sets.

It is sometimes argued that television is a force for good because it usually makes the point that crimes does not pay in the long run. That is true, but in the course of making that point there is likely to be considerable sex and violence of an interesting though extra-legal nature. Impressionable people seeing the process may decide that the game is worth the candle, not to mention the risk. However, crime does pay in television and it pays well. In the course of the Dodd hearings, a letter from one TV writer to another was introduced as "Exhibit 91." It started as follows: "Edward Gibbon devoted a lifetime to writing *The Decline and Fall of the Roman Empire.* For this monumental and superb classic he earned less than you and I are paid each week for the impeccable mediocrities we foist on the suffering television viewer. . . ."

Still, it could be argued that Gibbon was only writing *about* the fall of an empire, long after the fact, whereas some of our handsomely paid writers of TV mediocrities are actually contributing to our own nation's decline and fall by making decadence of one kind or another the in-thing.

Those who defend the violence that pervades television invariably get around to the argument that all literature portrays violence. It is found in the Bible, in Shakespeare, in the Greek tragedies, in the great Russian novels, and even in Mother Goose. Certainly there is violence in the great books and the great plays, and some of its is gory. There is, however, a significant difference. Those masterpieces were presented with artistry and perspective. The violence found in Shakespeare was set forth not as sensationalism, to shock and terrorize, but as a means of exposing the evil in human nature and of showing the suffering that follows when that evil surfaces. Noteworthy, in this connection, is the following, which appears in an analysis prepared for the Pastore committee:

"This, then, is the final difference: great literature employs violence in the service of reason; television violence panders not to reason, but to its opposite—the irrational side of human nature. Great literature makes the mind work; violence exploited for its own sake stirs up the instincts, the aggressive passions which must be controlled if man is to live in civilized society."

This country is not the only one that is faced with the problem. Even the Soviet Union finds television violence overdone, as witness the following poem, recently appearing in a Soviet nursery school journal, under the title "Is It Different at Your House?"

Nursery school is out for the day,
    Sonny is home—but refuses to play
Picture books, toys do not tempt him, you see
    He's waiting for Daddy to start the TV.

Whatever the picture, no matter how gory
    He won't be forbidden to follow the story.
His Mommie will tell you, why not, saints alive,
    He's not a teenager—he's only just 5!

And so he's permitted to view by the hour
    Whatever is beamed from the studio tower.
Agog, overwrought to the umpteenth degree
    He watches disasters and shootings with glee.

He's glued to his seat till the screen has gone dead
>And finally Mommie will tuck him in bed . . .
The house is in darkness, the family sleeps
>When the nightmares begin. The child tosses and weeps
He dreams of the chase, of sword and of fire
>He chokes, he has started to shake and perspire.

Next morning he's fretful, a whiner and mean
>And who is the villain? The TV machine.

So please keep in mind, all you daddies and mamas,
>Kids need children's programs, not bloodthirsty dramas.

CHAPTER EIGHT

The Kingmakers

NOT so many years ago Presidential candidates traveled about the country by rail, greeting crowds who gathered at sidings and saying a few more or less well-chosen words to them. The last of the major "whistle-stop" campaigns was that of President Harry S. Truman, running for reelection in 1948. Fighting an uphill battle against Thomas E. Dewey, Truman traveled more than 30,000 miles delivering hundreds of his famous "give 'em hell" speeches.

In today's campaigning a candidate can address himself to many more millions than Truman did, through a single television appearance. In a terse testimonial to the medium's effectiveness, Robert S. Kennedy once said he would rather have thirty seconds on network television than have his views set forth in every newspaper in the world.

However, television exacts a price for such exposure, and a very high price. Though not all of this is financial, TV costs have become so important in modern politicking that the day of the poor boy attaining high office in the United States is a thing of the past—unless the poor boy has a great many rich and influential friends who would like to see him in office. As matters now stand, only a candidate with the vast financial resources of a Kennedy or a Rockefeller can afford to pay his own way.

What can be accomplished with family riches was illustrated by the actions of the Kennedy family at the time Robert F. Kennedy

entered the Presidential primaries in 1968. This belated move inc-
ensed the followers of Senator Eugene McCarthy, and their anger
was not assuaged by the Kennedy family's spending spree. The senator's mother, Rose Kennedy, staunchly defended their investment in
high politics, saying: "It's our money and we're free to spend it in
any way we please. It's part of this campaign business. If you have
money, you spend it to win. And the more you can afford, the more
you'll spend. The Rockefellers are like us. We both have money to
spend on our campaigns. It's something that is not regulated. Therefore, it's not unethical."

Certainly such spending to buy office is not illegal under the law
as it now stands. But whether it is fair to candidates whose families
are not blessed with hundreds of millions of dollars is highly debata-
ble.

The great political sweepstakes of 1968—national, state and local
—are estimated to have cost more than a quarter-billion dollars.
That figure could have gone even higher but, as *U.S. News & World
Report* pointed out, "the politicians stopped spending because they
could beg or borrow no more money." The way in which the Democrats ran out of money and credit is reflected in their deficit of
$8,000,000, which Lawrence O'Brien was hired to help liquidate.

Dr. Herbert E. Alexander, director of the Citizens Research Foundation in Princeton, N.J., has stated that in 1968 the Presidential
candidates spent approximately $55 million as against $35 million in
1964. Much of this was spent in bitter primary campaigns waged by
Eugene McCarthy, Ronald Reagan, Nelson Rockefeller, Richard
Nixon, Robert F. Kennedy, Hubert Humphrey and George Rom-
ney. Nor was George Wallace a piker. His total expenditures came
to $5.8 million.

Much of this huge outpouring of money went into television and
radio. Dr. Alexander places the 1968 figure at $50 million.

Senator John Pastore uttered an understandable complaint when
he pointed out that there was little point in spending $2 million to
be elected to an office paying only $42,500 a year, and other political
spending makes as little economic sense. It is said to cost at least a
million dollars to run a statewide campaign in any of the nation's

large or medium states, and upwards of $100,000 for a campaign in a contested election for congressman. Some of Senator McCarthy's reported disillusionment with politics may be attributed to a report that his unsuccessful campaign cost more than $5 million, leaving the senator and his followers with an indebtedness of $400,000.

Faced with such formidable figures, politicians and others are trying to do something about the high cost of television campaigning. They feel, with justification, that they have been victimized. They not only pay the top rate for TV time but have to pay for it in advance. In a move to correct this, a bill prepared by Senator Pastore's Subcommittee on Communications provides for TV and radio debates between opposing candidates, but more important it provides that political time shall be sold at the "lowest unit rate" charged to anyone by the station.

This can mean a tremendous saving, since most regular advertisers receive discounts that are sometimes only a small fraction of what a one-time advertiser might pay. Amendments under consideration may mean further discounts, even on the "lowest unit rate," and placing a limit on the amount of money any candidate can spend on radio and TV. Other limitations being weighed would restrict the total amount of time any station could sell to a single candidate, including spot commercials of a minute or less.

The Twentieth Century Fund has come up with a different set of proposals. This plan calls for providing candidates with "Voters' Time" purchased with federal funds at half the usual rate. There would be at least six half-hour periods of prime time in the five weeks preceding an election and the political messages would be carried simultaneously by every radio and television station.

None of these plans has aroused any enthusiasm on the part of broadcasters. The idea of giving substantial discounts obviously does not appeal to them, and they probably visualize millions of viewers turning off their sets as politicians hold forth on all that cut-rate time. The Twentieth Century Fund proposal was cited as an imposition on viewers, since it gave them no choice during these half-hours but made them a captive audience for candidate X or Y. And there is no doubt that many TV viewers and radio listeners would resent finding X or Y holding forth on every channel.

If the industry and the politicians can work out some method of cutting the high cost of TV campaigning, it will solve only one political problem. The other is the one set forth by Spiro Agnew and mentioned in an earlier chapter: that the people who run Big Media demand conformity to their ideas, that they support politicians who go along with their ideas, and bitterly oppose those who disagree. This offers as good a reason as any for the way in which certain political faces keep showing up on television. It also may explain why certain politicians are either ignored or singled out for criticism and abuse. The way in which Lyndon Johnson was treated comes to mind, as does the vicious treatment accorded Barry Goldwater in 1964. However, there have been many others.

Probably the first coordinated press attack on a President was directed at President Hoover, long before television. The signals were called by Charles Michelson, a former newspaperman hired for the job by the Democratic National Committee. His job was to discredit Hoover. Michelson was able to persuade millions of Americans that Hoover was personally responsible for the hard times they were suffering, and that the only way to bring back good times was to turn him out and replace him with a Democrat. Unfortunately it was not that simple, and the falsity of the premise was eventually proved. Despite a succession of dramatic maneuvers, such as the NRA, the depression worsened. Prosperity returned only as an economic by-product of World War II.

Although Alfred E. Smith had earlier failed to gain the Presidency, he was the first Presidential candidate to be televised, the event taking place as he delivered his acceptance speech. The first President to speak before a TV camera was Franklin D. Roosevelt and the occasion was the opening of the New York World's Fair in 1939. TV convention coverage started the following year at the Republican National Convention, which nominated Wendell Willkie. Radio can take much of the credit for having made Willkie a national figure. One of the most popular programs of that time was a quiz show called *Information Please,* and Willkie appeared on it as a guest. His engaging personality and wit made a profound impression. Before long he was being discussed as a Presidential possibility, and at the convention his popular appeal won him the bid.

Liberals who wanted an unprecedented third term for FDR's administration sneered at Willkie as "a barefoot boy from Wall Street." President Roosevelt, whose third-term ambitions displeased many, received help of an electronic nature from a strategic quarter. Some of Mayor Kelly's "boys" stationed themselves in the Chicago convention hall basement and connected microphones to the public address system serving the delegates. Whenever Roosevelt's name was mentioned "the boys" broke into loud cheers, which were fed into the loudspeakers upstairs. Delegates were greatly impressed by this proof of President Roosevelt's tremendous popularity, and since the hoax was being broadcast, millions of Americans got the same impression. The President was of course nominated for a third term. At the time of his fourth-term election, a sampling of the electorate showed that 38 percent of the voters had been influenced by radio as against only 23 percent by the printed word.

Many reasons have been advanced for the Truman victory in 1948, after he had been counted out by many experts. However, it is possible that his slim victory margin may have been attained because Dewey did not take the advice of his image-makers. He had the services of a large advertising agency, Batten, Barton, Durstine & Osborne, available to him, but he disregarded their recommendations. They urged him to use a spot-announcement campaign on radio but he turned down the proposal and concentrated on formal broadcast speeches.

It was during the 1948–1952 term of President Truman that "McCarthyism" came to the fore, and millions of Americans came to know the senator through radio and television. Many liberals were disturbed as they saw how McCarthy was embarrassing people held in high esteem by them, but many other Americans were disturbed at something else. They became convinced that something was wrong with the news they were getting, since what they saw and heard on television often did not square with what they later read in their newspapers and magazines, or even heard discussed by commentators holding forth on the same stations.

Probably the most damaging blow against McCarthy was delivered by Edward R. Murrow on his *See It Now*. Many liberals hailed this as a milestone in television, but others saw it as a disturbing example of television's ability to distort when it wants to make a point. Murrow's presentation could be described as an animated Herblock cartoon. Writing in *Saturday Review* for April 24, 1954, Gilbert Seldes cited it as an example of the fallacy of equal time. The attack on McCarthy, he said, was "the product of some three years of experience in the handling of film clips, an art in which Murrow and his co-worker Fred Friendly have no peers." Given equal time by Murrow, McCarthy was no match for the masters and suffered accordingly. In protesting the program, Seldes, a liberal, was joined by liberal John Cogley of *Commonweal,* who said it "set a potentially dangerous precedent."

By way of contrast, Murrow's interview with J. Robert Oppenheimer was so laudatory that even Dorothy Schiff, the publisher of the ultra-liberal *New York Post* protested. In Mrs. Schiff's words, Murrow portrayed the scientist as "a hero and a martyr." No mention was made of the fact that Oppenheimer's wife, mistress and brother were Communists, that he had contributed substantial funds to the Party, and that he had lied under oath to security agents.

In view of such reporting, it is interesting to consider two statements about Murrow that appeared in a *New Yorker* Profile in 1953, written by Charles Wertenbaker. The author quoted a friend of Murrow's who said, "Ed never pushes his liberalism beyond a carefully calculated safety point." Another said, "He's much too clever to let you see what he's up to." Actually, Murrow was not that clever, and neither are his successors who consider him exemplary. Quite often, their liberalism is all too obvious.

In the 1952 Presidential campaign, personalities were more important than television as Adlai Stevenson was pitted against Dwight D. Eisenhower. Of the two, Stevenson was far more articulate, urbane and sophisticated. However, in 1952 the governor of Illinois was handicapped by his outspoken liberalism. Millions of Americans had become alarmed by charges of subversion in government, which had been underscored by such things as the Amerasia and Coplon spy cases, the McCarran hearings dealing with the Institute of Pacific Relations, and various aspects of the Korean War, notably the firing of General MacArthur.

Many voters decided they had had enough and felt that General Eisenhower would put an end to outrageous actions that many liberal leaders seemed to condone. Under President Eisenhower the country settled down; in 1956 he was reelected in a campaign in which television played only a minor role. The President was well aware of the importance of the medium, however, and was coached in its use.

In 1960 the role of television proved to be paramount when John F. Kennedy and Richard M. Nixon staged their historic series of four debates. These performances demonstrated the importance of the "image," as it is projected electronically. Nixon was of course aware of this, as he explains in his book *Six Crises:* "I knew, too, that how the candidates looked, to many viewers, was going to be a great deal more important than what they said."

On the first of the four debates, held on September 26, 1960, Nixon made a poor visual impression. He had been sick for weeks and he looked haggard. His dark beard was barely concealed by a light dusting of makeup, and allegedly on the advice on Henry Cabot Lodge, who could hardly be called on expert on the art of winning Presidential campaigns, he pulled his punches so as not to appear too aggressive.

John F. Kennedy, on the other hand, photographed well and he projected considerable charm and confidence. Confidence he should have had, for the efficient Kennedy staff had done his homework well for him. There was general agreement that the first of the debates went to Kennedy. Nixon did better in the other three but here the candidates were addressing smaller audiences. The first debate had a tremendous audience, estimated at 60 percent of all potential viewers, while the other three dropped off to an estimated 40 percent. To put it another way, approximately 20 million viewers who saw the first debate did not see the others.

Kennedy got an extra dividend from the debates, delivered by the media. As Nixon explains it in *Six Crises:* "Despite our best efforts, however, we were unable to make much impression on the press and radio commentators who were now spearheading the blitz. In the two weeks before Election Day, the newspapers and airwaves were full of predictions of everything from a close Kennedy victory to a Kennedy landslide."

What was being projected in print and over the air was a reflection in no small measure of the personal feelings of the press corps assigned to Vice President Nixon's campaign. Writing of this, Willard Edwards, Washington correspondent of the *Chicago Tribune,* stated:

> Ninety percent of the press corps, which ranged between 50 and 100 at various periods in the campaign, were all-out supporters of Kennedy. They were not only opposed to Nixon, they were outspoken in their hatred and contempt of him . . . it was loud and open. When Nixon was making a speech, there was a constant murmur of ridicule from many in the press rows just beneath the platform.

Such personal bias often seeps into the news as "interpretive reporting" and it is excused as such. There was a time when a reporter was supposed to present the facts and only the facts, leaving personal opinions for the editorial page, but now in many quarters the reporter is encouraged to "do his thing." The theory behind this seems to be that since no one can be strictly objective, why try? Let the reporter explain things as he sees them. The fallacy here is that this permits a reporter to be an advocate. He is allowed to embellish the facts with special pleading, putting things he likes in the best possible light and downgrading the things he opposes. In doing so he is able to apply the medium's tremendous leverage to move things his way.

On April 21, 1970, speaking before the American Newspaper Publishers Association in New York, Dr. S. I. Hayakawa appealed to the publishers "to assert again the values and responsibilities of objective journalism." In the same speech he urged them to end the present imbalance of liberal-arts students in journalism. Saying they had an "aristocratic, elitist bent" with "a profound contempt for democracy," he said they gave "a class bias to much of media coverage of the news."

Although interpretive reporting is held in high regard in certain places, it is this kind of news presentation that many Americans consider slanted. However, in its issue of December 31, 1969, *Variety,* the show-business magazine, strenuously protested Spiro Agnew's criticism of such journalism. "Analysis and interpretation," said *Variety,* are proper journalistic functions, and during the 1960s they became increasingly noticeable—until the Vice President stepped in.

"Until recently," said the article, "there seemed little question that the 'new journalism' of the 60's would at some point have a leavening effect on television news, if it wasn't doing so already. Then along came Agnew and it was apparent he stopped the process if in fact it was under way. . . . The resultant atmosphere was depressing and even frightening to TV newsmen."

Variety's annoyance is understandable since it has a show-business orientation. The "new journalism" it likes may provide better entertainment but quite often those touches of theater provide elements of distortion. Or at least the opportunity to distort. And though TV viewers like to be entertained, they will be better served if they get their news straight.

An interesting confirmation of one newscaster's bias was pointed out by National Review in its July 28, 1970, issue:

> Mr. Chet Huntley reveals in the current *Life* his secret thoughts. About Nixon: 1) "The shallowness of the man overwhelms me; the fact that he is President frightens me." On Spiro Agnew: 2) ". . . Agnew is appealing to the most base of elements. The networks almost created him, for God's sake." And on the network news programs: 3) "It deeply concerns me that 55 per cent of the American people are getting most of their news from TV. These are people who, for the most part, are being confronted with news for the first time. And these are the people who form the Agnew claque." And it occurs to us that all that gallimaufry adds up to is that 1) the people who like Agnew do so because 2) they get their news from the television networks and know that Agnew's criticism are just, and 3) were always able to see through the shallow impartiality of such as Chet Huntley.

Since George Washington's administration, Presidents of the United States have expressed bitterness at stings administered by

unfriendly and sometimes hostile newspapers. One of the most sensi-
tive of our Presidents was John F. Kennedy. He personally berated
Washington correspondents for critical stories they had written or
their papers had published, and other newspapermen were called to
account by Theodore Sorensen, Pierre Salinger, Robert F. Kennedy
and other members of the Kennedy family. Probably the most celebrated case of Presidential pique was the White House cancellation
of 22 subscriptions of the *New York Herald Tribune.*

Fletcher Knebel in a *Look* magazine article said that the Washington press corps took "almost as many lumps in 19 months of
Kennedy rule as during the three previous administrations put together." Even so, the Kennedy administration enjoyed a good press.
Segments of the communications media, notably television, were
almost ecstatic over the New Camelot that had come into being along
the Potomac, and the witty and elegant people that graced it. Joe
McGinniss in *The Selling of the President 1968* explained, "Camelot
was fun even for the peasants, as long as it was televised to their
huts."

There was a change when Lyndon B. Johnson succeeded President
Kennedy. Although at first his relations with the press were good,
there were some jarring notes as invidious comparisons were made
between the suave Kennedys and the more down-to-earth Johnsons.
To those who had been enthusiastic about the Kennedy way of doing
things, the Texans were uncouth interlopers who had no business in
the White House.

In a televised interview with Walter Cronkite, Mr. Johnson recalled this, saying: "Yes, I had many problems in my conduct of the
office, being contrasted with President Kennedy's conduct of the
office, with my manner of dealing with things and his manner, with
my accent and his accent, with my background and his background."
He told how, when he ran into difficulties, "there was a group in the
country, and very important and influential molders of public opinion, who I think genuinely felt that if President Kennedy had been
there, those things wouldn't have happened to him."

Even so, when the 1964 campaign pitted President Johnson
against Senator Barry Goldwater, that part of the media that really
mattered hesitated not at all in opting for the incumbent. For the

man from Arizona personified virtually everything that the liberals of the Eastern Establishment detested. He was a hawk on the Vietnam War, and believed that this country should get in and win. He opposed any concession to the Soviet Union that brought us nothing in return. He wanted a strong America and he made no secret of his devotion to this country.

In his book *Hysteria 1964,* Lionel Lokos has set forth in detail the types of attacks that were launched against Goldwater, and he identifies the primary attackers—the *New York Times,* the *Herald Tribune,* Walter Lippmann, Drew Pearson, CBS, NBC, the *New Yorker,* and other voices of the Eastern Establishment. Lokos shows how these and others hysterically accused Goldwater of being another Hitler, fomenting racial conflict, advocating a dangerous nuclear policy, seeking to destroy Social Security, being a lunatic, wrecking the Republican Party, trying to subvert labor unions and paving the way for a totalitarian government.

One of the most dishonest things shown on television was a paid commercial that purported to represent Goldwater's stand on nuclear warfare. The commercial showed a little girl in a field of daisies, and as she plucked the petals of one, a male voice counted down from ten to zero. Then an atomic explosion filled the screen, and a voice said, "These are the stakes. . . ."

Almost equally dishonest, and probably the most damaging of all the TV commercials, was one that used a theme that was echoed throughout the campaign. This showed a pair of hands ripping up a Social Security card. The message was that this was what a heartless Barry Goldwater had in store for the old folks. Actually, he had suggested that thought be given to making Social Security voluntary, without the compulsion of the present system.

Thanks to paid and unpaid messages of this sort, the country was saved from Barry Goldwater. But this failed to make Johnson's critics entirely happy, particularly when the President made it clear that he had no intention of aborting the war in Vietnam. Criticism of the President steadily built up into a deafening crescendo that drove him to announce in 1968 that he had no wish to try for reelection.

Richard M. Nixon had felt much the same way for the same reason when in 1962 he made his famous "farewell to politics" speech, in which he told reporters, "You don't have Nixon to kick around any more. Because, gentlemen, this is my last press conference."

Nixon had made himself highly unpopular with the liberal press long before this, on two counts, and both involved the Communist issue. One was the Alger Hiss case. Hiss had received substantial support from some of the nation's foremost opinion makers (Eleanor Roosevelt among them), who emphatically assured their readers and listeners that Hiss was as pure as the driven snow. These pundits had been proved wrong partly through Richard Nixon's efforts, and hell hath no fury like that of a pundit made to look ridiculous.

In *Six Crises,* Nixon said this "left a residue of hatred and hostility toward me—not only among the Communists but also among substantial segments of the press and the intellectual community—a hostility that remains even today." IIe also offended the liberal opinion makers when he called attention to the pro-Communist voting record of Helen Gahagan Douglas.

However, the press, like Alger Hiss, found Richard Nixon to be a tough adversary, one who tries to avoid repeating past mistakes. Well aware of the role that television had played in his loss of the 1960 election, he took steps to insure that there would be no repetition of past errors.

In his book *The Selling of the President 1968,* Joe McGinniss makes it appear that Richard Nixon placed himself in the hands of expert image-makers who packaged him as attractively as possible and sold him to television audiences as though he were a commercial product. A much different picture is presented by Frank Shakespeare, who directed the Nixon television campaign whereas McGinniss was limited to observing it. According to Shakespeare, "McGinniss was never present at any strategy conference or senior conference, or where we really were planning. He was quite often present, however, when what you might call the mechanics of television were being undertaken."

Shakespeare, a CBS senior vice president in 1967, decided to become active in politics and called on Nixon, then a lawyer in New York. After discussing the national and international situation, the pair talked about politics and television. Shakespeare continues:

> We talked about the necessity on TV to be what you are. TV, probably more than any other medium, can't be colored. You cannot, over a consistent period of time, be what you are not, because the ever-present glare of that eye will show you up eventually for what you really are.
>
> Out of all that conversation I became convinced that this was a man who was somewhat different from the public image of the man and so I decided that I would try to work with him as closely as I could during the campaign.

An effective format was developed for television early in the primaries, at a little town in New Hampshire, Hillsboro. Mr. Nixon sat down in the courthouse with six citizens, and the show was recorded without rehearsal as the townspeople talked over the issues with the candidate, with no holds barred. The Hillsboro format proved so successful that the concept was used throughout the primary campaign. For the national campaign the same general format was used but the panel of citizens was expanded to include Democrat and Wallace supporters. Some editing of the one-hour give-and-take tapes was done, but Shakespeare says that nothing substantive was deleted.

"The whole purpose of it was simply to take a man who had been represented to the people as something perhaps that he was not, and bring him into the living room. The end result of all this, for what it's worth, in my view, is that this man who eventually became President, gained a certain confidence with TV as a medium."

The McGinniss version of this, by dint of clever promotion, became a bestseller. It is interesting to speculate on what would have resulted if the author had attached himself to Hubert Humphrey's entourage as an apprentice image-maker. A clue is provided in a rather tasteless reference to the former Vice President. After reminding his readers that a person on television must be polite, remembering always that he is a guest in the nation's living rooms, McGinniss said, "Humphrey vomited on the rug."

Unable to divorce himself from President Johnson's position on Vietnam, Hubert Humphrey was extremely unpopular with the instant-peace element that favored such doves as Robert Kennedy, Eugene McCarthy and George McGovern. This was apparent in the demonstrations that rocked Chicago at the time of the Democratic National Convention. Humphrey was just one more manifestation of the hated Establishment, and so the demonstrators demanded, "Dump the Hump!"

There were few things that the so-called student leaders and their followers cared for but they were particularly resentful about the way in which the Democratic Party and the city of Chicago were doing things. And here the networks felt pretty much as the revolutionary element did. A Staff Report of a Special Subcommittee on Investigations of the House Committee on Interstate and Foreign Commerce makes this abundantly clear. Studying allegations that television news organizations were resentful of the Democratic Party and the city of Chicago, the report attempted to determine if there was animosity, and if so, was it reflected in biased news coverage.

The basis of the trouble was a strike of the International Brotherhood of Electrical Workers (IBEW) against the Illinois Bell Telephone Company. This prevented live coverage from Convention Hall and cnormously complicatcd the normally difficult task of television coverage of the proceedings. According to reports that appeared in television trade publications, the industry was convinced that Mayor Richard S. Daley and the Democratic Party went out of their way to hinder coverage. In addition to restrictions imposed by the electricians' strike, which it was believed that Mayor Daley encouraged, there were charges of police and fire department harassment of video trucks and personnel, live pickups were forbidden at strategic places, and cables were cut.

Some saw in all this a pattern to minimize live coverage outside Convention Hall, which might show violence. However, network officials were quoted in the report as saying that they looked upon such aggravations as "part of the broadcasting business" and certainly nothing that would cause bias.

A different attitude was strongly indicated by commentators and people they brought before the microphones. The report quotes Walter Cronkite as complaining that "the security here is worthy of an armed camp." Interviews with Paul Newman, Shirley MacLaine, Theodore Bikel, Arthur Miller and Jules Pfeiffer evoked their great unhappiness at security measures. "It provokes me to be hostile," remarked Miss MacLaine. Incidentally, the movie actress did not lack for television exposure at the convention. One observer, writing in *TV Guide,* reported that she was seen "24 times on one network in one evening." This report continued, " . . . she's no authority on politics, yet the commentators were asking her opinions on everything and then making no effort to try to balance them."

Which fact indicates one of the things wrong with television. A person who becomes well known as a comedienne, a baby doctor or a folk singer automatically seems to possess credentials as an expert on everything. One of the more amusing incidents described in the Staff Report again cited Shirley MacLaine:

"It was noted that, after Mayor Stokes' seconding speech for Vice President Humphrey, CBS's floor reporters again sought out Miss Shirley MacLaine for further commentary on the events downtown, which she had been viewing on a small television set in the Convention Hall."

The report went on to state, " . . . it would be possible to conclude that the networks had deliberately sought out for interviews those with known biased feelings against the conduct of the convention and the city government, some of whom would appear to have questionable credentials as political commentators." Although television thrives on the kind of conflict that can be stirred by dissidents, there were complaints that this was overdone as investigators "noted a tendency also to seek out and interview dissident delegates and other individuals for commentary."

One incident at the Democratic convention offered TV viewers a good example of the way in which television can give a totally distorted image. When the riots were at a peak and were being televised, CBS interviewed Mayor Daley at Convention Hall. The interview was interspersed with shots that had been taken 45 minutes earlier at Grant Park showing the violence there. The result was a TV presentation that was manifestly unfair to Mayor Daley.

As the *Chicago American* for August 30 described it, this showed "a picture of a smiling, obviously pleased Mayor Daley, with no explanation that there was no connection between the Grant Park films and the convention picture of Daley. The juxtaposition of the downtown violence to a picture of a smiling Mayor Daley created the undeniable impression that the mayor was an insensitive, sadistic political boss who had ordered his police to commit acts of brutality and was pleased as punch that his orders were being carried out."

The mayor was of course unaware of the role he had been given to play. The Staff Report said of this, "The use of this technique would appear to place a powerful, and possibly unfair, advantage at the disposal of the broadcaster in discrediting the views of those with whom he personally disagrees."

A different picture had been presented at the Republican National Convention, which was held earlier in August at Miami Beach. It was a no-nonsense convention, and the only conflict was the attempts by Nelson Rockefeller and Ronald Reagan to cut into Nixon's delegates. There was a riot but it was miles from the convention site, and there was no apparent connection with the proceedings there.

But even though television people were given no reason for frustration in the form of an electricians' strike, police harassment, inferior living accomodations and danger from flying objects, they were unhappy for another reason. Television has to march, as Theodore White says, motivated by conflict and violence, and since this was missing at Miami Beach, the men with the mikes and the cameras became bored. This boredom often showed, together with their feeling that those attending this convention were not their kind of people. They were looked upon as squares, and the squarest of them all was the man they picked to be the Party's nominee.

Television's contempt for the proceedings showed in one of those whiz-kid sessions in which TV people ponder great questions and "analyze" them. After Nixon made his acceptance speech, Edwin

Newman, Sander Vanocur, John Chancellor and Frank McGee participated in one of those sessions. Their opinions, totally lacking in any enthusiasm, could be summarized in Chancellor's annoyed remark: "But that's the same old Nixon speech we've heard, oh, thirty times."

There was another form of television influence—the frequent polls that were taken in an attempt to project the eventual outcome. In *The Making of the President 1968,* Theodore White tells of CBS's work along this line, with an interesting observation: "So elaborate was its count, its daily, almost hourly checks of individuals that, finally, in an illustration of the law of physics which says that an attempt to measure matter can change matter, the CBS count became a political factor in itself."

In this there was a parallel with what happened later at Chicago, where violence sometimes erupted when television crews put in an appearance.

Shortly after Nixon's election, Crosby S. Noyes wrote a column in the *Washington Star* in which he said that "the greatest problem and hazard" confronting the new administration would be the press. "When it comes to its treatment of Presidents," Noyes continued, American press is a monster. . . . An important segment of the press apparently has come to feel that it has a God-given mission to frustrate, hamstring and finally destroy the men . . . chosen to lead the nation."

This has been demonstrated time and again, and certainly Richard M. Nixon is no exception. The attacks kept building, and they reached a crescendo when the President announced that he was sending troops into Cambodia.

CHAPTER NINE

Cloud Cuckoo Land

MUCH of what we see on television brings to mind the legal disclaimer used with many motion pictures. Viewers are informed that what they are about to see is strictly fictional, and any resemblance to real life or real people, alive or dead, is purely coincidental, unintended and purely happenstance. Television might give some thought to running similar disclaimers prior to many programs and preceding every commercial.

Those messages from sponsors come first to mind. There is the crusading housewife, forever helping her neighbors by introducing them to the wonders of brand X, Y or Z. We have all met the noisy little menace who loves to break into quiet gatherings to inform his permissive daddy that he is running out of cavities. Familiar figures are the zombie-like couples who grunt and groan as they reach for a cigarette with strange bisexual properties, and the soda-pop addicts who behave as though their drinks had been spiked with LSD. There are the aggressive man-hunting females who stalk their prey with mouthwash, and family groups who act like fugitives from mental institutions.

Curiously, no matter how asinine these people are, they manage to live very well indeed. They have lovely homes, and an abundance of expensive household appliances. They drive expensive cars, entertain lavishly and travel extensively, first-class.

The list of ridiculous situations and characters found in commercials could be extended indefinitely, since every day brings a new crop. Few people take these vignettes of American life seriously, but unfortunately many of the distortions found in commercials, together with those that are so readily apparent on the non-commercial side of television, are taken literally in some quarters.

Occasionally advertisers have been reprimanded or punished for presenting misleading commercials. A manufacturer of razor blades or electric shavers will be called on to prove it if he says his product will remove the sand from sandpaper or the fuzz from a peach. A gasoline company is hauled up short if it claims that its product contains a unique wonder ingredient when in fact that same ingredient is used by other refiners. Misrepresentation of that sort is discouraged, but a far more serious kind of misrepresentation bothers television not at all.

That is the way in which commercial and non-commercial offerings on TV misrepresent not just something being offered for sale but this country and the American people. The serious harm that this can cause was described by John L. Parry, an official of Communications Associates, in an address to the Public Relations Society of America, at Los Angeles, November 25, 1969. Speaking of Negroes, he said that what comes over the air provided "the only means of escape from the intolerable," and "the most attractive of the latter-day underground railroads." But, he asked, what is it that they escape into?

> It is the commercialized, packaged version of white America we created for them, for all of us, the quantitative never-never land where there are no problems which cannot be swallowed away with a couple of Excedrin tablets, and where everyone makes it.
>
> You and I, who live in Whitetown, know that everybody doesn't live like that on our side of the tracks. . . . The blacks think it's because they're black and we're white that we won't let them in after they bought the ticket and said all the magic passwords.
>
> But we know—don't we? those of us in the white communications arts who make up those alluring messages and send them out to fill every waking moment of life—we know there is not much of a qualitative society even for whites atop Big Rock Candy Mountain.

A somewhat similar point was made by Dr. Margaret Mead, telling of the way television both creates and shatters myths in the minds of children. While the medium educates young people to look actuality in the face, she said, "subtle forms of distortion are, at the same time, spreading unreal and dangerous expectations." Others have criticized the emphasis that television places on material things. Labor-saving appliances, rich carpeting and expensive furnishings guarantee a happy home. A bigger car than your neighbor's provides proof of success. An adequate supply of pills, mouthwashes, deodorants and cosmetics assures continued health and sexual fulfillment.

It is not that simple, of course, and most people are aware that the real world is far different from the fantasyland created by TV. However, many of our young people refuse to accept the reality. They believe it is possible to eliminate the evils and the injustices and build a utopia with the same quick efficiency that stagehands show when they shift the scenes of a theatrical set. Others do not think in such terms but relate what they see on television to their own condition in life. They wonder why they are unable to have lovely homes like those that—they think—everyone else has. They wonder why they too cannot have all the fun and pleasure that—they think—everyone else has. And here we get those "unreal and dangerous expectations" that Dr. Mead referred to. The belief held by many that they are not getting a fair share can become dangerous when political medicine men promise to turn all their wonderful dreams into reality, in return for votes. When the demagogues fail, as they always do in the face of reality, disillusionment truly sets in. Unfortunately, "the system" has to bear the brunt of popular fury, not the venal politicos who promise the impossible.

Demagogues are able to get away with their outrageous promises because there is a regrettable lack of understanding of "the system." Many naive people have the notion that Washington creates money which is passed around to people and projects it happens to favor. If Washington really wanted to they think it could hand every poor family enough cash to buy a nice house and a new car, and then it could send them enough money every month to keep them well fed and happy. But, as those fellows on television keep saying, Washington can't do that because it prefers to waste the money fighting a war in Asia. And so all the poor people can't have all the good things that the government really owes them, and they become frustrated and go on a rampage.

Americans take great pride in their educational system and spend billions of dollars on it every year. Still, it has failed miserably to explain properly the system that provides all those billions for education and other things. Or maybe it does not have the necessary enthusiasm to pay tribute to the hard-working capitalistic goose that keeps laying golden eggs for it. Certainly the schools have become increasingly diffident and apologetic about the American way of life, and here is where television could do some remedial teaching. Unfortunately, this is not likely to happen as long as rock-ribbed liberals control the cultural heights, and television has in fact made matters worse by continually offering a distorted picture of America, past and present.

The way in which the history of our country is presented on television is a good case in point. We get a great many history lessons from the TV tube, but those that come from commercial stations are not very educational. Almost the entire sweep of this nation's history, from the time of Columbus to the present day, has been pruned, expurgated, condensed and edited so that it can be told within the limits of an inexpensive Hollywood set.

Everyone is familiar with this set because it keeps turning up on millions of TV tubes, time and again. There's a dusty winding street. On one side is the most important building in the town, the Longnoose Saloon, flanked by a general store, bank, hotel, sheriff's office and jail. On the other side of the street is the stagecoach depot, Ma Shook's boarding house, a millinery shop and maybe a low-grade saloon for buffalo hunters, sheepmen and other undesirables. Down yonder is a little church for the solid citizens, and back behind the barbershop is Terwilliger's livery stable. Props consist of a stagecoach, some bolts of calico for the general store, a few decks of playing cards, a number of white hats and black hats, a supply of booze and beer for the Longnoose, and a large assortment of long guns, Colts and Smith & Wessons. You also need some people, horses and longhorn steers.

Within the confines of such a set and with a relatively small investment, television keeps telling the story of this nation's past and the basic reason for its greatness. This is not "E Pluribus Unum" or anything like that. The message obviously is, "The hand that fans the trigger rules the world."

Some consider this a bit unbalanced. Bernard De Voto, the historian, discussed this popular art form as follows:

> The emphasis on westerns today is a make-believe on a national scale. So far as it relates to reality at all it dates back to a time period which lasted little more than 20 years and ended forever nearly 70 years ago. The gunmen who did most of the shooting and who are the Robin Hoods of the balladry were hired thugs, indistinguishable from metropolitan hoods of today and equally repulsive . . . the cowboy image is in great part phony, a counterfeit, and concentration on it obscures the great diversity of the West. Past or present, there is a lot more to the West than a cow outfit.

And though you would never realize it from television, there is a great deal more to American history than cowboys and Indians.

It is hard to become indignant over a form of entertainment that most Americans love, but such folklore implants some mischievous notions. Much of the talk we hear about America's violent past could stem from images of the wild and woolly west portrayed on cinema screens and TV tubes. These indeed show a violent America as fictional counterparts of the James Brothers, Billy the Kid, Wyatt Earp, Kid Curry and other gunslingers and lawmen mow down enemies, fight off redskins, hold up banks or uphold the law.

Only one other aspect of American history gets considerable and continuing attention: World War II, which, one gathers, was the only worthwhile war that the United States ever fought. Perhaps this is because it meets Lenin's definition of a "just" war. On the other hand, the wars in Korea and Vietnam, being directed against Communism, are "unjust" wars, to be opposed and certainly not glorified.

Equally strange is the way television's programmers view historical figures. To paraphrase the old saying, "Some are born great, some achieve greatness, while others are having greatness thrust upon them by those who fabricate history." In this kind of newthink, even those once considered great do not rate the esteem of people in the media who have their own ideas of what constitutes greatness. An indication of this was given in the program listings for February 12 and 22, as published in the *New York Times* on the preceding Sundays. These are detailed listings which give not only the name of the program but, if the program is important, some descriptive text as well.

Not once did the name of Abraham Lincoln appear in the February 12th listings.

Not once did the name of George Washington appear in the February 22nd listings.

This does not mean that somewhere along the line our two greatest Presidents were not given some attention on network television. But they were not singled out for any special tributes.

As against this, the following appeared in the listings for February 17:

> 8:30   (7) • "THE JOURNEY OF ROBERT F. KENNEDY," special ninety-minute film made for A.B.C. The journey begins with the funeral train as it passes the countryside on route to Washington, then reverts back to the happy times of Bobby as a boy and speeds on to his emerging as a new leader. John Huston is the narrator   (C)

Television's solicitude for those enshrined in its pantheon of heroes becomes amusingly obvious at times. James Reston reported in the *New York Times* that in the course of a discussion on the David Frost show, Senator George McGovern mentioned Senator Edward F. Kennedy's name and the audience booed. Although this reaction was significant, it was eliminated from the tape before the show was aired. A cynical person might call this censorship but actually it is only the sort of thing that Edwin Newman probably meant when he said that TV does not censor, it edits. Conservatives, being used to this sort of thing, made no outcry on this occasion.

On the other hand a lot of liberals did complain when CBS snipped some tape from a Merv Griffin show. On this occasion Carol Burnett had appeared on the Griffin show and called on viewers to write letters calling for an end to the war in Vietnam. She asked that the letters be sent to Mrs. Martin Luther King, who planned to deliver them to President Nixon. CBS said it was against policy to run such an appeal and deleted the reference. However, liberals looked upon this not as editing but as censoring.

In no area does television show greater ambivalence than in its portrayal of Negroes. For years the medium was almost lily white, except for a few stereotypes such as Amos 'n' Andy and Rochester, and appearances by such superb artists as Pearl Bailey, Louis Armstrong, Marian Anderson, Ella Fitzgerald and Duke Ellington. Then the policy changed with an abruptness that startled many viewers. Variety shows started featuring Negroes as regular members of the cast, dramatic shows became integrated, and new shows were developed to show blacks and whites working together. On news shows black reporters and commentators became commonplace, and commercials started using Negro models, giving Negroes long-delayed status as consumers.

All this has been to the good, though it sometimes seems as though there is an occasional false note as the camaraderie becomes a bit forced and shrill. But that may be merely another manifestation of the way things are done in show business, and there may be complete sincerity in television's integration policy.

Still, some of this racial harmony is negated by the distorted picture that TV often presents of black America and black Americans. Simeon Booker, in a radio broadcast over KYW, Philadelphia, on December 14, 1969, presented one aspect of this in describing a relatively minor incident, the Pigskin Club's 32nd annual awards, which had just been made in Washington. This club is made up of 500-plus members, predominantly black, and these men, he said, "include the brains and power of the black community on the eastern seaboard, from judges to attorneys, from college professors to businessmen." In the course of the session, the vital importance of teamwork was stressed, and, practicing what it preached, the Pigskin Club announced the selection of five white youths for its all-metropolitan high school team, picked from more than 135 institutions in the greater Washington area.

In the face of considerable racial turmoil and pessimism, the Pigskin Club's awards presented a ray of hope, a praiseworthy example of judging people by performance. Unfortunately, as Mr. Booker pointed out, this action by the nation's oldest, biggest and most distinguished black sports group was not considered worthy of coverage by any of the media. With a trace of bitterness, he concluded, "If blacks had rioted in the streets all the cameras and press would have been there."

The cameras and press would also have been out in force if the Black Panthers had turned up in their guerrilla outfits, prepared for a confrontation; and certainly a personal appearance by Stokeley Carmichael or the Panther minister of information, "Big Man," would have been considered worthy of coverage by the media. All of which shows how the media regard the true source of black power. Someone like Roy Wilkins, head of the NAACP, or Whitney M. Young, Jr., of the National Urban League, would probably get less attention.

In the intensive coverage of black unrest on certain campuses, in which black frustration is likely to be emphasized, a salient detail gets little if any attention. Negro enrollment in colleges increased 85 percent in five years, between 1964 and 1968. Thus it would appear that "the system" may not be as repressive of blacks as certain firebrands keep telling us over television.

Another common distortion perpetrated by television is the way in which Negro living conditions are invariably portrayed. If the emphasis is not on crime or violence, it is on filthy apartments and ramshackle houses. Rarely if ever are Negroes shown at peace with themselves and their neighbors, a credit in every way to the communities in which they live with whites or with other Negroes.

Millions of Americans thus see the worst of Negro life. Fearing this, they resist moves that would bring Negroes into white neighborhoods and white places of employment.

However, whites have as much reason to complain about television distortion as do blacks.

The most important distortions occur in presentations of "the big issues," as has been discussed earlier. In these, television has served to create the semblance of a house divided. It has magnified the actions and amplified the mouthings of small but vociferous minorities, and has given the impression that these people speak for most if not all Americans. Campus agitators, many of whom are not students, dominate television and their calls for violence are palmed off as the dissidence of all students. Gun-toting black militants, vowing to kill "whitey", are set forth as proxies for the 20,000,000 black citizens of the United States. At the time of the Cambodian invasion, television made it appear as though virtually every American was violently opposed to the President's action and wanted an immediate end to the war in Vietnam. But even as they played out this charade, polls of the general public showed its utter falseness.

However, in many other ways television makes little attempt to show things as they are; instead, life is presented as television people think it is or would like it to be. The distorted image of America and American thinking sometimes indicates that those people who control "the cultural heights" of Manhattan never stepped foot off the island, or, for that matter, never ventured far from midtown. For much of what appears on television is strongly tinctured with New York's traditional provincialism.

Nowhere is such thinking more in evidence than in TV commercials. The way in which women are so often presented in the sales messages is so outrageous that militant women's organizations are now demanding a change. This may cause those responsible to stop hiring off-Broadway bit players and scrawny models to portray American housewives and the women men are supposed to dream about in their fantasies. Next, television officials should take corrective action with regard to some of the men and children used in commercial pitches. With more credible casts, some of the commercials might become a bit more believable, but it would help more if there was less of that pseudo-sophistication and more good taste.

This is not to say that all commercials are poor. Many are tasteful and clever, and often show more imagination and professionalism than the programs they adorn. But all too often they are an insult to the viewer's intelligence and an imposition. Sometimes it seems as though the aim is to make the commercial so irritating that it is bound to be remembered. Sponsors who consider this good psychology should ask TV viewers what they think.

On a par with the vignettes of American life portrayed by commercials are the soap operas. Essentially the same kind of pop art that Bernard Macfadden used to dispense in his true-story epics, the TV versions differ from the master's offerings in one respect—they go on forever and ever. The conventional true story or romance, in print, has a beginning, a middle and an end. Once an electronic version gets under way it never stops. As fast as characters die of some loathsome disease, commit suicide, are dragged off to an insane asylum, become dope addicts, run off with the payroll, suffer delirium tremens, desert home and babies, go to jail, or walk the last mile to the gas chamber, new characters emerge to take their places. Theirs not to reason why, theirs but to do and die, and usually in a most agonizing manner.

It may be that there are some people in this land of ours who endure some of the trials and tribulations that are the daily lot of the poor souls shown on soap operas. Presumably there are neurotics aplenty of the type that flit across the TV screen during the afternoon hours. But as the westerns give the impression that the American past was a violent one, so the soap operas certainly would lead one to believe that present-day America is in toto a pretty sick society. Can it be that university professors and other pundits who proclaim that America is sick spend their afternoons looking at the soaps?

Such epics usually cut across broad segments of what soap writers may view as American life. The viewer gets to know the town's leading industrialist, the poor but honest mechanic, various members of the medical and legal professions, the frustrated and alcoholic wife, the playboy son who is more interested in girls than work, the assistant bookkeeper who may or may not be cheating his employer, and so on. Watch enough episodes and in time you will encounter every business, trade and profession listed in the yellow pages of your phone book.

But television offers another type of program of cloud-cuckoo nature. These are in-depth portrayals of professional people at work and at play (and sometimes it is hard to figure out which is which). TV's most popular profession is medicine, which is understandable because it provides a broad canvas on which to depict birth and death, joy and sadness, pain and happiness, bravery and cowardice, torment and tears, faith, hope, charity and other dramatic pigments.

Here we find nice old Doctor Muggsby in his clinic, surrounded by fellow idealists, all of them passionately dedicated to the principles laid down by Hippocrates. The clinic is obviously richly endowed, and whether you come to Doc Muggsby to have a cinder removed from your eye or to get a lobotomy, you get quick and pleasant service. No one even asks whether you have Blue Cross. And if you have any marital or financial problems, Doc will take time to straighten those out too.

Possibly TV script writers and producers go to someone like Doc Muggsby when they get a virus or feel a nervous breakdown coming on, but to most people the Muggsby Clinic is right smack in the middle of never-never land. Most of the people who make up the really sick society of ours—sick with aches and pains—make their way to a doctor's office that is usually crowded with patients. Hours later they are ushered into an utterly harassed and tired physician who does his best but doesn't have nearly as much time as Doc Muggsby to provide intensive care. The prescription he hands you may do the trick, but if you end up in the hospital it is a far cry from the kind of institution shown on the TV tube. If you are lucky or can wait, you may get a semi-private room, but do not count on having a lot of dedicated internes, nurses and administrative personnel dropping in to check your progress and maintain your morale. And there are no Dr. Muggsbys around to help you solve your personal problems. But then you will probably have time aplenty to work on them without interruptions from the staff.

American jurisprudence also gets considerable attention from those who provide television. In fact, it would probably be possible to run an entire TV network with only two sets. One, for historical drama, would be like the one that is used for *Gunsmoke*. The other would be a replica of a courtroom. (Here the jury box could serve for quiz shows, and the judge's bench should be impressive enough to suit most newscasters.)

Along with the courtroom setting go certain well-established principles of TV justice. One is that the prisoner at bar is not guilty but is only in the docket because he has been framed. The second principle taught at the TV School of Law is that without the help of an attorney such as Burl Ives, Raymond Burr, E. G. Marshall or possibly William J. Kunstler, the poor defendant is a shoo-in for the gas chamber. As every connoisseur of TV courtroom drama knows, a slick lawyer is a person's only hope to beat the kind of justice we have in this country.

Penitentiaries are full of people who have been railroaded there, whose only mistake was their selection of an incompetent counsel. For if they were not actually framed by relatives, friends or the cops, they might just as well have been, since they were only the unfortunate victims of their environment. Had they been given a little understanding and perhaps more generous relief checks, they would not have found it necessary to push heroin, gun down bank clerks, steal Cadillacs and otherwise fight back against a society that repressed and frustrated them.

Television does a great social service as it thus tries to educate us on the problems of these unfortunate victims of the system. Only a quibbler would suggest that maybe the medium ought to air some programs that would give equal time to telling the story of the victims of those victims of environment.

No discussion of television's fantasyland would be complete without some reference to Big Business as the medium presents it. The average tycoon, as shown on TV, would feel cramped and imposed upon if he had to swing his big deals in quarters used by the president of General Motors, A. T. & T., or Standard Oil. Surely none of those officials has such impressive office equipment, such well stocked bars and such well developed secretaries.

But then not many real-life tycoons are such swingers in the business world, acquiring mammoth corporations the way housewives load their carts in supermarkets.

For some reason television has a way of inflating everyone and everything out of all proportion, whether it be an Abbie Hoffman, a politician or a fictional creation. Currently one of the networks is presenting a series based on magazine publishing. Considerable emphasis is placed on a crime magazine, but to turn out this publication a building far more impressive than the Time-Life Building is required. But then TV's crime magazine has impact. The very mention of it makes law-enforcement officials snap to attention and causes criminals to cringe in terror. Maybe we could curb the crime wave in this country if there were such a magazine. As it is, we do not have a single crime magazine listed among the top 100 magazines.

It would not be realistic to call on television to "tell it like it is" with regard to these things, since viewers would find the actuality without much romance and glamour. Most magazines, for example, are turned out in small, sometimes dingy offices not at all like those found in Robert Stack's splendiferous establishment, and few magazine people are viewed as Ministers Plenipotentiaries of The Press, with the power to make or break others.

Courtrooms do provide drama, but if the process were anything like that shown on television, officials could charge jurors for the privilege of participating in the judicial process. And though there are occasional miscarriages of justice, there is usually a conscientious effort to be fair. If anything, the accused is likely to get a better break than he deserves, a fact that is indicated by the way in which so many criminals are turned loose.

Obviously it would be silly to attempt to entertain viewers with the truth, the whole truth and nothing but the truth. A year or so ago an off-Broadway group staged a performance that it billed as real life, and that it was. The stage served as an apartment and people drifted in and out of it doing the things that people do in apartments. There was no script and members of the cast did whatever came naturally. It was as dull an offering as could be imagined, and even avant-gardists found nothing in it to warrant their enthusiasm.

Television's programming problems are many. Filling all those hours is not too difficult, but the trick is to fill them with good material. This complicates the problem because there is no noticeable oversupply of good material. And there is likely to be considerable disagreement as to what is good. Many viewers would rate as good anything in the way of a sports program. Others might go for a news special or a quiz show, while the station's program director might have an entirely different idea of what is good. Thinking of the ratings, the director might decide that the best possible offering would be a re-run of an old episode of *The Untouchables* or a Humphrey Bogart movie of long ago.

It is a complex problem to satisfy a highly diversified audience and, to use a phrase favored by politicians, "there are no simple solutions." However, there may be a way out in a form of programming that has been sadly neglected. Curiously, something of this sort has been suggested by certain television officials, and though it is not expected to revolutionize television, it could make a significant difference. The general idea, which would not only "tell it like it is," but tell it as it should be told, will be discussed in the next chapter.

CHAPTER TEN

The Big Omissions

BY now everyone is aware that television is able to sell certain concepts, and in view of the way the liberal element dominates the medium, those concepts are usually liberal. This has drawn fire from conservatives who resent the anti-war propaganda, the attention given to radical rabble-rousers, the overemphasis on sex and violence, and a general tendency to downgrade this country by stressing the things that are wrong with it.

Most of the criticism of television, whether from viewers or from official investigating bodies, has been based on the things that are *put into* programs. What is seldom criticized is what television *leaves out* of its programming, and this is at least as important.

Television viewers saw and heard a great deal about the tragic demonstration at Kent State University, which left four students dead when fired on by National Guardsmen. They were shown the scene of the tragedy, and there was considerable discussion to the effect that Kent State students had done nothing to warrant such a reaction from the troops. Repercussions from other campuses were reported, considerable coverage was given to the funerals of the victims, and various spokesmen for the academic and political communities got into the act. Almost without exception these spokesmen blamed actions by President Nixon or "Agnew rhetoric" for inciting the Kent State students to riot.

Unfortunately, little attention was paid to some significant events that had led up to the fatal demonstration, and this was regrettable because these things added up to a far more interesting story than the one that TV presented. But television cannot be faulted too much for this, because even *The New York Times* for some reason flubbed this one. In its May 5th issue, the *Times* carried the headline, "60 Years of Quiet at Kent State are Shattered in Era of Protest," and went on to tell that "until recently the schools most serious demonstration was a 1958 panty raid on two women's dormitories the last day of the school year. . . ."

This was utterly false and misleading. The fact is that Kent State had been a hotbed of radical turmoil for almost two years prior to the fatal confrontation. SDS agitators had created so much havoc that the House Internal Security Committee in 1969 devoted two days to an investigation of SDS activites on that allegedly bucolic campus. If television had shown a little more enterprise than the *Times,* it could have come up with a revealing news special on this, based on 167 pages of testimony available at a modest charge from the Government Printing Office. And this could have been given a dramatic touch, the kind television likes, because one of the revolutionaries blown up in the Greenwich Village "bomb factory" was the leader of the first "rebellion" at Kent State. This fellow, Terry Robbins, was an SDS activist, and he had planned the Kent State offensive in two manuals that described an on-campus guerrilla campaign.

Had television gone into this, millions of people would have been given a much better understanding of what the National Guard was up against. This was no student gathering, upset because Spiro Agnew had insulted all those scholars found in the groves of academe. It was a threatening mob, manipulated by hard-core revolutionaries. The victims apparently were innocent bystanders who may not have been able to avoid being caught up in the action.

In an earlier chapter there was a reference to the fact that television seems to have a large stable of sacred cows in the form of prominent people who are treated with the utmost respect even when they say and do the most asinine things. However, there are also many subjects that must be treated with deference, and such glossing-over constitutes a form of distortion that can be dangerous.

For example, a few months ago television gave considerable attention to a group of young Puerto Ricans when they seized the First Spanish Methodist Church in Harlem and nailed the doors shut. Television viewers were told that the church had been illegally seized and the church trustees insisted that the occupiers get out. However, during the two weeks of the siege the youths, who called themselves the Young Lords, were given considerable TV exposure of a sympathetic nature. They were permitted to tell their story and explained that they had taken over the church because it had failed in its duty to the community. They said they intended to use it as a free breakfast center and school for the children of Spanish Harlem.

Unfortunately it was all misleading. Viewers were not told that these "idealists" were a former street gang that had turned revolutionary along Maoist lines. Nor were viewers told that many of them had extensive criminal records for narcotics offenses, sex crimes, assault and robbery. However, this sort of background no doubt helped them in their free breakfast program, since food for this was obtained from neighborhood merchants on an "or else" basis.

By omitting such pertinent details, the media left New York unprepared when in June 1970 the Young Lords went on a rampage through Harlem, vandalizing and looting stores because the police had the audacity to arrest one of their fuehrers.

Among the liberal element it is considered bad form to pay much attention to reports issued by the House Committee on Un-American Activities or the Senate Internal Security Committee; both are looked upon as a form of McCarthyism, beneath notice. However, study of these documents could provide leads and background information at least as informative as those now found in *The New York Times,* the *Washington Post* and other influential news organs. It would be interesting, for example, to know how many of those TV people who conduct interviews with such people as David Dellinger, Tom Hayden and Rennie Davis have ever read their testimony before the HCUA, in which testimony these revolutionaries express their thoughts on our present system and what they hope to do about it. Discussion of such material, with its frightening implications is left to anti-Communist publications, most of which are of small circulation.

Had they shown some initiative in this vital field, the networks could have presented a very significant news special on December 12, 1969, when the Tom Paine Awards Dinner was staged by the Communist-front National Emergency Civil Liberties Committee. More than 1,300 well-heeled radicals and liberals paid $17.50 apiece to attend this gala affair, but despite the prominence of some of the proletarians who attended, the major media ignored it. Alice Widener, writing in the conservative publication *Human Events,* told how the repressed and the frustrated gathered "to dine on lobster bisque, filet mignon, bombe glacé jubilee, [and] to cover presentation of NECLC awards to David Dellinger, Dr. Howard Levy and TV star Tom Smothers (for whom a stand-in accepted the award and read a message)."

Television viewers would have seen Black Panther Tom Jolly and his bodyguards. They could have viewed Leonard Boudin, father of Kathy Boudin who disappeared after the deadly bomb factory blew up in Greenwich Village. Boudin *Pere*, an NECLC counsel, told of various court victories by NECLC, some of them obtained "because the government surrendered." TV viewers might have been surprised at the obvious affluence of these people, many of whom detest the capitalist system that has treated them so generously. Exclusive of pledges, more than $32,000 in contributions was collected when a Marxist Cornell professor, Douglas Dowd, passed the hat.

Viewers would have been treated to a revealing performance by Dr. "Captain" Howard Levy, a former Army medical officer who spent 26 months in prison for refusing to obey military orders. The good doctor has been interviewed time and again by TV reporters and he comes across as a highly idealistic albeit mealymouthed martyr, willing to suffer because he hates war. However, at the Tom Paine Awards Dinner there was a different Levy. He delivered a hysterical harangue in which he used gutter profanity to express his violent feelings about the army, and called on the audience to join him in screaming the filthy word that seemed to obsess him. According to Miss Widener, the nice people obliged to his complete satisfaction.

Another star of this distinguished gathering was David Dellinger, who presented a somewhat different face from that of the elderly and sanctimonious youth leader who passionately loves peace, on a coast-to-coast basis. Miss Widener wrote, "He repeated every obscenity yelled in the Chicago courtroom by Black Panther Bobby Seale before he was sentenced to four years in jail for contempt of court. . . ."

Concluding her report, Miss Widener asked, "Where were the New York City newspapers and TV reporters? I don't know. But I do know that those on the NECLC dinner dais in the Hotel Americana ballroom constitute a kind of board of directors for violent revolution in our nation. They seem to enjoy privileged sanctuary from the press. Why?"

Miss Widener is not the only one who wonders why. When it comes to such characters, the media maintain a discreet silence if they are unable to say something nice about them or to present them as interesting or even attractive figures.

Television goes in for documentaries on significant subjects and occasionally it has produced some of merit. Most, however, are superficial and have little impact. And this is unfortunate, because without leaving Manhattan the networks could present some significant developments that are having a profound effect on the nation as a whole.

The status of the book-publishing business today would make a fascinating documentary—to cite one example. As it is, television barely touches on this subject, providing only forums where certain books can be huckstered. Why not show the background instead? Viewers surely should find it interesting to see how a book by, say, Jerry Rubin, Abbie Hoffman or Tom Hayden is produced and marketed.

How did these very busy people find the time to turn out books while doing so many other things, traveling to international conferences and commuting to numerous campuses? Were they helped by revolutionary ghost writers, and if so what does radical ectoplasm look like? How did they find publishers so readily when non-revolutionary authors usually run into problems in this respect? Maybe a look inside certain publishing offices might be enlightening, to see who contracts for such books and who edits them. Perhaps TV crews should set up their cameras in the book-review department of *The New York Times* and elsewhere, to get some idea as to how such books are selected for attention, and why certain reviewers are picked for certain books.

TV crews could then go into various bookstores and libraries where interviews with librarians and buyers might disclose what caused them to fill their counters and stacks with revolutionary merchandise of this nature. The program could end with interviews with college and high school students who have read such books. Did they find that this literature helped them to realize the utter rottenness of U.S. society, the sinfulness of fighting the Viet Cong and the North Vietnamese, the wickedness of our leaders, the necessity to overthrow the establishment, and so on?

While such TV specials and documentaries would be highly educational concerning the nature of the enemy within, they would suffer from a defect that is common to almost every program TV presents on the big issues of the day—the accent would be entirely on the negative.

What is needed, and what is missing from television today is accent on the positive. That is the *big* omission, probably the biggest of all.

In an editorial published on March 31, 1970, the *Wall Street Journal* noted this fact: "That American society is utterly undeserving of respect, then, has been the message poured out of our most prestigious universities, our most respected media, our largest cultural centers, our most successful political party. Indeed the message has been that American society is an object to kick. Scant wonder that youths or blacks or workers would decide to do a little kicking in their own manner."

If you think this is an exaggeration, *how long has it been since you have seen something on television which made you truly proud to be an American?*

What we get instead are programs that deal in flaws and defects, wrongs and repressions, corruption and injustice. We are fully informed concerning millions who are supposed to go to bed hungry every night, the terrible conditions in the ghettoes, the plight of non-union grapepickers, the pollution that threatens to engulf us, growing use of narcotics, political corruption, etc. There is considerably more to life in America than that, but as far as television is concerned, the good and decent things might as well be taking place on the far side of the moon.

This same myopia is apparent in the way—as mentioned in the previous chapter—that TV tells the story of our past largely in terms of western shoot-em-ups. Now surely this nation has produced men more deserving of the rapt attention given to such men as Matt Dillon and Ben Cartwright, admirable as they are. Why don't we see more portrayals of America's true heroes, most of whom achieved greatness with no violence whatever? Or is violence an absolute essential for television, regardless of the period?

Why, too, all the emphasis on what happened in a relatively brief period of time, in the West alone? It would seem that a few other aspects of this nation's history also deserve attention. The crowds that travel to Williamsburg, Old Sturbridge and Mystic Seaport to see those restorations of colonial days strongly suggest a tremendous interest in those times. Throngs of visitors to the historical shrines of the Revolutionary War and the Civil War indicate the ties of millions of Americans to those events of the past. And why not, since many of their forebears were involved in them? Yet none of these is considered worthy of much attention by the people who hack out television scripts or by those who order them. Some more or less authentic history occasionally surfaces in the form of an old movie —usually a very old movie shown very late at night—but that is about it.

Several weeks before the Vice President made his critical remarks about television, an interesting article written by Edith Efron was published in *TV Guide*, for September 27, 1969. It anticipated some of Mr. Agnew's criticism and a now-famous phrase was part of the title, "The Silent Majority Comes into Focus." Miss Efron's piece told of "simmering anger" on the part of the public, fed up with what it was being told by irresponsible leftists and radicals in the medium. Conceding that there was a problem, certain network officials were quoted to the effect that changes were called for and changes would be made. Instead of constantly knocking the United States, there would be a positive approach, and viewers would be shown the good things about their country.

If this different attitude has found expression on television, it has been so subtle as to escape general notice. Certainly liberals have been given no reason for complaints because of a rash of flagwaving and chauvinism on the networks. A few sporadic attempts have been made to tell the story of America's past, but none has been inspired. On February 28, 1970, NBC presented a one-hour special for children entitled *The Boston Spy Story,* and there was another shot at American history when a cartoon version was presented starring Mister Magoo. This was more Magoo than history and as far as instilling an understanding of our nation was concerned, both shows were an utter waste of time and effort. The kiddies would have been as well served with some Bugs Bunny cartoons or the Ritz Brothers.

When plans for the 1970–1971 television were announced by the networks, there was little indication that any of that patriotic fervor hinted at in the *TV Guide* article had survived any conference-room sessions. There was only one series mentioned with a title having any historical overtones, *The Young Rebels,* to be presented over ABC. This was described as being about a guerrilla band in the Revolutionary War, and it could be estimable. On the other hand, considering how television does things, we may find that it is the sort of thing that could use Jerry Rubin, Tom Hayden and Stokeley Carmichael as guest stars.

Otherwise, things are going to be the same as ever on the networks. A few new shows were announced, but most will be holdovers— situation comedies, stories about dedicated lawyers and doctors, action adventure stories, westerns, lots of sports, variety shows, quizzes, etc. In other words, your TV screen will look pretty much as it did last year and the year before that. And you will look in vain for anything that may arouse any latent chauvinism. Television people are above exploiting such primitive feelings as love of country.

The medium's apathetic attitude toward patriotism was again indicated on May 30, 1970. In observing Memorial Day, many millions of Americans displayed the flag, visited cemeteries and listened to sermons and speeches concerning our honored dead. The Associated Press reported that sales of Old Glory had spurted in the weeks before the holiday, with gains of 100 percent over the preceding year. However, television seemed oblivious to these straws—or flags—in the wind. In the Sunday edition of *The New York Times* covering the holiday, Memorial Day was not mentioned once in the TV program listings. Nor was it mentioned in *TV Guide's* listings for the metropolitan New York area. TV coverage was provided in the form of some news shots showing parades and memorial services, and these were interspersed with portrayals of the surrender-now element proclaiming messages that, as usual, should have been addressed to Hanoi.

The strangest aspect of this neglect is that, time and again, the American people have shown that they love material that deals with their past and gives them justified pride in their heritage. A long list of successful stage productions and motion pictures could be presented as evidence of this but a few will suffice.

Today, while most Broadway and off-Broadway theatrical productions deal in what has been called "septic-tank art," one that doesn't is an outstanding success—1776, which is unabashed patriotism. Bob Considine described it as "a deep breath of fresh air on the fetid Broadway scene." Sherman Edwards, whose idea it was, met discouragement on every hand as he tried to bring it into being. Producers told him that patriotism was box-office poison, but theatergoers had a different idea and the show is now on its way to being an all-time hit. Predictions are that it will still be running in 1976.

As was mentioned in an earlier chapter, John Wayne's motion picture *The Green Berets* was produced only because of Wayne's dogged determination. When it was finally screened, certain liberal critics went into a frenzy of denunciation. Probably the worst of these denunciations was the one published by *The New York Times.* However, the *Times* subsequently reported that as of January 1969

The Green Berets "is turning into one of the most successful movies released by Warner Brothers–Seven Arts in the last five years." Prior to that report, *U.S. News & World Report* made a comparison of the film with another hit *The Graduate.* It told that *The Graduate* had been popular with college students, many of whom had seen it two or three times. "But another big success at the box-office," the report said, "was *The Green Berets,* an unabashedly patriotic film produced by John Wayne, Hollywood's super-American. Exhibitors report that working-class youngsters lined up to see that film, often two or three times, while showing little interest in *The Graduate.*"

So there may be hope for America.

This is not a new phenomenon. Many motion pictures that have dealt with patriotic themes and American history have become classics and fantastic moneymakers as well. *Gone With the Wind,* made in 1939, is still being shown and has grossed more than $70,000,000. The classic *Birth of a Nation,* made in 1915, is still being screened but no longer for general audiences because of its content, which would be explosive today. Other great historic films include *The Covered Wagon, How the West Was Won, Drums Along the Mohawk, Cimarron, The Alamo, Northwest Passage, The Longest Day, Sergeant York,* and others. There is no need to point out that today's films usually concern themselves with more intimate matters, and today one would look hard to find a movie that would make anyone feel optimistic about the human race, let alone our country. Still, if inspiring films are again produced, there is obviously a market for them. They might indeed bring many erstwhile moviegoers back to the theaters.

From the comments of New York–based critics and from statements published in the trade press covering show biz generally and television in particular, it is obvious that the American people are a puzzlement to dispensers of entertainment. The artistic merits of such works as *Oh, Calcutta, Hair, I Am Curious Yellow* and a play extolling the late Rosenbergs, they can appreciate. What they cannot understand is why so many Americans are partial to Lawrence Welk, Liberace, the *Beverly Hillbillies,* Red Skelton and other unsophisticates. Why, they even went for *Hee Haw!* That ultra-rural program was put on by CBS as a replacement for the Smothers Brothers, and there is a theory that the move was made with malice aforethought: "If they can't take Dick and Tom, let 'em eat corn!"

Cornball it was, but *Hee Haw* proved so popular that TV sophisticates were aghast. A *New York Times* writer set forth the thesis that the show was CBS's version of a Southern strategy, and damned it with the observation that it represented "the Spiro Agnew of the CBS lineup." So much for *Times* humor.

More understanding was shown by J. D. Nicola, a writer for Catholic Press Features:

> Perhaps the popularity of *Hee Haw* and Glen Campbell and Johnny Cash . . . tells us something about the average American's desire to hold onto the good things in an age of increasing sophistication and technology: Earthy, clean (albeit square) humor instead of sophisticated "adult" humor; folksy soloists with a single twangy guitar instead of a bearded quintet with a truckful of electronic musical gadgets and flashing lights and words you can't understand.

This is not intended as an argument for more of the same to fill the present void in television's vast wasteland. The popularity of these shows may instead be taken as a reaction to much of the material that has been dealt out by people who feel they have a mission to make all America like what they happen to like.

Possibly a clue as to what can and should be done was offered by a special titled *It Couldn't Be Done,* which was sponsored by the Bell System, on April 2, 1970. This saluted several great Americans who had done the seemingly impossible.

Narrated by Lee Marvin, the program told how these men had conceived and built such achievements as the Panama Canal, Hoover Dam, the Golden Gate Bridge, the monument at Mount Rushmore and the Holland Tunnel. Lee Mendelson, who produced the show, said:

"In the light of current national self-criticism and self-doubt, a television reminder of American know-how can perhaps persuade more and more people to feel that if we can build these impossible projects, surely we can succeed in building bridges between mens' minds and mens' hearts."

Here again response from the viewing public was enthusiastic, but regrettably this was just one show, not even a "pilot" that might presage other shows of this nature.

On the face of it there is a public that is avid for programs of this sort, but one might almost believe that there is an arbitrary censorship that keeps such programs at an absolute minimum. Possibly a clue to network thinking in this respect can be found in an experience of Samuel Goldwyn, in the old movie days. Goldwyn movies were popular and they made money for him, but reviewers disliked them. Concerned about this, Goldwyn brought a half-dozen screen and stage critics to Hollywood to tell his writers and directors how to upgrade their product. As told in Benjamin B. Hampton's *A History of the Movies,* these people made significant changes.

> These sophisticates strenuously and sarcastically condemned as "melodrama" and "hokum" all suggestions of widely popular themes and treatments, and Miss Mathis permitted herself to be convinced that movie audiences were ready to assimilate a higher class of ration. The studio steadily swung away from the showman ingredients of screen construction, and most of its offerings became smart, modernistic themes selected to win the approval of the intelligentsia.

The result was that while many of the pictures were technically excellent, they were unsuitable for large audiences. The author reports, "The corporation succumbed and its properties passed into a merger of several companies."

No one can accuse television of being unmindful of large audiences, and it does everything it can to appeal to them, even to opening itself to the criticism that it reduces its programs to a low common denominator. Yet in its attempts to reach millions, it consistently ignores subjects that would seem to guarantee large audiences.

Under the Communications Act, licensees have the responsibility of arranging their program structure so that their operations will be in the public interest. This, however, is broadly interpreted and many broadcasters believe that they have earned the right to their licenses by such gestures as running "public-service announcements," by an occasional broadcast from city hall, or by presenting an important speech.

How much more meaningful it would be if television set out to give the people of this country a better understanding and appreciation of these United States. This would not require the exaggerated kind of flagwaving that sophisticates deride. All that is needed is an honest portrayal of this country, with the good presented along with the bad. There is enough good in this country so that no one need worry about the outcome of this particular battle for the minds of men.

CHAPTER ELEVEN

What They Should Do

TELEVISION broadcasters, the "they" of this chapter heading, have often been criticized, but never has there been such an outpouring of criticism as in the past year or so. Much of this echoed Vice President Agnew's comments concerning biased news, but other aspects of television have come under attack from many quarters. Among the things that many TV viewers find distasteful are:

- Undue emphasis on sex and violence
- Crime made attractive and offered as a solution to human problems
- Lack of respect shown for parental authority
- Sneers at accepted moral, social and ethical ideals
- Smut and vulgarity
- Ridicule of the sanctity of marriage and a casual view of divorce
- Contemptuous references to law enforcement and police
- Crime techniques presented in detail
- Murder justified for revenge
- Illicit sex presented as commendable
- Overemphasis on the use of liquor
- Inadequate costuming of performers
- Suggestive gestures by dancers and performers
- Use of horror for its own sake

Viewers are not the only ones who think that these things are out of place on the television screen. The foregoing items are a few quotations taken almost verbatim from the Television Code of the National Association of Broadcasters, an extensive listing of subjects to be avoided by broadcasters, together with subjects to be given attention. The Code, presented in full in Appendix B of this book, is deserving of study. It will be found that, like the Preamble to the Charter of the United Nations, there is a marked difference between its aims and the way in which those aims are implemented.

Network broadcasting represents a tremendous concentration of power, and network heads are conscious of the power they wield. This was implicit in the way the network heads reacted to the Agnew criticism. There was no concession that they might be at fault, but in this case at least they were shown to be out of step with others who are important to the industry. Some of the biggest "names" in newscasting conceded that there was bias in the news, and NBC must have been distressed to learn that 60 percent of its own affiliates felt likewise. Most disturbing of all was the way the public reacted. In view of this, the three network heads obviously represented a small minority, even though they were joined by a vociferous group of media people, many of whom were as vulnerable to the same criticism as the networks.

This kind of reaction by broadcasting officialdom is nothing new. When Senate committees chaired by Kefauver, Dodd and Pastore concluded that television paid too much attention to sex and violence and that this was contributing to juvenile delinquency, network heads refused to be convinced. Long after the Kefauver committee first showed a relationship between television violence and violence in real life, portrayals of TV violence continued and actually increased. However, public resentment relayed largely through official channels finally got through to network policy makers and recently there has been a change for the better. Although you can still see plenty of murder and other violence on television, much of it is likely to be in repeats of old shows. In more recent programs, the violence is likely to be implied, and minus the gory details of past performances.

But why the long delay in curtailing television violence? Back in 1944, Harry M. Warner, president of Warner Bros. Studios, showed an awareness of cause and effect that is often missing in television programming. Said Mr. Warner: "Whether a producer makes a picture for pleasure or for profit, for pure entertainment or for pure educating—or just for art's sake—he is up against the incontrovertible fact that his picture will produce some effect, for good or bad, on its audiences."

Thanks in no small measure to the stimulus provided by Spiro Agnew, it is possible to detect an improvement in television news. This is not to say that bias has been eliminated, but newscasters are a bit more circumspect. Furthermore, affiliated stations are less inclined to take everything that is offered to them by the networks, and this has aroused the ire of liberals in the media who point to this as "proof" that station owners have been intimidated by the Vice President's "threats." Actually one may assume that affiliated stations see no point in conforming to network preferences when what the networks choose to give them can get them in trouble with the people in the communities they are supposed to serve. Aware of an aroused public, station owners have reason to be wary, because they are the ones who stand to lose the most if the networks give them programs that annoy or outrage viewers. They are the ones who can lose their valuable licenses if protests become strong enough. It should be kept in mind that the networks themselves are not licensed, only the relatively few stations they themselves own and operate.

Individual stations will be showing more independence of the networks for another reason. Starting in the fall of 1971, under a recent FCC ruling, stations affiliated with networks in the top 50 markets will be required to limit network programs to no more than three hours of prime evening time. Up to four hours of prime-time programs are now provided by the networks, and the ruling is designed to encourage stations to reflect more community activity and interests in their programming. Quite conceivably, casualties of this ruling will probably be network programs that have brought criticism to the stations.

Thus, although the networks have tremendous power, they are not beyond the reach of an aroused public. It has been assumed by many people, and many broadcasters, that station licenses are granted in perpetuity—requiring only a routine renewal every three years—but this concept is being widely challenged. There is greater awareness that the airwaves belong to the public, and if a particular station fails to provide proper service, the license can be taken away and given to someone who will.

Even a broadcaster's property right, represented in his investment in transmitting equipment, studios, etc., is not considered as important as it once was. For one thing, a TV station is usually so profitable that costs of a physical plant are quickly written off. For another, viewers have a far greater investment in radio and TV than broadcasters have. In 1968 Consumers Union estimated that Americans had invested $20 billions in receiving sets (a figure that has unquestionably increased greatly since then because of a vast flow of color TV sets into homes). Another $3 billions had been invested in antennas, and maintenance calls were estimated at another $1.25 billions a year. The point was also made that the public contributes to TV in another way, by buying enough goods to justify the billions spent yearly by advertisers to plug their wares on the air.

Thus, broadcasters would appear to have an obligation to try a little harder than they usually do. As a matter of fact, they have a legal duty to operate *in the public interest.* In return for a $150 fee covering a three-year term, the licensee is supposed to "consider the tastes, needs and desires of the public he is licensed to serve and should exercise conscientious efforts not only to ascertain them but also to carry them out as well as he reasonably can."

The way in which television interprets this led Judge Warren Burger, when he was on the U.S. Court of Appeals, to say, "After nearly five decades of operation the broadcast industry does not seem to have grasped the simple fact that a broadcast license is a public trust subject to termination for breach of duty."

However, *they* may decide it is necessary to make some necessary changes at this time for economic reasons. Television for a number of years has enjoyed a boom, but from all indications there are changes ahead. When cigarette advertising goes off the air in 1971 it will mean a cut of approximately 10 percent in total ad revenues. The gradual end of inflation will bring other curtailments. A slackening of car buying is being reflected in plans to cut down on commercials that tell you how easy it is to own the longest, lowest, fastest, most powerful, largest and most luxurious automobile on your block. And there are hints of other advertising cutbacks. This means greater competition for advertising dollars, and television will be further handicapped if advertisers feel that they are appealing to people who have a chip on their shoulders because of some of the things they see on the tube.

That chip could be easily removed if *they* made a fairly simple concession. Frustrated viewers are usually reasonable people who make no "non-negotiable demands," of the sort they keep hearing about on television. They merely ask that the programs they get over their airwaves be presented with greater objectivity. Specifically, they want an end to propaganda that persists in plugging the liberal and far-left concepts that are favored by so many television people. Viewers are willing to sit still for interminable commercials offering all sorts of products, but they refuse to serve as captive audiences for ideas they consider objectionable.

This kind of huckstering is not going to be stopped by circulating interoffice memoranda to station employees calling on them to stop making propaganda over the air. As Frank Shakespeare pointed out, most of these people try to be fair and they think they are fair, even though they are not. The necessary solution in television is likely to be that employed by Shakespeare to restore some needed objectivity to the United States Information Agency. Finding that the personnel was predominantly liberal he leavened it with some conservatives. However, any conservatives who go to work in network television or with many stations had better be rugged individuals. They will find the atmosphere pretty chilly, if not antagonistic.

There is another change *they* could make, to show the viewing public that they sincerely mean to provide better balance in the news. They could sign up a few conservative newscasters and commentators. At the present time William F. Buckley, Jr., is the only known conservative on a network and that network is a secondary one, largely improvised. Probably as much as anything else this Johnny-one-note aspect of network television convinces the Silent Majority that the medium has no use for the conservative viewpoint.

They could do something else to convince the Silent Majority of good faith. Many viewers have become dubious of the lack of objectivity that is apparent in some news specials. Aware of this, Thomas Petry, of WCNY-TV, Syracuse, gave one such message some added meaning. Mr. Petry had long been annoyed at the left-wing bias in material emanating from New York City liberals who are highly influential in programming for educational television. His annoyance came to a head when in April 1970 he was offered a special NET documentary on Fidel Castro that he and his staff considered blatant pro-Castro propaganda.

The station's first reaction was to refuse to run it because of its background. The film, *Fidel,* had been produced by one Saul Landau, a long-time apologist for the Castro regime and a person highly regarded in far-left circles. Other Landau films on Cuba that had been broadcast over NET stations had drawn strong public and congressional protests.

On second thought, Petry decided on another course. An outspoken advocate of balanced programming, he realized that the Castro film gave him an opportunity to give viewers a rounded picture of Communist Cuba and also to provide a lesson on propaganda techniques. He therefore obtained two other films dealing with Cuba. One of these, *Hitler in Havana,* was a strongly anti-Communist, anti-Castro portrayal of the tyranny now rampant in Cuba and the plight of those who have fled from it. The other was a historical offering titled *Cuba Night,* a CBS feature covering conditions in Cuba from the time of Castro's childhood until a few years ago.

The program built on these three films constituted an object lesson in the presentation of controversial subjects. The three films, with commentary by experts on Cuba, lasted from 9 p.m. until midnight on April 7, and at the end of that in-depth showing, WCNY-TV viewers had a very good idea of Castro and what he has done in

Cuba. They also had at least a glimmering of what is back of some of the stuff they see and hear concerning Cuba and what has happened there.

Few if any commercial television stations could devote three hours to this, vital as the subject is. However, even in much shorter periods they could provide the kind of rounded picture that Mr. Petry did, to the benefit of the viewing public and their own reputations for fairness. In passing, it might be mentioned that Thomas Petry has been trying to enlist other ETV stations in a move for greater objectivity. Many stations have joined in this but he is receiving little support from those that have the greatest influence over National Educational Television's overall policies.

At the risk of making themselves unpopular, television officials sometimes do take steps against those who abuse their facilities. CBS, for example, showed commendable courage in deciding that it had had enough of the Smothers Brothers brand of social and political commentary, on a program that was supposed to provide entertainment. Similar fortitude was shown by the American Telephone and Telegraph Company in an incident involving Simon & Garfunkel.

The phone company decided to sponsor a special featuring this very popular pair, but when the utility realized what it was getting into it withdrew and sold the show to Alberto Culver, the toiletry manufacturer. This brought the following reaction from Jack Gould in *The New York Times:*

> Mother Bell seems hypersensitive because the special contained no great revelation of the feelings of Simon & Garfunkel. They prefer love-making at the Woodstock Music Festival to killing in Vietnam, and can't forget just yet President Kennedy, Senator Robert F. Kennedy, the mule train hunger march on Washington and the strike of grape pickers in California. Apparently A.T. & T. wanted to buy only "entertainment" and get [*sic*] an editorial in the bargain.

On the face of it, Ma Bell obviously did figure on buying only a pair of entertainers, not some messages aimed at the hearts of liberals. Sam Goldwyn is reputed to have told his writers, "If you want to send messages, use Western Union." The phone company may have reasoned, similarly, that it had no need for a couple of messenger boys. In any case, it takes courage for a sponsor to turn down something of this sort since strong disapproval may be expected from those who favor such propagandizing.

It may be assumed that some of the things we see on television are there not because of a desire to propagandize but because those responsible simply did not know any better. The member of a TV crew who respectfully solicits comments from a "student leader" may not be aware that the fellow is actually a traveling agitator who has no connection at all with the campus being agitated, and may in fact have a record of arrests for troublemaking. The black militant whose views are solicited may be under criminal charges at the moment he is urging others, via TV, to join him in further criminality.

And those who will pass on this videotape may know little if anything more about their subjects than the camera crews did.

It would appear that the networks could use better research facilities and personnel with some expertise in agitators and subversives, if only to protect themselves against the charge that they irresponsibly increase the potential of troublemakers. The admirable biographical and subject index of *The New York Times* could serve as a model for network research facilities (even if *Times* people seem to make selective use of this vast reservoir of background information in writing their stories). At the very least, the networks should have available—and consult—reports of official investigative bodies so that a check can be made on the people who show up on tapes or who make themselves available for TV exposure. This would permit them to be properly introduced to viewers, if the networks considered them worthy of a forum.

They could also use a little more common sense in news coverage. No editor of a backwoods country weekly would think of seeking out the village idiot for interviews on world and national affairs. Yet sophisticated network people aim their cameras and poke their microphones in the direction of obvious paranoiacs, soliciting their incoherent observations on military strategy, morality, university administration, the political climate, jurisprudence, and other subjects.

In the previous chapter the point was made that television showed little interest in presenting programs of a positive nature, to show some of the things that are right with this country, its institutions and its people.

Every year, starting in April or May, television enters the doldrums, a period of mental hibernation for the medium. This is a time of year when anything goes and the vast wasteland becomes even more drab and forbidding. We see the re-runs of re-runs, and other reminders of the oldest and worst aspects of television. Now and then a summer replacement of merit is scheduled, but for the most part there is little of value to be seen for days on end.

They could do something about this. Here indeed is an opportunity to offer something new and worthwhile—shows of a truly positive nature. Here is where some of that dead time could be enlivened with programs that would give Americans a better understanding and appreciation of their heritage. Here is where television could place the accent where it belongs, on the positive, and help build some needed unity in this country of ours.

Some time ago the irrepressible Al Capp suggested that "every institution of learning in America add one more course—love of country."

If television were to act on this suggestion, the Silent Majority would have little to complain about.

CHAPTER TWELVE

What You Can Do

NICHOLAS Johnson, of the FCC, who has strong opinions concerning television, once said, "I think quite frankly that at the present time there is very little danger of intimidation of the mass media. My own feeling is quite the contrary, that the mass media, the networks in particular, broadcasting in particular, are probably now beyond the check of any institution in our society. The President, the Congress of the United States, the FCC, the foundations and universities are reluctant even to get involved. I think they may now be so powerful that they're beyond the check of anyone."

It sometimes *seems* as though television has reached a point where it is "beyond the check of any institution in our society," but that is not so. *You* can still exercise control over the medium by recognizing that it is your airwaves that are being used by broadcasters and by insisting that they use them in the public interest, as required by law.

However, to exercise control, the Silent Majority must be less reticent than it has been to date. It is not enough to make an occasional show of strength to register approval or disapproval of some action taken by television. There must be continuing interest in the medium and intelligent expressions of that interest.

A lesson applicable to television can be learned from recent campus disturbances. We have seen how a small but determined and articulate group can shut down a great university when the masses of students are apathetic. A radical minority presumes to speak for tens of thousands of students, and getting away with that audacity, it makes demands and commitments in the name of all the others.

This, incidentally, is a variation of an old Communist tactic that was often used to take over a union or some other organization. Although few in numbers, the comrades would so arrange and conduct themselves in a meeting hall that they gave the impression of being far more numerous than they really were. Working as a team, the Communists would then disrupt the meeting, using violence where necessary, and non-Communists would leave in disgust. Then the Reds would take over, pass resolutions, elect officers and sometimes even authorize the use of the organization's funds for their own purposes.

The point is that the democratic process can be utterly destroyed if the great majority of Americans let disruptive minorities get away with their attempts to seize control of strategic points. If the American people were to assert themselves, emphatically and forcefully, they could quickly put an end to many of the abuses that have developed because of general indifference and apathy. The American people have indeed been too tolerant of too many things for too long.

Television has contributed to this by presenting in sympathetic terms certain concepts that are unacceptable to the great majority of conservative Americans. When such concepts—usually products of the liberal left—are presented, they should not be accepted with equanimity but challenged and the challenge should be made by many. Conditioned by ratings, television operates "by the numbers." If only a few people take the trouble to express their likes and dislikes to broadcasters, we can expect no change. If many express their feelings, as they did at the time Spiro Agnew spoke out, the results may be as important in network planning as the Nielsen ratings.

Volume is not everything, however. If reports by some network people are true, much of the mail that poured into networks, stations and individuals following the Agnew criticism would have been better if left unmailed. Some was described as vituperative, with name-calling that reflected bigotry, and it merely antagonized those who received it.

As one who has been on the receiving end of considerable mail on a wide range of controversial subjects over almost two decades, I can speak with some authority on the matter. No one takes seriously a scurrilous letter, but attention is given to the one that deals in specifics and offers intelligent criticism or suggestions. So if you are writing to a station or a network to complain about a program or performer, be as specific as you can. What was it that aroused your anger? What was said or what was done? In this connection, if you go in for TV-watching with the feeling that a certain program may give you cause for complaint, makes notes. Or better yet, use a tape recorder to get it all.

Sometimes a questioning letter can be effective. If a certain commentator says something that sounds dubious to you, ask the station or network about it. Why did he say what he did, in just that way? Doesn't that fellow do quite a bit of that sort of thing? Haven't others criticized him for it? Has he ever taken a different position?

Obviously it is not just the news that can raise questions. One can legitimately question the way in which such people as Joan Baez, Pete Seeger, Stokeley Carmichael, Abbie Hoffman and others of that genus keep turning up as honored guests on influential network shows. Is this done as a matter of policy? Who pulls what strings to get such exposure? *Is it in the public interest* to permit these people to spread their propaganda? One can certainly question the things that these people inevitably talk about and viewers should ask why, under the Fairness Doctrine, the networks are not under an obligation to offer equal time to counter their expressions.

The viewer who becomes annoyed at certain aspects of television has a powerful weapon in the Fairness Doctrine, presented in full in an appendix of this book. Under this doctrine "equal opportunities" are supposed to be made available to present contrasting viewpoints of public importance. Thus if a station sets forth a premise that you think is wrong, you can call on it for the opportunity to present your side of the issue. Stations that present editorials often solicit opposing points of view, but even if they do not, the dissenting viewer can demand the right to rebut the station's expressed position.

Those public-service announcements telling that cigarette smoking is harmful are the result of the Fairness Doctrine, and stand as a testimonial to its effectiveness. John Banzhaf, a New York lawyer, protested to the FCC about cigarette advertising, saying that all those commercials represented only one point of view, that of the tobacco industry. He insisted that, to counter this, information be made available to show the hazards of smoking. He made his point, as millions know.

Under the Fairness Doctrine it would seem that viewers would have the right to see programs that would offset the many that are presented showing this nation in the worst possible light. This is a matter that might be worth looking into. Viewers can certainly ask for a little patriotism to be presented on their airwaves under the provisions of the Fairness Doctrine.

While they are at it, they would also be justified in calling on stations and networks to install some conservatives, not just in news departments but elsewhere, to help provide some balance, or fairness, or objectivity throughout the medium. To keep Bill Buckley from becoming lonesome as the only avowed conservative seen nationally on TV, it ought to be possible to draft such qualified people as John Chamberlain, David Lawrence, Henry J. Taylor, Irene Corbally Kuhn, James Kilpatrick, Maj. Gen. Thomas Lane, Victor Riesel and others. All these people have followings, from newspaper columns and other writings, so no television buildup would be necessary.

Who should get your complaints, recommendations or, when occasion warrants, the kudos that may be in order?

Most of these can be set forth in letters, but there are other channels. A personal approach is often more effective. A station's program director may prefer a personal discussion if you approach him with something specific, in the way of either a complaint or a suggestion. He will probably show more interest if you are presenting more than your own personal opinion, and can show that you speak for others besides yourself.

If you are a member of an organization that feels as you do about certain aspects of broadcasting, make your views known as a group. If your organization feels that a visit to a station is in order, set up a committee to go in a body. If your organization wishes to present its views to a network, it should do so officially, perhaps through a formal resolution.

There was a time when complaints to sponsors could be highly effective. Advertisers who invested a lot of money in broadcasting did so to create good will for themselves and the products they were offering. To protect their investment, they usually insisted that their programs be free of anything or anyone that would arouse resentment.Thus there was a time when people with records of activity in subversive organizations were anathema. Sponsors wanted no part of them because they knew how deeply most Americans resented them. But today all of that is changed. People with extensive records of Communist and pro-Communist affiliations and activities keep turning up on television, where they are often effusively welcomed. Some brazenly spout the current Party line. Ironically, in doing so these people undermine the very system that makes commercial broadcasting possible.

One reason for this is that sponsors no longer have the control they once exercised. Just as very few politicians, with the exception of such as Edward Kennedy or Nelson Rockefeller, have the financial resources to buy a great deal of network time, so with business. Not many manufacturers can afford, week after week, the kind of "hours" they used to sponsor on radio. Not only is TV time very expensive, but mounting a television production is an extremely costly operation. A program is therefore usually sold on a "participating" basis. American Motors will buy a few spots, Maxwell House a few more, and Fresca, Listerine, Alka-Seltzer and others will also come in. These sponsors and their agencies know in a general way what they are buying but they have little if any control of the content.

Responsibility is thus diffused. If a notorious rabble-rouser turns up on a program and a sponsor gets a few complaints, he can shrug them off, express due concern, and pass the complaints along to the network and his ad agency. However, if there are enough complaints, the sponsor may truly become alarmed. His remarks to the network may take on an edge, and he might start looking for another agency, one that will keep him out of hot water.

Naturally, liberals detest the very idea of a sponsor exercising any control over what he buys. This is put down as a form of thought control, which of course is *their* province. On the other hand, there is no reason why consumers should patronize an advertiser who offends them with an objectionable program. The person who is offended obviously has every right to tell the sponsor of his annoyance, even to the point of informing him that he has no intention of buying any more of his products.

In various public appearances and in his book *How to Talk Back to Your TV Set,* Nicholas Johnson advocates a rather extreme check on the medium. His suggestion is in the form of a reminder that if a station does a poor job, it can have its license taken away. This, he says, is "the citizen's ultimate control over broadcast programming."

In recent years groups have been challenging the right of stations to have their licenses renewed, but most of the challenges have come from liberals. The United Church of Christ took the lead in this field by an action against Jackson, Mississippi, station WLBT-TV, which allegedly excluded Negroes from its facilities and promoted segregationist views. In Media, Pa., a group of local organizations took legal action against radio station WXUR because they felt it carried too much right-wing political programming, without opposing viewpoints. In Los Angeles a group called on the FCC not to renew the license of KHJ-TV because they said it was not providing adequate service. A union in Ashtabula, Ohio, petitioned the FCC not to renew the licenses of radio stations in the area because the stations would not carry paid advertisements calling on consumers to boycott a certain store.

Indicating the trend, organizations that are interesting themselves in television in this respect include the American Civil Liberties Union, the Anti-Defamation League, the Institute for American Democracy (to combat "hate programming"), the United Church of Christ and the AFL-CIO.

It is interesting and perhaps significant to note the position of the usually critical Mr. Johnson to one highly controversial group of stations: "Many communities have the blessings of community-supported noncommercial stations. The Pacifica Foundation operates radio stations WBAI in New York, KPFA in Berkeley, and KPRK in Los Angeles. It has recently begun a new station in Houston."

If Mr. Johnson means to imply that the Pacifica Foundation operation is a blessing, there are many who feel differently. In *Barron's* for April 6, 1970, the publication's Washington editor, Shirley Scheibla, said this: "According to FCC files and the *Congressional Record,* programs broadcast recently over wholly-owned Pacifica stations have featured regular news commentaries by identified Communists and Black Panthers, tapes made by Radio Hanoi, Red Chinese propaganda and advocacy of blowing up police stations and fire houses." The article cited a long list of complaints in proof of the Pacifica Foundation's ultra-leftist propagandizing.

From all indications, however, Nicholas Johnson, an orthodox liberal, views such broadcasting with complete equanimity. The only broadcasters whose license renewals call for scrutiny or challenge are those that show signs of a conservative bias.

The kind of challenge suggested by Johnson constitutes an insidious form of censorship, and one that should concern broadcasters much more than Spiro Agnew's critical comments. With ultra-liberal outfits policing the airwaves and threatening non-conforming stations with the loss of their licenses, we may find even more of a liberal bias in the months and years ahead.

If this threat should develop, it is essential that conservatives be prepared to provide a countervailing force. A good starting place for this would be to challenge the licenses of Pacifica Foundation stations, and in doing so challenge those members of the FCC who have permitted and encouraged the growth of this chain.

More important than all this, however, is something else. To repeat what has been said before, there should be a greater emphasis on positive things. Listeners—you—must demand programs that build up instead of tearing down, and insist on programs that will show our nation as it really is. For, conceding some faults, it has a multitude of virtues that have been taken too much for granted or overlooked entirely. Children especially should be told about these virtues, so that they will grow up with the aim of building a better

America instead of seeking to tear down two centuries of work and sacrifice.

Public demand for good programming should be reinforced by public support when television does fulfill its promise. And in this area considerable criticism can be aimed at conservatives. One reason why we are deluged with smutty films and stage shows and far-left books is that such offerings earn money for their producers. People who like to think of themselves as liberals are certainly liberal patrons of such mental merchandise.

On the other hand, all too often conservatives fail to support those who seek to strengthen conservatism. Theater owners insist that they show X-rated films because movies suitable for family showing usually attract small audiences. Bookstores display as bestsellers the works of writers promoting liberal ideas because such books are bought, whereas conservative books often languish on the shelves. American business spends hundreds of millions advertising in media that are often unfriendly to business and to conservatism generally. Meanwhile, a magazine such as *National Review,* which staunchly supports the free-enterprise system, has few of America's giant corporations among its advertisers. Buyers of advertising space give various reasons for this, but the most cogent is likely to be, "Well, it's a matter of policy."

It is also likely to be a matter of economics. If something produces results, that is all that really matters. I once heard the advertising manager of a large New York concern explain why she had recommended a large advertising schedule for an openly Communistic newspaper. She herself was a very conservative Republican, as was the entire management of the company that employed her. There was certainly no sympathy for Communism in that setup; but, as she put it, "When we advertise in the ——— we can count on making sales, especially sales to retail outlets."

As the saying goes, that's business, and such thinking must be taken into account in dealing with television. The broadcaster is interested in maintaining and increasing his revenues, and sponsors will keep spending money in the medium as long as it successfully moves merchandise. What goes on the air is likely to be incidental to this.

If television offends or transgresses, and makes a great many people angry enough to complain to broadcasters, sponsors, government officials or to other media, there may be second thoughts about what is being aired. And that can bring about changes, as in the past.

But, again, that is the negative aspect. There are many times when television does some very fine things and these should be noted too. Viewers should be as quick to express approval as they are to condemn, and those expressions should go to everyone responsible for the good things.

It could mean better television.

Appendix A

===============

The text of Vice President Spiro Agnew's attack on media bias, delivered at Des Moines, Iowa, November 13, 1969.

Tonight I want to discuss the importance of the television news medium to the American people. No nation depends more on the intelligent judgment of its citizens. No medium has a more profound influence over public opinion. Nowhere in our system are there fewer checks on vast power. So, nowhere should there be more conscientious responsibility exercised than by the news media. The question is, Are we demanding enough of our television news presentations? And are the men of this medium demanding enough of themselves?

Monday night a week ago, President Nixon delivered the most important address of his Administration, one of the most important of our decade. His subject was Vietnam. His hope was to rally the American people to see the conflict through to a lasting and just peace in the Pacific. For 32 minutes, he reasoned with a nation that has suffered almost a third of a million casualties in the longest war in its history.

When the President completed his address—an address, incidentally, that he spent weeks in the preparation of—his words and policies were subjected to instant analysis and querulous criticism. The audience of 70 million Americans gathered to hear the President of the United States was inherited by a small band of network commentators and self-appointed analysts, the majority of whom expressed in one way or another their hostility to what he had to say.

It was obvious that their minds were made up in advance. Those who recall the fumbling and groping that followed President Johnson's dramatic disclosure of his intention not to seek another term have seen these men in a genuine state of nonpreparedness. This was not it.

One commentator twice contradicted the President's statement about the exchange of correspondence with Ho Chi Minh. Another challenged the President's abilities as a politician. A third asserted that the President was following a Pentagon line. Others, by the expression on their faces, the tone of their questions and the sarcasm of their responses, made clear their sharp disapproval.

To guarantee in advance that the President's plea for national unity would be challenged, one network trotted out Averell Harriman for the occasion. Throughout the President's message, he waited in the wings. When the President concluded, Mr. Harriman recited perfectly. He attacked the Thieu Government as unrepresentative; he criticized the President's speech for various deficiencies; he twice issued a call to the Senate Foreign Relations Committee to debate Vietnam once again; he stated his belief that the Vietcong or North Vietnamese did not really want a military takeover of South Vietnam; and he told a little anecdote about a "very, very responsible" fellow he had met in the North Vietnamese delegation.

All in all, Mr. Harriman offered a broad range of gratuitous advice challenging and contradicting the policies outlined by the President of the United States. Where the President had issued a call for unity, Mr. Harriman was encouraging the country not to listen to him.

A word about Mr. Harriman. For 10 months he was America's chief negotiator at the Paris peace talks—a period in which the United States swapped some of the greatest military concessions in the history of warfare for an enemy agreement on the shape of the bargaining table. Like Coleridge's Ancient Mariner, Mr. Harriman seems to be under some heavy compulsion to justify his failure to anyone who will listen. And the networks have shown themselves willing to give him all the air time he desires.

Now every American has a right to disagree with the President of the United States and to express publicly that disagreement. But the President of the United States has a right to communicate directly with the people who elected him, and the people of this country have the right to make up their own minds and form their own opinions about a Presidential address without having a President's words and thoughts characterized through the prejudices of hostile critics before they can even be digested.

When Winston Churchill rallied public opinion to stay the course against Hitler's Germany, he didn't have to contend with a gaggle of commentators raising doubts about whether he was reading public opinion right, or whether Britain had the stamina to see the war through.

When President Kennedy rallied the nation in the Cuban missile crisis, his address to the people was not chewed over by a roundtable of critics who disparaged the course of action he'd asked America to follow.

The purpose of my remarks tonight is to focus your attention on this little group of men who not only enjoy a right of instant rebuttal to every Presidential address, but, more importantly, wield a free hand in selecting, presenting and interpreting the great issues in our nation.

First, let's define that power. At least 40 million Americans every night, it's estimated, watch the network news. Seven million of them view A.B.C., the remainder being divided between N.B.C. and C.B.S.

According to Harris polls and other studies, for millions of Americans the networks are the sole source of national and world news. In Will Rogers's observation, what you knew was what you read in the newspaper. Today for growing millions of Americans, it's what they see and hear on their television sets.

Now how is this network news determined? A small group of men, numbering perhaps no more than a dozen anchormen, commentators and executive producers, settle upon the 20 minutes or so of film and commentary that's to reach the public. This selection is made from the 90 to 180 minutes that may be available. Their powers of choice are broad.

They decide what 40 to 50 million Americans will learn of the day's events in the nation and in the world.

We cannot measure this power and influence by the traditional democratic standards, for these men can create national issues overnight.

They can make or break by their coverage and commentary a moratorium on the war.

They can elevate men from obscurity to national prominence within a week. They can reward some politicians with national exposure and ignore others.

For millions of Americans the network reporter who covers a continuing issue—like the ABM or civil rights—becomes, in effect, the presiding judge in a national trial by jury.

It must be recognized that the networks have made important contributions to the national knowledge—for news, documentaries and specials. They have often used their power constructively and creatively to awaken the public conscience to critical problems. The networks made hunger and black lung disease national issues overnight. The TV networks have done what no other medium could have done in terms of dramatizing the horrors of war. The networks have tackled our most difficult social problems with a directness and an immediacy that's the gift of their medium. They focus the nation's attention on its environmental abuses—on pollution in the Great Lakes and the threatened ecology of the Everglades.

But it was also the networks that elevated Stokely Carmichael and George Lincoln Rockwell from obscurity to national prominence.

Nor is their power confined to the substantive. A raised eyebrow, an inflection of the voice, a caustic remark dropped in the middle of a broadcast can raise doubts in a million minds about the veracity of a public official or the wisdom of a Government policy.

One Federal Communications Commissioner considers the powers of the networks equal to that of local state and Federal Governments all combined. Certainly it represents a concentration of power over American public opinion unknown in history.

Now what do Americans know of the men who wield this power? Of the men who produce and direct the network news, the nation knows practically nothing. Of the commentators, most Americans know little other than that they reflect an urbane and assured presence seemingly well-informed on every important matter.

We do know that to a man these commentators and producers live and work in the geographical and intellectual confines of Washington, D.C., or New York City, the latter of which James Reston terms the most unrepresentative community in the entire United States.

Both communities bask in their own provincialism, their own parochialism.

We can deduce that these men read the same newspapers. They draw their political and social views from the same sources. Worse, they talk constantly to one another, thereby providing artificial reinforcement to their shared viewpoints.

Do they allow their biases to influence the selection and presentation of the news? David Brinkley states objectivity is impossible to normal human behavior. Rather, he says, we should strive for fairness.

Another anchorman on a network news show contends, and I quote: "You can't expunge all your private convictions just because you sit in a seat like this and a camera starts to stare at you. I think your program has to reflect what your basic feelings are. I'll plead guilty to that."

Less than a week before the 1968 election, this same commentator charged that President Nixon's campaign commitments were no more durable than campaign balloons. He claimed that, were it not for the fear of hostile reaction, Richard Nixon would be giving into, and I quote him exactly, "his natural instinct to smash the enemy with a club or go after him with a meat axe."

Had this slander been made by one political candidate about another, it would have been dismissed by most commentators as a partisan attack. But this attack emanated from the privileged sanctuary of a network studio and therefore had the apparent dignity of an objective statement.

The American people would rightly not tolerate this concentration of power in Government.

Is it not fair and relevant to question its concentration in the hands of a tiny, enclosed fraternity of privileged men elected by no one and enjoying a monopoly sanctioned and licensed by Government?

The views of the majority of this fraternity do not—and I repeat, not—represent the views of America.

That is why such a great gulf existed between how the nation received the President's address and how the networks reviewed it.

Not only did the country receive the President's address more warmly than the networks, but so also did the Congress of the United States.

Yesterday, the President was notified that 300 individual Congressmen and 50 Senators of both parties had endorsed his efforts for peace.

As with other American institutions, perhaps it is time that the networks were made more responsive to the views of the nation and more responsible to the people they serve.

Now I want to make myself perfectly clear. I'm not asking for Government censorship or any other kind of censorship. I'm asking whether a form of censorship already exists when the news that 40 million Americans receive each night is determined by a handful of men responsible only to their corporate employers and is filtered through a handful of commentators who admit to their own set of biases.

The questions I'm raising here tonight should have been raised by others long ago. They should have been raised by those Americans who have traditionally considered the preservation of freedom of speech and freedom of the press their special provinces of responsibility.

They should have been raised by those Americans who share the view of the late Justice Learned Hand that right conclusions are more likely to be gathered out of a multitude of tongues than through any kind of authoritative selection.

Advocates for the networks have claimed a First Amendment right to the same unlimited freedoms held by the great newspapers of America.

[But the situations are not identical. Where The New York Times reaches 800,000 people, N.B.C. reaches 20 times that number on its evening news. [The average weekday circulation of The Times in October was 1,012,367; the average Sunday circulation was 1,523,-558.] Nor can the tremendous impact of seeing television film and hearing commentary be compared with reading the printed page.]

A decade ago, before the network news acquired such dominance over public opinion, Walter Lippman spoke to the issue. He said there's an essential and radical difference between television and printing. The three or four competing television stations control virtually all that can be received over the air by ordinary television sets. But besides the mass circulation dailies, there are weeklies, monthlies, out-of-town newspapers and books. If a man doesn't like his newspaper, he can read another from out of town or wait for a weekly news magazine. It's not ideal, but it's infinitely better than the situation in television.

There if a man doesn't like what the networks are showing, all he can do is turn them off and listen to a phonograph. Networks he stated which are few in number have a virtual monopoly of a whole media of communications.

The newspapers of mass circulation have no monopoly on the medium of print.

Now a virtual monopoly of a whole medium of communication is not something that democratic people should blindly ignore. And we are not going to cut off our television sets and listen to the phonograph just because the airways belong to the networks. They don't. They belong to the people.

As Justice Byron White wrote in his landmark opinion six months ago, it's the right of the viewers and listeners, not the right of the broadcasters, which is paramount.

Now it's argued that this power presents no danger in the hands of those who have used it responsibly. But, as to whether or not the networks have abused the power they enjoy, let us call as our first witness former Vice President Humphrey and the city of Chicago. According to Theodore White, television's intercutting of the film from the streets of Chicago with the current proceedings on the floor of the convention created the most striking and false political picture of 1968—the nomination of a man for the American Presidency by the brutality and violence of merciless police.

If we are to believe a recent report of the House of Representatives Commerce Committee, then television's presentation of the violence in the streets worked an injustice on the reputation of the Chicago police. According to the committee findings, one network in particular presented, and I quote, "a one-sided picture which in large measure exonerates the demonstrators and protesters." Film of provocations of police that was available never saw the light of day while the film of a police response which the protesters provoked was shown to millions.

Another network showed virtually the same scene of violence from three separate angles without making clear it was the same scene. And, while the full report is reticent in drawing conclusions, it is not a document to inspire confidence in the fairness of the network news.

Our knowledge of the impact of network news on the national mind is far from complete, but some early returns are available. Again, we have enough information to raise serious questions about its effect on a democratic society. Several years ago Fred Friendly, one of the pioneers of network news, wrote that its missing ingredients were conviction, controversy and a point of view. The networks have compensated with a vengeance.

And in the networks' endless pursuit of controversy, we should ask: What is the end value—to enlighten or to profit? What is the end result—to inform or to confuse? How does the ongoing exploration for more action, more excitement, more drama serve our national search for internal peace and stability.

Gresham's Law seems to be operating in the network news. Bad news drives out good news. The irrational is more controversial than the rational. Concurrence can no longer compete with dissent.

One minute of Eldridge Cleaver is worth 10 minutes of Roy Wilkins. The labor crisis settled at the negotiating table is nothing compared to the confrontation that results in a strike—or better yet, violence along the picket lines.

Normality has become the nemesis of the network news. Now the upshot of all this controversy is that a narrow and distorted picture of America often emerges from the televised news.

A single, dramatic piece of the mosaic becomes in the minds of millions the entire picture. And the American who relies upon television for his news might conclude that the majority of American students are embittered radicals. That the majority of black Americans feel no regard for their country. That violence and lawlessness are the rule rather than the exception on the American campus.

We know that none of these conclusions is true.

Perhaps the place to start looking for a credibility gap is not in the offices of the Government in Washington but in the studios of the networks in New York.

Television may have destroyed the old stereotypes, but has it not created new ones in their places?

What has this passionate pursuit of controversy done to the politics of progress through local compromise essential to the functioning of a democratic society?

The members of Congress or the Senate who follow their principles and philosophy quietly in a spirit of compromise are unknown to many Americans, while the loudest and most extreme dissenters on every issue are known to every man in the street.

How many marches and demonstrations would we have if the marchers did not know that the ever-faithful TV cameras would be there to record their antics for the next news show?

We've heard demands that Senators and Congressmen and judges make known all their financial connections so that the public will know who and what influences their decisions and their votes. Strong arguments can be made for that view.

But when a single commentator or producer, night after night, determines for millions of people how much of each side of a great issue they are going to see and hear, should he not first disclose his personal views on the issue as well?

In this search for excitement and controversy, has more than equal time gone to the minority of Americans who specialize in attacking the United States—its institutions and its citizens?

Tonight I've raised questions. I've made no attempt to suggest the answers. The answers must come from the media men. They are challenged to turn their critical powers on themselves, to direct their energy, their talent and their conviction toward improving the quality and objectivity of news presentation.

They are challenged to structure their own civic ethics to relate their great responsibilities they hold.

And the people of America are challenged, too, challenged to press for responsible news presentations. The people can let the networks know that they want their news straight and objective. The people can register their complaints on bias through mail to the networks and phone calls to local stations. This is one case where the people must defend themselves; where the citizen, not the Government, must be the reformer; where the consumer can be the most effective crusader.

By way of conclusion, let me say that every elected leader in the United States depends on these men of the media. Whether what I've said to you tonight will be heard and seen at all by the nation is not my decision, it's not your decision, it's their decision.

In tomorrow's edition of The Des Moines Register, you'll be able to read a news story detailing what I've said tonight. Editorial comment will be reserved for the editorial page, where it belongs.

Should not the same wall of separation exist between news and comment on the nation's networks?

Now, my friends, we'd never trust such power, as I've described, over public opinion in the hands of an elected Government. It's time we questioned it in the hands of a small and unelected elite.

The great networks have dominated America's airwaves for decades. The people are entitled to a full accounting of their stewardship.

Appendix B

National Association of Broadcasters Code*

PREAMBLE

Television is seen and heard in every type of American home. These homes include children and adults of all ages, embrace all races and all varieties of religious faith, and reach those of every educational background. It is the responsibility of television to bear constantly in mind that the audience is primarily a home audience, and consequently that television's relationship to the viewers is that between guest and host.

The revenues from advertising support the free, competitive American system of telecasting and make available to the eyes and ears of the American people the finest programs of information, education, culture and entertainment. By law the television broadcaster is responsible for the programing of his station. He, however, is obliged to bring his positive responsibility for excellence and good taste in programing to bear upon all who have a hand in the production of programs, including networks, sponsors, producers of film and of live programs, advertising agencies, and talent agencies.

The American businesses which utilize television for conveying their advertising messages to the home by pictures with sound, seen free-of-charge on the home screen, are reminded that their responsibilities are not limited to the sale of goods and the creation of a favorable attitude toward the sponsor by the presentation of entertainment. They include, as well, responsibility for utilizing television to bring the best programs, regardless of kind, into American homes.

Television and all who participate in it are jointly accountable to

*Preamble through Part VIII.

the American public for respect for the special needs of children, for community responsibility, for the advancement of education and culture, for the acceptability of the program materials chosen, for decency and decorum in production, and for propriety in advertising. This responsibility cannot be discharged by any given group of programs, but can be discharged only through the highest standards of respect for the American home, applied to every moment of every program presented by television.

In order that television programing may best serve the public interest, viewers should be encouraged to make their criticisms and positive suggestions known to the television broadcasters. Parents in particular should be urged to see to it that out of the richness of television fare, the best programs are brought to the attention of their children.

I. ADVANCEMENT OF EDUCATION AND CULTURE

1. Commercial television provides a valuable means of augmenting the educational and cultural influences of schools, institutions of higher learning, the home, the church, museums, foundations, and other institutions devoted to education and culture.

2. It is the responsibility of a television broadcaster to call upon such institutions for counsel and cooperation and to work with them on the best methods of presenting educational and cultural materials by television. It is further the responsibility of stations, networks, advertising agencies and sponsors consciously to seek opportunities for introducing into telecasts factual materials which will aid in the enlightenment of the American public.

3. Education via television may be taken to mean that process by which the individual is brought toward informed adjustment to his society. Television is also responsible for the presentation of overtly instructional and cultural programs, scheduled so as to reach the viewers who are naturally drawn to such programs, and produced so as to attract the largest possible audience.

4. The television broadcaster should be thoroughly conversant with the educational and cultural needs and desires of the community served.

5. He should affirmatively seek out responsible and accountable educational and cultural institutions of the community with a view toward providing opportunities for the instruction and enlightenment of the viewers.

6. He should provide for reasonable experimentation in the development of programs specifically directed to the advancement of the community's culture and education.

7. It is in the interest of television as a vital medium to encourage and promote the broadcast of programs presenting genuine artistic or literary material, valid moral and social issues, significant controversial and challenging concepts and other subject matter involving adult themes. Accordingly, none of the provisions of this code, including those relating to the responsibility toward children, should be construed to prevent or impede their broadcast. All such programs, however, should be broadcast with due regard to the composition of the audience. The highest degree of care should be exercised to preserve the integrity of such programs and to ensure that the selection of themes, their treatment and presentation are made in good faith upon the basis of true instructional and entertainment values, and not for the purposes of sensationalism, to shock or exploit the audience or to appeal to prurient interests or morbid curiosity.

II. RESPONSIBILITY TOWARD CHILDREN

1. The education of children involves giving them a sense of the world at large. It is not enough that only those programs which are intended for viewing by children shall be suitable to the young and immature. In addition, those programs which might be reasonably expected to hold the attention of children and which are broadcast during times of the day when children may be normally expected to constitute a substantial part of the audience should be presented with due regard for their effect on children.

2. Such subjects as violence and sex shall be presented without undue emphasis and only as required by plot development or character delineation. Crime should not be presented as attractive or as a solution to human problems, and the inevitable retribution should be made clear.

3. The broadcaster should afford opportunities for cultural growth as well as for wholesome entertainment.

4. He should develop programs to foster and promote the commonly accepted moral, social and ethical ideals characteristic of American life.

5. Programs should reflect respect for parents, for honorable behavior, and for the constituted authorities of the American community.

6. Exceptional care should be exercised with reference to kidnapping or threats of kidnapping of children in order to avoid terrorizing them.

7. Material which is excessively violent or would create morbid suspense, or other undesirable reactions in children, should be avoided.

8. Particular restraint and care in crime or mystery episodes involving children or minors, should be exercised.

III. COMMUNITY RESPONSIBILITY

1. A television broadcaster and his staff occupy a position of responsibility in the community and should conscientiously endeavor to be acquainted fully with its needs and characteristics in order better to serve the welfare of its citizens.

2. Requests for time for the placement of public service announcements or programs should be carefully reviewed with respect to the character and reputation of the group, campaign or organization involved, the public interest content of the message, and the manner of its presentation.

IV. GENERAL PROGRAM STANDARDS

1. Program materials should enlarge the horizons of the viewer, provide him with wholesome entertainment, afford helpful stimulation, and remind him of the responsibilities which the citizen has towards his society. The intimacy and confidence placed in television demand of the broadcaster, the network and other program sources that they be vigilant in protecting the audience from deceptive program practices.

2. Profanity, obscenity, smut and vulgarity are forbidden, even when likely to be understood only by part of the audience. From time to time, words which have been acceptable, acquire undesirable meaning, and telecasters should be alert to eliminate such words.

3. Words (especially slang) derisive of any race, color, creed, nationality or national derivation, except wherein such usage would be for the specific purpose of effective dramatization such as combating prejudice, are forbidden, even when likely to be understood only by part of the audience. From time to time, words which have been acceptable, acquire undesirable meanings, and telecasters should be alert to eliminate such words.

4. Racial or nationality types shall not be shown on television in such a manner as to ridicule the race or nationality.

5. Attacks on religion and religious faiths are not allowed. Reverence is to mark any mention of the name of God, His attributes and powers. When religious rites are included in other than religious programs the rites shall be accurately presented. The office of minister, priest or rabbi shall not be presented in such a manner as to ridicule or impair its dignity.

6. Respect is maintained for the sanctity of marriage and the value of the home. Divorce is not treated casually as a solution for marital problems.

7. In reference to physical or mental afflictions and deformities, special precautions must be taken to avoid ridiculing sufferers from similar ailments and offending them or members of their families.

8. Excessive or unfair exploitation of others or of their physical or mental afflictions shall not be presented as praiseworthy.

The presentation of cruelty, greed and selfishness as worthy motivations is to be avoided.

9. Law enforcement shall be upheld and, except where essential to the program plot, officers of the law portrayed with respect and dignity.

10. Legal, medical and other professional advice, diagnosis and treatment will be permitted only in conformity with law and recognized ethical and professional standards.

11. The use of animals both in the production of television programs and as part of television program content shall at all times,

be in conformity with accepted standards of humane treatment.

12. Care should be exercised so that cigarette smoking will not be depicted in a manner to impress the youth of our country as a desirable habit worthy of imitation.

13. Criminality shall be presented as undesirable and unsympathetic. The condoning of crime and the treatment of the commission of crime in a frivolous, cynical or callous manner is unacceptable.

The presentation of techniques of crime in such detail as to invite imitation shall be avoided.

14. The presentation of murder or revenge as a motive for murder shall not be presented as justifiable.

15. Suicide as an acceptable solution for human problems is prohibited.

16. Illicit sex relations are not treated as commendable.

Sex crimes and abnormalities are generally unacceptable as program material.

The use of locations closely associated with sexual life or with sexual sin must be governed by good taste and delicacy.

17. Drunkenness should never be presented as desirable or prevalent.

The use of liquor in program content shall be de-emphasized. The consumption of liquor in American life, when not required by the plot or for proper characterization, shall not be shown.

18. Narcotic addiction shall not be presented except as a vicious habit. The administration of illegal drugs will not be displayed. The use of hallucinogenic drugs shall not be shown or encouraged as desirable or socially acceptable.

19. The use of gambling devices or scenes necessary to the development of plot or as appropriate background is acceptable only when presented with discretion and in moderation, and in a manner which would not excite interest in, or foster, betting nor be instructional in nature.

20. Telecasts of actual sport programs at which on the scene betting is permitted by law should be presented in a manner in keeping with federal, state and local laws, and should concentrate on the subject as a public sporting event.

21. Program material pertaining to fortune-telling, occultism, as-

trology, phrenology, palm-reading, numerology, mind-reading or character-reading, is unacceptable when presented for the purpose of fostering belief in these subjects.

22. Quiz and similar programs that are presented as contests of knowledge, information, skill or luck must, in fact, be genuine contests and the results must not be controlled by collusion with or between contestants, or any other action which will favor one contestant against any other.

23. No program shall be presented in manner which through artifice or simulation would mislead the audience as to any material fact. Each broadcaster must exercise reasonable judgment to determine whether a particular method of presentation would constitute a material deception, or would be accepted by the audience as normal theatrical illusion.

24. The appearances or dramatization of persons featured in actual crime news will be permitted only in such light as to aid law enforcement or to report the news event.

25. The use of horror for its own sake will be eliminated; the use of visual or aural effects which would shock or alarm the viewer, and the detailed presentation of brutality or physical agony by sight or by sound are not permissible.

26. Contests may not constitute a lottery.

27. The costuming of all performers shall be within the bounds of propriety and shall avoid such exposure or such emphasis on anatomical detail as would embarrass or offend home viewers.

28. The movements of dancers, actors, or other performers shall be kept within the bounds of decency, and lewdness and impropriety shall not be suggested in the positions assumed by performers.

29. Camera angles shall avoid such views of performers as to emphasize anatomical details indecently.

30. The use of the television medium to transmit information of any kind by the use of the process called "subliminal perception," or by the use of any similar technique whereby an attempt is made to convey information to the viewer by transmitting messages below the threshold of normal awareness, is not permitted.

31. The broadcaster shall be constantly alert to prevent activities

that may lead to such practices as the use of scenic properties, the choice and identification of prizes, the selection of music and other creative program elements and inclusion of any identification of commercial products or services, their trade names or advertising slogans, within a program dictated by factors other than the requirements of the program itself. The acceptance of cash payments or other considerations in return for including any of the above within the program is prohibited except in accordance with Sections 317 and 508 of the Communications Act.

32. A television broadcaster should not present fictional events or other non-news material as authentic news telecasts or announcements, nor should he permit dramatizations in any program which would give the false impression that the dramatized material constitutes news. Expletives, (presented aurally or pictorially) such as "flash" or "bulletin" and statements such as "we interrupt this program to bring you . . ." should be reserved specifically for news room use. However, a television broadcaster may properly exercise discretion in the use in non-news programs of words or phrases which do not necessarily imply that the material following is a news release.

33. Program content should be confined to those elements which entertain or inform the viewer and to the extent that titles, teasers and credits do not meet these criteria, they should be restricted or eliminated.

34. The creation of a state of hypnosis by act or demonstration on the air is prohibited and hypnosis as an aspect of "parlor game" antics to create humorous situations within a comedy setting cannot be used.

V. TREATMENT OF NEWS AND PUBLIC EVENTS NEWS

1. A television station's news schedule should be adequate and well-balanced.

2. News reporting should be factual, fair and without bias.

3. A television broadcaster should exercise particular discrimination in the acceptance, placement and presentation of advertising in news programs so that such advertising should be clearly distinguisheable from the news content.

4. At all times, pictorial and verbal material for both news and comment should conform to other sections of these standards, wherever such sections are reasonably applicable.

5. Good taste should prevail in the selection and handling of news:

Morbid, sensational or alarming details not essential to the factual report, especially in connection with stories of crime or sex, should be avoided. News should be telecast in such a manner as to avoid panic and unnecessary alarm.

6. Commentary and analysis should be clearly identified as such.

7. Pictorial material should be chosen with care and not presented in a misleading manner.

8. All news interview programs should be governed by accepted standards of ethical journalism, under which the interviewer selects the questions to be asked. Where there is advance agreement materially restricting an important or newsworthy area of questioning, the interviewer will state on the program that such limitation has been agreed upon. Such disclosure should be made if the person being interviewed requires that questions be submitted in advance or if he participates in editing a recording of the interview prior to its use on the air.

9. A television broadcaster should exercise due care in his supervision of content, format, and presentation of newscasts originated by his station, and in his selection of newscasters, commentators, and analysts.

PUBLIC EVENTS

1. A television broadcaster has an affirmative responsibility at all times to be informed of public events, and to provide coverage consonant with the ends of an informed and enlightened citizenry.

2. The treatment of such events by a television broadcaster should provide adequate and informed coverage.

VI. CONTROVERSIAL PUBLIC ISSUES

1. Television provides a valuable forum for the expression of responsible views on public issues of a controversial nature. The television broadcaster should seek out and develop with accountable

individuals, groups and organizations, programs relating to controversial public issues of import to his fellow citizens; and to give fair representation to opposing sides of issues which materially affect the life or welfare of a substantial segment of the public.

2. Requests by individuals, groups or organizations for time to discuss their views on controversial public issues, should be considered on the basis of their individual merits, and in the light of the contribution which the use requested would make to the public interest, and to a well-balanced program structure.

3. Programs devoted to the discussion of controversial public issues should be identified as such. They should not be presented in a manner which would mislead listeners or viewers to believe that the program is purely of an entertainment, news, or other character.

4. Broadcasts in which stations express their own opinions about issues of general public interest should be clearly identified as editorials. They should be unmistakably identified as statements of station opinion and should be appropriately distinguished from news and other program material.

VII. POLITICAL TELECASTS

1. Political telecasts should be clearly identified as such. They should not be presented by a television broadcaster in a manner which would mislead listeners or viewers to believe that the program is of any other character.

(Ref.: Communications Act of 1934, as amended, Secs. 315 and 317, and FCC Rules and Regulations, Secs. 3.654, 3.657, 3.663, as discussed in NAB's "A Political Catechism.")

VIII. RELIGIOUS PROGRAMS

1. It is the responsibility of a television broadcaster to make available to the community appropriate opportunity for religious presentations.

2. Telecasting which reaches men of all creeds simultaneously should avoid attacks upon religion.

3. Religious programs should be presented respectfully and accurately and without prejudice or ridicule.

4. Religious programs should be presented by responsible individuals, groups and organizations.

5. Religious programs should place emphasis on broad religious truths, excluding the presentation of controversial or partisan views not directly or necessarily related to religion or morality.

6. In the allocation of time for telecasts of religious programs the television station should use its best efforts to apportion such time fairly among the representative faith groups of its community.

Appendix C

[FCC 64-611]

APPLICABILITY OF THE FAIRNESS DOCTRINE IN THE HANDLING OF CONTROVERSIAL ISSUES OF PUBLIC IMPORTANCE

PART I—INTRODUCTION

It is the purpose of this Public Notice to advise broadcast licensees and members of the public of the rights, obligations, and responsibilities of such licensees under the Commission's "fairness doctrine", which is applicable in any case in which broadcast facilities are used for the discussion of a controversial issue of public importance. For this purpose, we have set out a digest of the Commission's interpretative rulings on the fairness doctrine. This Notice will be revised at appropriate intervals to reflect new rulings in this area. In this way, we hope to keep the broadcaster and the public informed of pertinent Commission determinations on the fairness doctrine, and thus reduce the number of these cases required to be referred to the Commission for resolution. Before turning to the digest of the rulings, we believe some brief introductory discussion of the fairness doctrine is desirable.

The basic administrative action with respect to the fairness doctrine was taken in the Commission's 1949 Report, Editorializing by Broadcast Licensees, 13 FCC 1246; Vol. 1, Part 3, R.R. 91–201.[1]

---

[1] Citations in "R.R." refer to Pike & Fischer, Radio Regulations. The above report thus deals not only with the question of editorializing but also the requirements of the fairness doctrine.

This report is attached hereto because it still constitutes the Commission's basic policy in this field.[2]

Congress recognized this policy in 1959. In amending Section 315 so as to exempt appearances by legally qualified candidates on certain news-type programs from the "equal opportunities" provision, it was stated in the statute that such action should not be construed as relieving broadcasters "* * * from the obligation imposed upon them under this Act to operate in the public interest and to afford reasonable opportunity for the discussion of conflicting views on issues of public importance" (Public Law 86–274, approved September 14, 1959, 73 Stat. 557).[3] The legislative history[4] establishes that this provision "is a restatement of the basic policy of the 'standard of fairness' which is imposed on broadcasters under the Communications Act of 1934" (H. Rept. No. 1069, 86th Cong., 1st Sess., p. 5).

While Section 315 thus embodies both the "equal opportunities" requirement and the fairness doctrine, they apply to different situations and in different ways. The "equal opportunities" requirement relates solely to use of broadcast facilities by candidates for public office. With certain exceptions involving specified news-type programs, the law provides that if a licensee permits a person who is a legally qualified candidate for public office to use a broadcast station, he shall afford equal opportunities to all other such candidates for that office in the use of the station. The Commission's Public Notice on Use of Broadcast Facilities by Candidates for Public Office, 27 Fed. Reg. 10063 (October 12, 1962), should be consulted with respect to "equal opportunities" questions involving political candidates.

The fairness doctrine deals with the broader question of affording reasonable opportunity for the presentation of contrasting view-

[2]The report (par. 6) also points up the responsibility of broadcast licensees to devote a reasonable amount of their broadcast time to the presentation of programs dealing with the discussion of controversial issues of public importance. See Appendix A.

[3]The full statement in Section 315(a) reads as follows: "Nothing in the foregoing sentence [i.e., exemption from equal time requirements for news-type programs] shall be construed as relieving broadcasters, in connection with the presentation of newscasts, news interviews, news documentaries, and on-the-spot coverage of news events, from the obligation imposed upon them under this chapter to operate in the public interest and to afford reasonable opportunity for the discussion of conflicting views on issues of public importance."

[4]See Appendix B.

points on controversial issues of public importance. Generally speaking, it does not apply with the precision of the "equal opportunities" requirement. Rather, the licensee, in applying the fairness doctrine, is called upon to make reasonable judgments in good faith on the facts of each situation—as to whether a controversial issue of public importance is involved, as to what viewpoints have been or should be presented, as to the format and spokesmen to present the viewpoints, and all the other facets of such programming. See par. 9, Editorializing Report. In passing on any complaint in this area, the Commission's role is not to substitute its judgment for that of the licensee as to any of the above programming decisions, but rather to determine whether the licensee can be said to have acted reasonably and in good faith. There is thus room for considerably more discretion on the part of the licensee under the fairness doctrine than under the "equal opportunities" requirement.

INTERPRETATIVE RULINGS—COMMISSION PROCEDURE

We set forth below a digest of the Commission's rulings on the fairness doctrine. References, with citations, to the Commission's decisions or rulings are made so that the researcher may, if he desires, review the complete text of the Commission's ruling. Copies of rulings may be found in a "Fairness Doctrine" folder kept in the Commission's Reference Room.

In an area such as the fairness doctrine, the Commission's rulings are necessarily based upon the facts of the particular case presented, and thus a variation in facts might call for a different or revised ruling. We therefore urge that interested persons, in studying the rulings for guidance, look not only to the language of the ruling but the specific factual context in which it was made.

It is our hope, as stated, that this Notice will reduce significantly the number of fairness complaints made to the Commission. Where complaint is made to the Commission, the Commission expects a complainant to submit specific information indicating (1) the particular station involved; (2) the particular issue of a controversial nature discussed over the air; (3) the date and time when the program was carried; (4) the basis for the claim that the station has presented only one side of the question; and (5) whether the station has afforded, or has plans to afford, an opportunity for the presentation of contrasting viewpoints.[5] (Lar Daly, 19 R.R. 1104, March 24, 1960; cf. Cullman Bctg. Co., FCC 63–849, Sept. 18, 1963.)

If the Commission determines that the complaint sets forth sufficient facts to warrant further consideration, it will promptly advise the licensee of the complaint and request the licensee's comments on the matter. Full opportunity is given to the licensee to set out all programs which he has presented, or plans to present, with respect to the issue in question during an appropriate time period. Unless additional information is sought from either the complainant or the licensee, the matter is then usually disposed of by Commission action. (Letter of September 18, 1963 to Honorable Oren Harris, FCC 63–851.)

Finally, we repeat what we stated in our 1949 Report:

* * * It is this right of the public to be informed, rather than any right on the part of the Government, any broadcast licensee or any individual member of the public to broadcast his own particular views on any matter, which is the foundation stone of the American system of broadcasting.

PART II—COMMISSION RULINGS

A. *Controversial Issue of Public Importance.*

1. *Civil rights as controversial issue.* In response to a Commission inquiry, a station advised the Commission, in a letter dated March 6, 1950, that it had broadcast editorial programs in support of a National Fair Employment Practices Commission on January 15–17, 1950, and that it had taken no affirmative steps to encourage and implement the presentation of points of view with respect to these matters which differed from the point of view expressed by the station.

Ruling. The establishment of a National Fair Employment Practices Commission constitutes a controversial question of public im-

[5]The complainant can usually obtain this information by communicating with the station.

portance so as to impose upon the licensee the affirmative duty to aid and encourage the broadcast of opposing views. It is a matter of common knowledge that the establishment of a National Fair Employment Practices Commission is a subject that has been actively controverted by members of the public and by members of the Congress of the United States and that in the course of that controversy numerous differing views have been espoused. The broadcast by the station of a relatively large number of programs relating to this matter over a period of three days indicates an awareness of its importance and raises the assumption that at least one of the purposes of the broadcasts was to influence public opinion. In our report In the Matter of Editorializing by Broadcast Licensees, we stated that:

* * * In appraising the record of a station in presenting programs concerning a controversial bill pending before the Congress of the United States, if the record disclosed that the licensee had permitted only advocates of the bill's enactment to utilize its facilities to the exclusion of its opponents, it is clear that no independent appraisal of the bill's merits by the commission would be required to reach a determination that the licensee had misconstrued its duties and obligations as a person licensed to serve the public interest.

In light of the foregoing the conduct of the licensee was not in accord with the principles set forth in the report. (New Broadcasting Co. (WLIB), 6 R.R. 258, April 12, 1950.)

2. *Political spot announcements.* In an election an attempt was made to promote campaign contributions to the candidates of the two major parties through the use of spot announcements on broadcast stations. Certain broadcast stations raised the question whether the airing of such announcements imposed an obligation under Section 315 of the Act and/or the fairness doctrine to broadcast such special announcements for all candidates running for a particular office in a given election.

Ruling. The "equal opportunities" provision of Section 315 applies only to uses by candidates and not to those speaking in behalf of or against candidates. Since the above announcements did not contemplate the appearance of a candidate, the "equal opportunities" provision of Section 315 would not be applicable. The fairness doctrine is, however, applicable. (Letter to Lawrence M. C. Smith, FCC 63–358, 25 R.R. 291, April 17, 1963.) See Ruling No. 13.

3. *"Reports to the People".* The complaint of the Chairman of the Democratic State Committee of New York alleged that an address by Governor Dewey over the facilities of the stations affiliated with the CBS network on May 2, 1949, entitled "A Report to the People of New York State," was political in nature and contained statements of a controversial nature. The CBS reply stated, in substance, that it was necessary to distinguish between the reports made by holders of office to the people whom they represented and the partisan political activities of the individuals holding office.

Ruling. The Commission recognizes that public officials may be permitted to utilize radio facilities to report on their stewardship to the people and that "the mere claim that the subject is political does not automatically require that the opposite political party be given equal facilities for a reply." On the other hand, it is apparent that so-called reports to the people may constitute attacks on the opposite political party or may be a discussion of a public controversial issue. Consistent with the views expressed by the Commission in the Editorializing Report, it is clear that the characterization of a particular program as a report to the people does not necessarily establish such a program as noncontroversial in nature so as to avoid the requirement of affording time for the expression of opposing views. In that Report, we stated "* * * that there can be no one all embracing formula which licensees can hope to apply to insure the fair and balanced presentation of all public issues * * *. The licensee will in each instance be called upon to exercise his best judgment and good sense in determining what subjects should be considered, the particular format of the programs to be devoted to each subject, the different shades of opinion to be presented, and the spokesmen for each point of view." The duty of the licensee to make time available for the expression of differing views is invoked where the facts and circumstances in each case indicate an area of controversy and differences of opinion where the subject matter is of public importance. In the light of the foregoing, the Commission concludes that "it does not appear that there has been the abuse of judgment on the part of [CBS] such as to warrant holding a hearing on its applications for renewal of license." (Paul E. Fitzpatrick, 6 R.R. 543, July 21, 1949; (see also, California Democratic State Central Committee, Public Notice 95873, 20 R.R. 867.869, October 31, 1960.))

4. *Controversial issue within service area.* A station broadcast a statement by the President of CBS opposing pay TV; two newscasts containing the views of a Senator opposed to pay TV; one newscast reporting the introduction by a Congressman of an anti-pay TV bill; a half-hour network program on pay TV in which both sides were represented, followed by a ten-minute film clip of a Senator opposing pay TV; a half-hour program in which a known opponent of pay TV was interviewed by interrogators whose questions in some instances indicated an opinion by the questioner favorable to pay TV. In a hearing upon the station's application for modification of its construction permit, an issue was raised whether the station had complied with the requirements of the fairness doctrine. The licensee stated that while nationally pay TV was "certainly" a controversial issue, it regarded pay TV as a local controversial issue only to a very limited extent in its service area, and therefore it was under no obligation to take the initiative to present the views of advocates of pay TV.

Ruling. The station's handling of the pay TV question was improper. It could be inferred that the station's sympathies with the opposition to pay TV made it less than a vigorous searcher for advocates of subscription television. The station evidently thought the subject of sufficient general interest (beyond its own concern in the matter) to devote broadcast time to it, and even to preempt part of a local program to present the views of the Senator in opposition to pay TV immediately after the balanced network discussion program, with the apparent design of neutralizing any possible public sympathy for pay TV which might have arisen from the preceding network forum. The anti-pay TV side was represented to a greater extent on the station than the other, though it cannot be said that the station choked off the expression of all views inimical to its interest. A licensee cannot excuse a one-sided presentation on the basis that the subject matter was not controversial in its service area, for it is only through a fair presentation of all facts and arguments on a particular question that public opinion can properly develop. (In re The Spartan Radiocasting Co., 33 F.C.C., 765, 771, 794–795, 802–803, November 21, 1962.)

5. *Substance of broadcast.* A number of stations broadcast a program entitled "Living Should Be Fun", featuring a nutritionist giving comment and advice on diet and health. Complaint was made that the program presented only one side of controversial issues of public importance. Several licensees contended that a program dealing with the desirability of good health and nutritious diet should not be placed in the category of discussion of controversial issues.

Ruling. The Commission cannot agree that the program consisted merely of the discussion of the desirability of good health and nutritious diet. Anyone who listened to the program regularly—and station licensees have the obligation to know what is being broadcast over their facilities—should have been aware that at times controversial issues of public importance were discussed. In discussing such subjects as the flouridation of water, the value of krebiozen in the treatment of cancer, the nutritive qualities of white bread, and the use of high potency vitamins without medical advice, the nutritionist emphasized the fact that his views were opposed to many authorities in these fields, and on occasions on the air, he invited those with opposing viewpoints to present such viewpoints on his program. A licensee who did not recognize the applicability of the fairness doctrine failed in the performance of his obligations to the public. (Report on "Living Should be Fun" Inquiry, 33 F.C.C. 101, 107, 23 R.R. 1599, 1606, July 18, 1962.)

6. *Substance of broadcast.* A station broadcast a program entitled "Communist Encirclement" in which the following matters, among others, were discussed: socialist forms of government were viewed as a transitory form of government leading eventually to communism; it was asserted that this country's continuing foreign policy in the

Far East and Latin America, the alleged infiltration of our government by communists, and the alleged moral weakening in our homes, schools and churches have all contributed to the advance of international communism. In response to complaints alleging one-sided presentation of these issues, the licensee stated that since it did not know of the existence of any communist organizations or communists in its community, it was unable to afford opportunity to those who might wish to present opposing views.

Ruling. In situations of this kind, it was not and is not the Commission's intention to require licensees to make time available to communists or the communist viewpoint. But the matters listed above raise controversial issues of public importance on which persons other than communists hold contrasting views. There are responsible contrasting viewpoints on the most effective methods of combatting communism and communist infiltration. Broadcast of proposals supporting only one method raises the question whether reasonable opportunity has been afforded for the expression of contrasting viewpoints. (Letter to Tri-State Broadcasting Company, Inc., April 26, 1962 (staff letter).)

7. *Substance of broadcast.* In 1957, a station broadcast a panel discussion entitled "The Little Rock Crisis" in which several public officials appeared, and whose purpose, a complainant stated, was to stress the maintenance of segregation and to express an opinion as to what the Negro wants or does not want. A request for time to present contrasting viewpoints was refused by the licensee who stated that the program was most helpful in preventing trouble by urging people to keep calm and look to their elected representatives for leadership, that it was a report by elected officials to the people, and that therefore no reply was necessary or advisable.

Ruling. If the matters discussed involved no more than urging people to remain calm, it can be urged that no question exists as to fair presentation. However, if the station permitted the use of its facilities for the presentation of one side of the controversial issue of racial integration, the station incurred an obligation to afford a reasonable opportunity for the expression of contrasting views. The fact that the proponents of one particular position were elected officials did not in any way alter the nature of the program or remove the applicability of the fairness doctrine. See Ruling No. 3. (Lamar Life Insurance Co., FCC 59–651, 18 R.R. 683, July 1, 1959.)

8. *National controversial issues.* Stations broadcast a daily commentary program six days a week, in three of which views were expressed critical of the proposed nuclear weapons test ban treaty. On one of the stations the program was sponsored six days a week and on the other one day a week. A national committee in favor of the proposed treaty requested that the stations afford free time to present a tape of a program containing viewpoints opposed to those in the sponsored commentary program. The stations indicated, among other things, that it was their opinion that the fairness doctrine is applicable only to local issues.

Ruling. The keystone of the fairness doctrine and of the public interest is the right of the public to be informed—to have presented to it the "conflicting views of issues of public importance." Where a licensee permits the use of its facilities for the expression of views on controversial local or national issues of public importance such as the nuclear weapons test ban treaty, he must afford reasonable opportunities for the presentation of contrasting views by spokesmen for other responsible groups. (Letter to Cullman Broadcasting Co., Inc., FCC 63–849, September 18, 1963.) See Rulings No. 16 and 17 for other aspects of the Cullman decision.

B. *Licensee's obligation to afford reasonable opportunity for the presentation of contrasting viewpoints.*

9. *Affirmative duty to encourage.* In response to various complaints alleging that a station had been "one-sided" in its presentations on controversial issues of public importance, the licensee concerned rested upon its policy of making time available, upon request, for "the other side."

Ruling. The licensee's obligations to serve the public interest cannot be met merely through the adoption of a general policy of not refusing to broadcast opposing views where a demand is made of the station for broadcast time. As the Commission pointed out in the Editorializing Report (par. 9):

* * * If, as we believe to be the case, the public interest is best served in a democracy through the ability of the people to hear expositions of the various positions taken by responsible groups and individuals on particular topics and to choose between them, it is evident that broadcast licensees have an affirmative duty generally to encourage and implement the broadcast of all sides of controversial public issues over their facilities, over and beyond their obligation to make available on demand opportunities for the expression of opposing views. It is clear that any approximation of fairness in the presentation of any controversy will be difficult if not impossible of achievement unless the licensee plays a conscious and positive role in bringing about balanced presentation of the opposing viewpoints.

(John J. Dempsey, 6 R.R. 615, August 16, 1950; Editorializing Report, par. 9) (See also Metropolitan Bctg. Corp., Public Notice 82386, 19 R.R. 602, 604, December 29, 1959.)

10. *Non-delegable duty.* Approximately 50 radio stations broadcast a program entitled "Living Should Be Fun", featuring a nutritionist giving comment and advice on diet and health. The program was syndicated and taped for presentation, twenty-five minutes a day, five days a week. Many of the programs discussed controversial issues of public importance. In response to complaints that the stations failed to observe the requirements of the fairness doctrine, some of the licensees relied upon (i) the nutritionist's own invitation to those with opposing viewpoints to appear on his program or (ii) upon the assurances of the nutritionist or the sponsor that the program fairly represented all responsible contrasting viewpoints on the issues with which it dealt, as an adequate discharge of their obligations under the fairness doctrine.

Ruling. Those licensees who relied solely upon the assumed built-in fairness of the program itself, or upon the nutritionist's invitation to those with opposing viewpoints, cannot be said to have properly discharged their responsibilities. Neither alternative is likely to produce the fairness which the public interest demands. There could be many valid reasons why the advocate of an opposing viewpoint would be unwilling to appear upon such a program. In short, the licensee may not delegate his responsibilities to others, and particularly to an advocate of one particular viewpoint. As the Commission said in our Report in the Matter of Editorializing by Broadcast Licensees, "It is clear that any approximation of fairness in the presentation of any controversy will be difficult if not impossible of achievement unless the licensee plays a conscious and positive role in bringing about balanced presentation of the opposing viewpoints." (Report on "Living Should Be Fun" Inquiry, 33 FCC 101, 107, 23 R.R. 1599, 1606, July 18, 1962.)

11. *Reliance upon other media.* In January 1958, the issue of subscription television was a matter of public controversy, and it was generally known that the matter was the subject of Congressional hearings being conducted by the House and Senate Interstate and Foreign Commerce Committees. On Monday, January 27, 1958, between 9:30 and 10:00 p.m., WSOC-TV broadcast the Program "Now It Can Be Tolled" (simultaneously with the other Charlotte television station, WBTV), a program consisting of a skit followed by a discussion in which the president of WSOC-TV and the vice president and general manager of Station WBTV were interviewed by employees of the two stations. The skit and interview were clearly weighted against subscription TV, and in the program the station made clear its preference for the present TV system. On Saturday, February 1, 1958, WSOC-TV presented for 15 minutes, beginning at 3:35 p.m., a film clip in which a United States Representative discussed subscription television and expressed his opposition thereto. From January 24 to January 30, 1958, inclusive, WSOC-TV presented a total of 43 spot announcements, all of them against subscription television, and urged viewers, if they opposed it, to write their Congressmen without delay to express their opposition. WSOC-TV did not broadcast any programs or announcements presenting a viewpoint favorable to subscription television although on February 28, 1958, the station did (together with the management of Station WBTV) send a telegram to the three chief subscription television groups, offering them joint use of the two Charlotte stations, without charge, at a time mutually agreeable to all parties concerned, for the purpose of putting on a program by the proponents of pay TV. This offer was refused by Skiatron, one of the three groups. In its reply

to the Commission's inquiry, the station referred to "the large amount of publicity already given by the Pay-TV proponents in newspapers, magazines and by direct mail," and asserted that its decision in this matter was taken "in an effort to furnish the public with the opposing viewpoints on the subject * * *"

Ruling. The station's broadcast presentation of the subscription TV issue was essentially one-sided, and, taking into account the circumstances of the situation existing at the time, the station did not make any timely effort to secure the presentation of the other side of the issue by responsible representatives. It is the Commission's view that the requirement of fairness, as set forth in the Editorializing Report, applies to a broadcast licensee irrespective of the position which may be taken by other media on the issue involved; and that the licensee's own performance in this respect, in and of itself, must demonstrate compliance with the fairness doctrine. (Letter to WSOC Broadcasting Co., FCC 58–686, 17 R.R. 548, 550, July 16, 1958.)

C. *Reasonable opportunity for the presentation of contrasting viewpoints.*

12. *"Equal time" not required.* Licensee broadcast over its several facilities on October 28, 1960, a 30-minute documentary concerning a North Dakota hospital. The last five minutes of the program consisted of an interview of the Superintendent of the hospital and the Chairman of the Board of Administration for State Institutions who responded to charges that the complainant, a candidate for the office of Attorney General of North Dakota, had publicly leveled against the Superintendent and Chairman concerning the administration of the hospital. On November 4, 1960 and at about the same viewing time as the preceding documentary, complainant's 30-minute broadcast was aired over the Stations in which complainant presented his allegations about the professional, administrative, and disciplinary conditions at the hospital and a state training school. The following day (November 5) licensee presented a 30-minute documentary on the state training school, the last five minutes of which consisted of a discussion of the charges made by complainant on his November 4 program by a spokesman for the opposing political party, and by the interviewees of the October 28 program. Licensee refused com-

plaintant's request for "equal time" to reply to the November 5 broadcast.

Ruling. In view of the fact that the "equal opportunities" requirement of Section 315 becomes applicable only when an opposing candidate for the same office has been afforded broadcast time, and that the complainant's political opponent did not appear on any of the programs in question (and, in fact, was never mentioned during the broadcast of these programs), the Commission reviewed the matter in light of the fairness doctrine. Unlike the "equal opportunities" requirement of Section 315, the fairness doctrine requires that where a licensee affords time over his facilities for an expression of one opinion on a controversial issue of public importance, he is under obligation to insure that proponents of opposing viewpoints are afforded a reasonable opportunity for the presentation of such views. The Commission concludes that on the facts before it, the licensee's actions were not inconsistent with the principles enunciated in the Editorializing Report. (Hon. Charles L. Murphy, FCC 62–737, 23 R.R. 953, July 13, 1962.)

13. *"Equal time" not required.* During a state-wide election an attempt was made to promote bipartisan campaign contributions, particularly for the candidates of the two major parties running for Governor and Senator, through the use of spot announcements on broadcast stations. Several stations raised the question whether the broadcast of these announcements would impose upon them the obligation, under the fairness doctrine, to broadcast such special announcements for all candidates running for a particular office in a given election.

Ruling. If there were only the two candidates of the major parties for the office in question, fairness would obviously require that these two be treated roughly the same with respect to the announcements. But it does not follow that if there were, in addition, so-called minority party candidates for the office of Senator, these candidates also would have to be afforded a roughly equivalent number of similar announcements. In such an event, the licensee would be called upon to make a good faith judgment as to whether there can reasonably be said to be a need or interest in the community calling for some provision of announcement time to these other parties or candidates and, if so, to determine the extent of that interest or need and the appropriate way to meet it. In short, the licensee's obligation under the fairness doctrine is to afford a reasonable opportunity for the presentation of opposing views in the light of circumstances—an obligation calling for the same kind of judgment as in the case where party spokesmen (rather than candidates) appear. (Letter to Mr. Lawrence M. C. Smith, FCC 63–658, April 18, 1963.)

14. *No necessity for presentation on same program.* In the proceedings leading to the Editorializing Report, it was urged, in effect, that contrasting viewpoints with respect to a controversial issue of public importance should be presented on the same program.

Ruling. The commission concluded that any rigid requirement in this respect would seriously limit the ability of the licensees to serve the public interest. "Forums and roundtable discussions, while often excellent techniques of presenting a fair cross section of differing viewpoints on a given issue, are not the only appropriate devices for radio discussion, and in some circumstances may not be particularly appropriate or advantageous." (Par. 8, Editorializing Report.)

15. *Overall performance on the issue.* A licensee presented a program in which views were expressed critical of the proposed nuclear weapons test ban treaty. The licensee rejected a request of an organization seeking to present views favorable to the treaty, on the ground, among others, that the contrasting viewpoint on this issue had already been presented over the station's facilities in other programming.

Ruling. The licensee's overall performance is considered in determining whether fairness has been achieved on a specific issue. Thus, where complaint is made, the licensee is afforded the opportunity to set out all the programs, irrespective of the programming format, which he has devoted to the particular controversial issue during the appropriate time period. In this case, the Commission files contained no complaints to the contrary, and therefore, if it was the licensee's good faith judgment that the public had had the opportunity fairly to hear contrasting views on the issue involved in his other programming, it appeared that the licensee's obligation pursuant to the fairness doctrine had been met. (Letter to Cullman Bctg. Co., FCC 63–849, September 18, 1963; Letter of September 20, 1963, FCC 63–851, to Honorable Oren Harris.)

D. *Limitations which may reasonably be imposed by the licensee.*

16. *Licensee discretion to choose spokesman.* See Ruling 8 for facts.

Ruling. Where a licensee permits the use of its facilities for the expression of views on controversial local or national issues of public importance such as the nuclear weapons test ban treaty, he must afford reasonable opportunities for the presentation of contrasting views by spokesmen for other responsible groups. There is, of course, no single method by which this obligation is to be met. As the Editorializing Report makes clear, the licensee has considerable discretion as to the techniques or formats to be employed and the spokesmen for each point of view. In the good faith exercise of his best judgment, he may, in a particular case, decide upon a local rather than regional or national spokesmen—or upon a spokesman for a group which also is willing to pay for the broadcast time. Thus, with the exception of the broadcast of personal attacks (see Part E), there is no single group or person entitled as a matter of right to present a viewpoint differing from that previously expressed on the station. (Letter to Cullman Broadcasting Co., Inc., FCC 63–849, September 18, 1963.)

17. *Non-local spokesman; paid sponsorship.* See Ruling 8 for facts. The stations contended that their obligation under the fairness doctrine extended only to a local group or its spokesman, and also inquired whether they were required to give free time to a group wishing to present viewpoints opposed to those aired on a sponsored program.

Ruling. Where the licensee has achieved a balance presentation of contrasting views, either by affording time to a particular group or person of its own choice or through its own programming, the licensee's obligations under the fairness doctrine—to inform the public— will have been met. But, it is clear that the public's paramount right to hear opposing views on controversial issues of public importance cannot be nullified by either the inability of the licensee to obtain paid sponsorship of the broadcast time or the licensee's refusal to consider requests for time to present a conflicting viewpoint from an organization on the sole ground that the organization has no local chapter. In short, where the licensee has chosen to broadcast a sponsored program which for the first time presents one side of a controversial issue, has not presented (or does not plan to present) contrasting viewpoints in other programming, and has been unable to obtain paid sponsorship for the appropriate presentation of the opposing viewpont or viewpoints, he cannot reject a presentation otherwise suitable to the licensee—and thus leave the public uninformed—on the ground that he cannot obtain paid sponsorship for that presentation. (Letter to Cullman Broadcasting Co., Inc., FCC 63–849, September 18, 1963.)

18. *Unreasonable limitation; refusal to permit appeal not to vote.* A station refused to sell broadcast time to the complainant who, as a spokesman for a community group, was seeking to present his point of view concerning a bond election to be held in the community; the station had sold time to an organization in favor of the bond issue. The complainant alleged that the station had broadcast editorials urging people to vote in the election and that his group's position was that because of the peculiarities in the bond election law (more than 50 percent of the electorate had to vote in the election for it to be valid), the best way to defeat the proposed measure was for people not to vote in the election. The complainant alleged, and the station admitted, that the station refused to sell him broadcast time because the licensee felt that to urge people not to vote was improper.

Ruling. Because of the peculiarities of the state election law, the sale of broadcast time to an organization favoring the bond issue, and the urging of listeners to vote, the question of whether to vote became an issue. Accordingly, by failing to broadcast views urging listeners not to vote, the licensee failed to discharge the obligations imposed upon him by the Commission's Report on Editorializing. (Letter to Radio Station WMOP, January 21, 1962 (staff ruling).)

19. *Unreasonable limitation; insistence upon request from both parties to dispute.* During the period of a labor strike which involved a matter of paramount importance to the community and to the

nation at large, a union requested broadcast time to discuss the issues involved. The request was denied by the station solely because of its policy to refuse time for such discussion unless both the union and the management agreed, in advance, that they would jointly request and use the station, and the management of the company involved in the strike had refused to do so.

Ruling. In view of the licensee's statement that the issue was "of paramount importance to the community * * *," the licensee's actions were not in accordance with the principles enunciated in the Editorializing Report, specifically that portion of par. 8, which states that:

* * * where the licensee has determined that the subject is of sufficient import to receive broadcast attention, it would obviously not be in the public interest for spokesmen for one of the opposing points of view to be able to exercise a veto power over the entire presentation by refusing to broadcast its position. Fairness in such circumstances might require no more than that the licensee make a reasonable representation of the particular position and if it fails in this effort, to continue to make available its facilities to the spokesmen for such position in the event that, after the original programs are broadcast, they then decide to avail themselves of a right to present their contrary opinion.

(Par. 8, Report on Editorializing by Broadcast Licensees; The Evening News Ass'n (WWJ), 6 R.R. 283, April 21, 1950.)

E. *Personal Attack Principle.*

20. *Personal attack.* A newscaster on a station, in a series of broadcasts, attacked certain county and state officials, charging them with nefarious schemes and the use of their offices for personal gain, attaching derisive epithets to their names, and analogizing their local administration with the political methods of foreign dictators. At the time of renewal of the station's license, the persons attacked urged that the station had been used for the licensee's selfish purposes and to vent his personal spite. The licensee denied the charge, and asserted that the broadcasts had a factual basis. On several occasions,

the persons attacked were invited to use the station to discuss the matters in the broadcasts.

Ruling. Where a licensee expresses an opinion concerning controversial issues of public importance, he is under obligation to see that those holding opposing viewpoints are afforded a reasonable opportunity for the presentation of their views. He is under a further obligation not to present biased or one-sided news programming (viewing such programming on an overall basis) and not to use his station for his purely personal and private interests. Investigation established that the licensee did not subordinate his public interest obligations to his private interests, and that there was "a body of opinion" in the community "that such broadcasts had a factual basis."

As to the attacks, the *Editorializing Report* states that "* * * elementary considerations of fairness may dictate that time be allocated to a person or group which has been specifically attacked over the station, where otherwise no such obligation would exist * * *" In this case, the attacks were of a highly personal nature, impugning the character and honesty of named individuals. In such circumstances, the licensee has an affirmative duty to take all appropriate steps to see to it that the persons attacked are afforded the fullest opportunity to respond. Here, the persons attacked knew of the attacks, were generally apprised of their nature, and were aware of the opportunities afforded them to respond. Accordingly, the license was renewed. (Clayton W. Mapoles, FCC 62–501, 23 R.R. 586, May 9, 1962.)

21. *Personal attack.* For a period of five days, September 18–22, a station broadcast a series of daily editorials attacking the general manager of a national rural electric cooperative association in connection with a pending controversial issue of public importance. The manager arrived in town on September 21 for a two-day stay and, upon being informed of the editorials, on the morning of September 22d sought to obtain copies of them. About noon of the same day, the station approached the manager with an offer of an interview to respond to the statements made in the editorials. The manager stated, however, that he would not have had time to prepare ade-

quately a reply which would require a series of broadcasts. He complained to the Commission that the station had acted unfairly.

Ruling. Where, as here, a station's editorials contain a personal attack upon an individual by name, the fairness doctrine requires that a copy of the specific editorial or editorials shall be communicated to the person attacked either prior to or at the time of the broadcast of such editorials so that a reasonable opportunity is afforded that person to reply. This duty on the part of the station is greater where, as here, interest in the editorials was consciously built up by the station over a period of days and the time within which the person attacked would have an opportunity to reply was known to be so limited. The Commission concludes that in failing to supply copies of the editorials promptly to the manager and delaying in affording him the opportunity to reply to them, the station had not fully met the requirements of the Commission's fairness doctrine. (Billings Bctg. Co., FCC 62–736. 23 R.R. 951, July 13, 1962.)

22. *No personal attack merely because individual is named.* A network program discussed the applicability of Section 315 to appearances by candidates for public office on TV newscasts and the Commission's decision holding that the mayoralty candidate, Lar Daly, was entitled to equal time when the Mayor of Chicago appeared on a newscast. The program contained the editorial views of the President of CBS opposing the interpretation of the Commission and urging that Section 315 not apply to newscasts. Three other persons on the program expressed contrasting points of view. Lar Daly's request that he be afforded time to reply to the President of CBS, because he was "directly involved" in the Commission's decision which was discussed over the air and because he was the most qualified spokesman to present opposing views, was denied by the station. Did the fairness doctrine require that his request be granted?

Ruling. It was the newscast question involved in the Commission's decision, rather than Lar Daly, which was the controversial issue which was presented. Since the network presented several spokesmen, all of whom appeared qualified to state views contrasting with those expressed by the network President, the network fulfilled its obligation to provide a "fair and balanced presentation of an important public issue of a controversial nature." (Lar Daly, 19 R.R. 1103, at 1104, Mar. 24, 1960.)[6]

23. *Licensee involvement in personal attack.* It was urged that in Mapoles, Billings, and Times-Mirror (see Rulings 20, 21, 25), the station was, in effect, "personally involved"; that the personal attack principle should be applied only when the licensee is personally involved in the attack upon a person or group (i.e., through editorals or through station commentator programming), and not where the attack is made by a party unconnected with the station.

Ruling. Under fundamental communications policy, the licensee, with the exception of appearances of political candidates subject to the equal opportunities requirement of Section 315, is fully responsible for all matter which is broadcast over his station. It follows that when a program contains a personal attack, the licensee must be fully aware of the contents of the program, whatever its source or his actual involvement in the broadcast. The crucial consideration, as the Commission stated in Mapoles, is that "his broadcast facilities [have been] used to attack a person or group." (Letter of September 18, 1963 to Douglas A. Anello, FCC 63–850.)

24. *Personal attack—no tape or transcript.* In the same inquiry as above (Ruling 23), the question was also raised as to the responsibility of the licensee when his facilities are used for a personal attack in a program dealing with a controversial issue of public importance and the licensee has no transcript or tape of the program.

Ruling. Where a personal attack is made and no script or tape is available, good sense and fairness dictate that the licensee send as accurate a summary as possible of the substance of the attack to the person or group involved. (Letter of September 18, 1963 to Douglas A. Anello, FCC 63–850.)

[6]As seen from the above rulings, the personal attack principle is applicable where there are statements, in connection with a controversial issue of public importance, attacking an individual's or group's integrity, character, or honesty or like personal qualities, and not when an individual or group is simply named or referred to. Thus, while a definitive Commission ruling must await a complaint involving specific facts—see introduction, p. 3, the personal attack principle has not been applied where there is simply stated disagreement with the views of an individual or group concerning a controversial issue of public importance. Nor is it necessary to send a transcript or summary of the attack, with an offer of time for response, in the case of a personal attack upon a foreign leader, even assuming such an attack occurred in connection with a controversial issue of public importance.

25. *Personal attacks on, and criticism of, candidate; partisan position on campaign issues.* In more than 20 broadcasts, two station commentators presented their views on the issues in the 1962 California gubernatorial campaign between Governor Brown and Mr. Nixon. The views expressed on the issues were critical of the Governor and favored Mr. Nixon, and at times involved personal attacks on individuals and groups in the gubernatorial campaign, and specifically on Governor Brown. The licensee responded that it had presented opposing viewpoints but upon examination there were two instances of broadcasts featuring Governor Brown (both of which were counterbalanced by appearances of Mr. Nixon) and two instances of broadcasts presenting viewpoints opposed to two of the issues raised by the above-noted broadcasts by the commentators. It did not appear that any of the other broadcasts cited by the station dealt with the issues raised as to the gubernatorial campaign.

Ruling. Since there were only two instances which involved the presentation of viewpoints concerning the gubernatorial campaign, opposed to the more than twenty programs of the commentators presenting their views on many different issues of the campaign for which no opportunity was afforded for the presentation of opposing viewpoints, there was not a fair opportunity for presentation of opposing viewpoints with respect to many of the issues discussed in the commentators' programs. The continuous, repetitive opportunity afforded for the expression of the commentators' viewpoints on the gubernatorial campaign, in contrast to the minimal opportunity afforded to opposing viewpoints, violated the right of the public to a fair presentation of views. Further, with respect to the personal attacks by the one commentator on individuals and groups involved in the gubernatorial campaign, the principle in Mapoles and Billings should have been followed. In the circumstances, the station should have sent a transcript of the pertinent continuity on the above programs to Governor Brown and should have offered a comparable opportunity for an appropriate spokesman to answer the broadcasts. (Times-Mirror, FCC 62–1130, 24 R.R. 404, Oct. 26, 1962; FCC 62–1109, 24 R.R. 407, Oct. 19, 1962.)

26. *Personal attacks on, and criticism of, candidates; partisan posi-*

tion on campaign issues—appropriate spokesman. See facts above. The question was raised whether the candidate has the right to insist upon his own appearance, to respond to the broadcasts in question.

Ruling. Since a response by a candidate would, in turn, require that equal opportunities under Section 315 be afforded to the other legally-qualified candidates for the same office, the fairness doctrine requires only that the licensee afford the attacked candidate an opportunity to respond through an appropriate spokesman. The candidate should, of course, be given a substantial voice in the selection of the spokesman to respond to the attack or to the statement of support. (Times-Mirror Bctg. Co., FCC 62–1130, 24 R.R. 404, 406, Oct. 19, 1962, Oct. 26, 1962.)

27. *Personal attacks on, and criticism of, candidate; partisan position on campaign issues.* During the fall of an election year, a news commentator on a local affairs program made several critical and uncomplimentary references to the actions and public positions of various political and non-partisan candidates for public office and of the California Democratic Clubs and demanded the resignation of an employee of the staff of the County Superintendent of Schools. In response to a request for time to respond by the local Democratic Central Committee, and after negotiations between the licensee and the complaining party, the licensee offered two five-minute segments of time on November 1 and 2, 1962, and instructed its commentator to refrain from expressing any point of view on partisan issues on November 5, or November 6, election eve and election day, respectively.

Ruling. On the facts of this case, the comments of the news commentator constituted personal attacks on candidates and others and involved the taking of a partisan position on issues involved in a race for political office. Therefore, under the ruling of the Times-Mirror case, the licensee was under an obligation to "send a transcript of the pertinent continuity in each such program to the appropriate candidates immediately and [to] offer a comparable opportunity for an appropriate spokesman to answer the broadcast." However, upon the basis of the showing, the licensee's offer of time, in response to the request, was not unreasonable under the fairness doctrine. (Letter to The McBride Industries, Inc., FCC 63–756, July 31, 1963.)

F. Licensee Editorializing.

28. *Freedom to editorialize.* The Editorializing Report and the 1960 Programming Statement, while stating that the licensee is not required to editorialize, make clear that he is free to do so, but that if he does, he must meet the requirements of the fairness doctrine.

Adopted: July 1, 1964.

FEDERAL COMMUNICATIONS COMMISSION,

[SEAL]   BEN F. WAPLE,
                    Secretary.

Appendix A

EDITORIALIZING BY BROADCAST LICENSEES

REPORT OF COMMISSION

1. This report is issued by the Commission in connection with its hearings on the above entitled matter held at Washington, D.C., on March 1, 2, 3, 4, and 5 and April 19, 20, and 21, 1948. The hearing had been ordered on the Commission's own motion on September 5, 1947, because of our belief that further clarification of the Commission's position with respect to the obligations of broadcast licensees in the field of broadcasts of news, commentary and opinion was advisable. It was believed that in view of the apparent confusion concerning certain of the Commission's previous statements on these vital matters by broadcast licensees and members of the general public, as well as the professed disagreement on the part of some of these persons with earlier Commission pronouncements, a reexamination and restatement of its views by the Commission would be desirable. And in order to provide an opportunity to interested per-

sons and organizations to acquaint the Commission with their views, prior to any Commission determination, as to the proper resolution of the difficult and complex problems involved in the presentation of radio news and comment in a democracy, it was designated for public hearing before the Commission en banc on the following issues:

1. To determine whether the expression of editorial opinions by broadcast station licensees on matters of public interest and controversy is consistent with their obligations to operate their stations in the public interest.

2. To determine the relationship between any such editorial expression and the affirmative obligation of the licensees to insure that a fair and equal presentation of all sides of controversial issues is made over their facilities.

2. At the hearings testimony was received from some 49 witnesses representing the broadcasting industry and various interested organizations and members of the public. In addition, written statements of their position on the matter were placed into the record by 21 persons and organizations who were unable to appear and testify in person. The various witnesses and statements brought forth for the Commission's consideration, arguments on every side of both of the questions involved in the hearing. Because of the importance of the issues considered in the hearing, and because of the possible confusion which may have existed in the past concerning the policies applicable to the matters which were the subject of the hearings, we have deemed it advisable to set forth in detail and at some length our conclusions as to the basic considerations relevant to the expression of editorial opinion by broadcast licensees and the relationship of any such expression to the general obligations of broadcast licensees with respect to the presentation of programs involving controversial issues.

3. In approaching the issues upon which this proceeding has been held, we believe that the paramount and controlling consideration is the relationship between the American system of broadcasting carried on through a large number of private licensees upon whom devolves the responsibility for the selection and presentation of program material, and the Congressional mandate that this licensee responsibility is to be exercised in the interests of, and as a trustee for the public at large which retains ultimate control over the channels of radio and television communications. One important aspect of this relationship, we believe, results from the fact that the needs and interests of the general public with respect to programs devoted to news

commentary and opinion can only be satisfied by making available to them for their consideration and acceptance or rejection, of varying and conflicting views held by responsible elements of the community. And it is in the light of these basic concepts that the problems of insuring fairness in the presentation of news and opinion and the place in such a picture of any expression of the views of the station licensee as such must be considered.

4. It is apparent that our system of broadcasting, under which private persons and organizations are licensed to provide broadcasting service to the various communities and regions, imposes responsibility in the selection and presentation of radio program material upon such licensees. Congress has recognized that the requests for radio time may far exceed the amount of time reasonably available for distribution by broadcasters. It provided, therefore, in section 3 (h) of the Communications Act that a person engaged in radio broadcasting shall not be deemed a common carrier. It is the licensee, therefore, who must determine what percentage of the limited broadcast day should appropriately be devoted to news and discussion or consideration of public issues, rather than to the other legitimate services of radio broadcasting, and who must select or be responsible for the selection of the particular news items to be reported or the particular local, state, national or international issues or questions of public interest to be considered, as well as the person or persons to comment or analyze the news or to discuss or debate the issues chosen as topics for radio consideration, "The life of each community involves a multitude of interests some dominant and all pervasive such as interest in public affairs, education and similar matters and some highly specialized and limited to few. The practical day-to-day problem with which every licensee is faced is one of striking a balance between these various interests to reflect them in a program service which is useful to the community, and which will in some way fulfill the needs and interests of the many." Capital Broadcasting Company, 4 Pike & Fischer, R.R. 21; The Northern Corporation (WMEX), 4 Pike & Fischer, R.R. 333, 338. And both the Commission and the Courts have stressed that this responsibility devolves upon the individual licensees, and can neither be delegated by the licensee or any network or other person or group, or be unduly fettered by contractual arrangements restricting the licensee in his free exercise of his independent judgments. National Broadcasting Company v. United States, 319 U.S. 190 (upholding the Commission's Chain Broadcasting Regulations, §§3.101–3.108, 3.231–3.238, 3.631–3.638), Churchill Tabernacle v. Federal Communications Commission, 160 F. 2d 244 (See, Rules and Regulations, §§3.109, 3.239, 3.639); Allen T. Simmons

v. Federal Communications Commission, 169 F. 2d 670, certiorari denied 335 U.S. 846.

5. But the inevitability that there must be some choosing between various claimants for access to a licensee's microphone, does not mean that the licensee is free to utilize his facilities as he sees fit or in his own particular interests as contrasted with the interests of the general public. The Communications Act of 1934, as amended, makes clear that licenses are to be issued only where the public interest, convenience or necessity would be served thereby. And we think it is equally clear that one of the basic elements of any such operation is the maintenance of radio and television as a medium of freedom of speech and freedom of expression for the people of the nation as a whole. Section 301 of the Communications Act provides that it is the purpose of the Act to maintain the control of the United States over all channels of interstate and foreign commerce. Section 326 of the Act provides that this control of the United States shall not result in any impairment of the right of free speech by means of such radio communications. It would be inconsistent with these express provisions of the Act to assert that, while it is the purpose of the Act to maintain the control of the United States over radio channels, but free from any regulation or condition which interferes with the right of free speech, nevertheless persons who are granted limited rights to be licensees of radio stations, upon a finding under Sections 307(a) and 309 of the Act that the public interest, convenience, or necessity would be served thereby, may themselves make radio unavailable as a medium of free speech. The legislative history of the Communications Act and its predecessor, the Radio Act of 1927 shows, on the contrary, that Congress intended that radio stations should not be used for the private interest, whims, or caprices of the particular persons who have been granted licenses, but in manner which will serve the community generally and the various groups which make up the community.[2] And the courts have consis-

[2]Thus in the Congressional debates leading to the enactment of the Radio Act of 1927, Congressman (later Senator) White stated (67 Cong. Rec. 5479, March 12, 1926):

We have reached the definite conclusion that the right of all our people to enjoy this means of communication can be preserved only by the repudiation of the idea underlying the 1912 law that anyone who will, may transmit and by the assertion in its stead of the doctrine that the right of the public to service is superior to the right of any individual to use the ether * * * the recent radio conference met this issue squarely. It recognized that in the present state of scientific development there must be a limitation upon the number of broadcasting stations and it recommended that licenses should be issued only to those stations whose operation would render a benefit to the public, are necessary in the public interest or would contribute to the development of the art. This principle was approved by every witness before your committee. We have written it into the bill. *If enacted into law, the broadcasting privilege will not be a right of selfishness. It will rest upon an assurance of public interest to be served.* [Emphasis added.]

tently upheld Commission action giving recognition to and fulfilling that intent of Congress. KFAB Broadcasting Association v. Federal Radio Commission, 47 F. 2d 670; Trinity Methodist Church, South v. Federal Radio Commission, 62 F. 2d 850, certiorari denied, 288 U.S. 599.

6. It is axiomatic that one of the most vital questions of mass communication in a democracy is the development of an informed public opinion through the public dissemination of news and ideas concerning the vital public issues of the day. Basically, it is in recognition of the great contribution which radio can make in the advancement of this purpose that portions of the radio spectrum are allocated to that form of radio communications known as radio-broadcasting. Unquestionably, then, the standard of public interest, convenience and necessity as applied to radio-broadcasting must be interpreted in the light of this basic purpose. The Commission has consequently recognized the necessity for licensees to devote a reasonable percentage of their broadcast time to the presentation of news and programs devoted to the consideration and discussion of public issues of interest in the community served by the particular station. And we have recognized, with respect to such programs, the paramount right of the public in a free society to be informed and to have presented to it for acceptance or rejection the different attitudes and viewpoints concerning those vital and often controversial issues which are held by the various groups which make up the community. [3] It is this right of the public to be informed, rather than any right on the part of the government, any broadcast licensee or any individual member of the public to broadcast his own particular views on any matter, which is the foundation stone of the American system of broadcasting.

And this view that the interest of the listening public rather than the private interests of particular licensees was reemphasized as recently as June 9, 1948 in a unanimous report of the Senate Committee on Interstate and Foreign Commerce on S. 1333 (80th Cong.) which would have amended the present Communications Act in certain respects. See S. Rep't No. 1567, 80th Cong., 2d Sess., pp. 1415.

7. This affirmative responsibility on the part of broadcast licensees to provide a reasonable amount of time for the presentation over their facilities of programs devoted to the discussion and consideration of public issues has been reaffirmed by this Commission in a long series of decisions. The United Broadcasting Company (WHKC) case, 10 F.C.C. 675, emphasized that this

[3]Cf., Thornhill v. Alabama, 310 U.S. 88, 95, 102; Associated Press v. United States, 326 U.S. 1, 20.

duty includes the making of reasonable provision for the discussion of controversial issues of public importance in the community served, and to make sufficient time available for full discussion thereof. The Scott case, 3 Pike & Fischer, Radio Regulation 259, stated our conclusions that this duty extends to all subjects of substantial importance to the community coming within the scope of free discussion under the First Amendment without regard to personal views and opinions of the licensees on the matter, or any determination by the licensee as to the possible unpopularity of the views to be expressed on the subject matter to be discussed among particular elements of the station's listening audience. Cf., National Broadcasting Company v. United States, 319 U.S. 190; Allen T. Simmons, 3 Pike & Fischer, R.R. 1029, affirmed; Simmons v. Federal Communications Commission, 169 F. 2d 670, certiorari denied, 335 U.S. 846; Bay State Beacon, 3 Pike & Fischer, R.R. 1455, affirmed; Bay State Beacon v. Federal Communications Commission, U.S. App. D.C., decided December 20, 1948; Petition of Sam Morris, 3 Pike & Fischer, R.R. 154; Thomas N. Beach, 3 Pike & Fischer R.R. 1784. And the Commission has made clear that in such presentation of news and comment the public interest requires that the licensee must operate on a basis of overall fairness, making his facilities available for the expression of the contrasting views of all responsible elements in the community on the various issues which arise. Mayflower Broadcasting Co., 8 F.C.C. 333; United Broadcasting Co. (WHKC), 10 F.C.C. 515; Cf. WBNX Broadcasting Co., Inc., 4 Pike & Fischer, R.R. 244 (Memorandum Opinion). Only where the licensee's discretion in the choice of the particular programs to be broadcast over his facilities is exercised so as to afford a reasonable opportunity for the presentation of all responsible positions on matters of sufficient importance to be afforded radio time can radio be maintained as a medium of freedom of speech for the people as a whole. These concepts, of course, do restrict the licensee's freedom to utilize his station in whatever manner he chooses but they do so in order to make possible the maintenance of radio as a medium of freedom of speech for the general public.

8. It has been suggested in the course of the hearing that licensees have an affirmation obligation to insure fair presentation of all sides of any controversial issue before any time may be allocated to the discussion or consideration of the matter. On the other hand, arguments have been advanced in support of the proposition that the licensee's sole obligation to the public is to refrain from suppressing or excluding any responsible point of view from access to the radio. We are of the opinion, however, that any

rigid requirement that licensees adhere to either of these extreme prescriptions for proper station programming techniques would seriously limit the ability of licensees to serve the public interest. Forums and roundtable discussions, while often excellent techniques of presenting a fair cross section of differing viewpoints on a given issue, are not the only appropriate devices for radio discussion, and in some circumstances may not be particularly appropriate or advantageous. Moreover, in many instances the primary "controversy" will be whether or not the particular problem should be discussed at all; in such circumstances, where the licensee has determined that the subject is of sufficient import to receive broadcast attention, it would obviously not be in the public interest for spokesmen for one of the opposing points of view to be able to exercise a veto power over the entire presentation by refusing to broadcast its position. Fairness, in such circumstances might require no more than that the licensee make a reasonable effort to secure responsible representation of the particular position and, if it fails in this effort, to continue to make available its facilities to the spokesmen for such position in the event that, after the original programs are broadcast, they then decide to avail themselves of a right to reply to present their contrary opinion. It should be remembered, moreover that discussion of public issues will not necessarily be confined to questions which are obviously controversial in nature, and in many cases, programs initiated with no thought on the part of the licensee of their possibly controversial nature will subsequently arouse controversy and opposition of a substantial nature which will merit presentation of opposing views. In such cases, however, fairness can be preserved without undue difficulty since the facilities of the station can be made available to the spokesmen for the groups wishing to state views in opposition to those expressed in the original presentation when such opposition becomes manifest.

9. We do not believe, however, that the licensee's obligations to serve the public interest can be met merely through the adoption of a general policy of not refusing to broadcast opposing views where a demand is made of the station for broadcast time. If, as we believe to be the case, the public interest is best served in a democracy through the ability of the people to hear expositions of the various positions taken by responsible groups and individuals on particular topics and to choose between them, it is evident that broadcast licensees have an affirmative duty generally to encourage and implement the broadcast of all sides of controversial public issues over their facilities, over and beyond their obligation to make available on demand opportunities for the expression of opposing views. It is clear that any

approximation of fairness in the presentation of any controversy will be difficult if not impossible of achievement unless the licensee plays a conscious and positive role in bringing about balanced presentation of the opposing viewpoints.

10. It should be recognized that there can be no one all embracing formula which licensees can hope to apply to insure the fair and balanced presentation of all public issues. Different issues will inevitably require different techniques of presentation and production. The licensee will in each instance be called upon to exercise his best judgment and good sense in determining what subjects should be considered, the particular format of the programs to be devoted to each subject, the different shades of opinion to be presented, and the spokesmen for each point of view. In determining whether to honor specific requests for time, the station will inevitably be confronted with such questions as whether the subject is worth considering, whether the viewpoint of the requesting party has already received a sufficient amount of broadcast time, or whether there may not be other available groups or individuals who might be more appropriate spokesmen for the particular point of view than the person making the request. The latter's personal involvement in the controversy may also be a factor which must be considered, for elementary considerations of fairness may dictate that time be allocated to a person or group which has been specifically attacked over the station, where otherwise no such obligation would exist. Undoubtedly, over a period of time some licensees may make honest errors of judgment. But there can be no doubt that any licensee honestly desiring to live up to its obligation to serve the public interest and making a reasonable effort to do so, will be able to achieve a fair and satisfactory resolution of these problems in the light of the specific facts.

11. It is against this background that we must approach the question of "editorialization"—the use of radio facilities by the licensees thereof for the expression of the opinions and ideas of the licensee on the various controversial and significant issues of interest to the members of the general public afforded radio (or television) service by the particular station. In considering this problem it must be kept in mind that such editorial expression may take many forms ranging from the overt statement of position by the licensee in person or by his acknowledged spokesmen to the selection and presentation of news editors and commentators sharing the licensee's general opinions or the making available of the licensee's facilities, either free of charge or for a fee to persons or organizations reflecting the licensee's viewpoint either generally or with respect to specific issues. It should also

be clearly indicated that the question of the relationship of broadcast editorialization, as defined above, to operation in the public interest, is not identical with the broader problem of assuring "fairness" in the presentation of news, comment or opinion, but is rather one specific facet of this larger problem.

12. It is clear that the licensee's authority to determine the specific programs to be broadcast over his station gives him an opportunity, not available to other persons, to insure that his personal viewpoint on any particular issue is presented in his station's broadcasts, whether or not these views are expressly identified with the licensee. And, in absence of governmental restraint, he would, if he so chose, be able to utilize his position as a broadcast licensee to weight the scales in line with his personal views, or even directly or indirectly to propagandize in behalf of his particular philosophy or views on the various public issues to the exclusion of any contrary opinions. Such action can be effective and persuasive whether or not it is accompanied by any editorialization in the narrow sense of overt statement of particular opinions and views identified as those of licensee.

13. The narrower question of whether any overt editorialization or advocacy by broadcast licensees, identified as such is consonant with the operaton of their stations in the public interest, resolves itself, primarily into the issue of whether such identification of comment or opinion broadcast over a radio or television station with the licensee, as such, would inevitably or even probably result in such over-emphasis on the side of any particular controversy which the licensee chooses to espouse as to make impossible any reasonably balanced presentation of all sides of such issues or to render ineffective the available safeguards of that over-all fairness which is the essential element of operation in the public interest. We do not believe that any such consequence is either inevitable or probable, and we have therefore come to the conclusion that overt licensee editorialization, within reasonable limits and subject to the general requirements of fairness detailed above, is not contrary to the public interest.

14. The Commission has given careful consideration to contentions of those witnesses at the hearing who stated their belief that any overt editorialization or advocacy by broadcast licensee is *per se* contrary to the public interest. The main arguments advanced by these witnesses were that overt editorialization by broadcast licensees would not be consistent with the attainment of balanced presentations since there was a danger that the institutional good will and the production resources at the disposal of broadcast licensees would inevitably influence public opinion in favor of the

positions advocated in the name of the licensee and that, having taken an open stand on behalf of one position in a given controversy, a licensee is not likely to give a fair break to the opposition. We believe, however, that these fears are largely misdirected, and that they stem from a confusion of the question of overt advocacy in the name of the licensee, with the broader issue of insuring that the station's broadcasts devoted to the consideration of public issues will provide the listening public with a fair and balanced presentation of differing viewpoints on such issues, without regard to the particular views which may be held or expressed by the licensee. Considered, as we believe they must be, as just one of several types of presentation of public issues, to be afforded their appropriate and non-exclusive place in the station's total schedule of programs devoted to balanced discussion and consideration of public issues, we do not believe that programs in which the licensee's personal opinions are expressed are intrinsically more or less subject to abuse than any other program devoted to public issues. If it be true that station good will and licensee prestige, where it exists, may give added weight to opinion expressed by the licensee, it does not follow that such opinion should be excluded from the air any more than it should in the case of any individual or institution which over a period of time has built up a reservoir of good will or prestige in the community. In any competition for public acceptance of ideas, the skills and resources of the proponents and opponents will always have some measure of effect in producing the results sought. But it would not be suggested that they should be denied expression of their opinions over the air by reason of their particular assets. What is against the public interest is for the licensee "to stack the cards" by a deliberate selection of spokesmen for opposing points of view to favor one viewpoint at the expense of the other, whether or not the views of those spokesmen are identified as the views of the licensee or of others. Assurance of fairness must in the final analysis be achieved, not by the exclusion of particular views because of the source of the views, or the forcefulness with which the view is expressed, but by making the microphone available, for the presentation of contrary views without deliberate restrictions designed to impede equally forceful presentation.

15. Similarly, while licensees will in most instances have at their disposal production resources making possible graphic and persuasive techniques for forceful presentation of ideas, their utilization for the promulgation of the licensee's personal viewpoints will not necessarily or automatically lead to unfairness or lack of balance. While uncontrolled utilization of such resources for the partisan ends of the licensee might conceivably lead to

serious abuses, such abuses could as well exist where the station's resources are used for the sole use of his personal spokesmen. The prejudicial or unfair use of broadcast production resources would, in either case, be contrary to the public interest.

16. The Commission is not persuaded that a station's willingness to stand up and be counted on these particular issues upon which the licensee has a definite position may not be actually helpful in providing and maintaining a climate of fairness and equal opportunity for the expression of contrary views. Certainly the public has less to fear from the open partisan than from the covert propagandist. On many issues, of sufficient importance to be allocated broadcast time, the station licensee may have no fixed opinion or viewpoint which he wishes to state or advocate. But where the licensee, himself, believes strongly that one side of a controversial issue is correct and should prevail, prohibition of his expression of such position will not of itself insure fair presentation of that issue over his station's facilities, nor would open advocacy necessarily prevent an overall fair presentation of the subject. It is not a sufficient answer to state that a licensee should occupy the position of an impartial umpire, where the licensee is in fact partial. In the absence of a duty to present all sides of controversial issues, overt editorialization by station licensees could conceivably result in serious abuse. But where, as we believe to be the case under the Communications Act, such a responsibility for a fair and balanced presentation of controversial public issues exists, we cannot see how the open espousal of one point of view by the licensee should necessarily prevent him from affording a fair opportunity for the presentation of contrary positions or make more difficult the enforcement of the statutory standard of fairness upon any licensee.

17. It must be recognized, however, that the licensee's opportunity to express his own views as part of a general presentation of varying opinions on particular controversial issues, does not justify or empower any licensee to exercise his authority over the selection of program material to distort or suppress the basic factual information upon which any truly fair and free discussion of public issues must necessarily depend. The basis for any fair consideration of public issues, and particularly those of a controversial nature, is the presentation of news and information concerning the basic facts of the controversy in as complete and impartial a manner as possible. A licensee would be abusing his position as public trustee of these important means of mass communication were he to withhold from expression over his facilities relevant news or facts concerning a controversy or to slant or

distort the presentation of such news. No discussion of the issues involved in any controversy can be fair or in the public interest where such discussion must take place in a climate of false or misleading information concerning the basic facts of the controversy.

18. During the course of the hearings, fears have been expressed that any effort on the part of the Commission to enforce a reasonable standard of fairness and impartiality would inevitably require the Commission to take a stand on the merits of the particular issues considered in the programs broadcast by the several licensees, as well as exposing the licensees to the risk of loss of license because of "honest mistakes" which they may make in the exercise of their judgment with respect to the broadcasts of programs of a controversial nature. We believe that these fears are wholly without justification, and are based on either an assumption of abuse of power by the Commission or a lack of proper understanding of the role of the Commission, under the Communications Act, in considering the program service of broadcast licensees in passing upon applications for renewal of license. While this Commission and its predecessor, the Federal Radio Commission, have, from the beginning of effective radio regulation in 1927, properly considered that a licensee's overall program service is one of the primary indicia of his ability to serve the public interest, actual consideration of such service has always been limited to a determination as to whether the licensee's programming, taken as a whole, demonstrates that the licensee is aware of his listening public and is willing and able to make an honest and reasonable effort to live up to such obligations. The action of the station in carrying or refusing to carry any particular program is of relevance only as the station's actions with respect to such programs fits into is overall pattern of broadcast service, and must be considered in the light of its other program activities. This does not mean, of course, that stations may, with impunity, engage in a partisan editorial campaign on a particular issue or series of issues provided only that the remainder of its program schedule conforms to the statutory norm of fairness; a licensee may not utilize the portion of its broadcast service which conforms to the statutory requirements as a cover or shield for other programming which fails to meet the minimum standards of operation in the public interest. But it is clear that the standard of public interest is not so rigid that an honest mistake or error in judgment on the part of a licensee will be or should be condemned where his overall record demonstrates a reasonable effort to provide a balanced presentation of comment and opinion on such issues. The question is necessarily one of the reasonableness of the station's actions, not whether any

absolute standard of fairness has been achieved. It does not require any appraisal of the merits of the particular issue to determine whether reasonable efforts have been made to present both sides of the question. Thus, in appraising the record of a station in presenting programs concerning a controversial bill pending before the Congress of the United States, if the record disclosed that the licensee had permitted only advocates of the bill's enactment to utilize its facilities to the exclusion of its opponents, it is clear that no independent appraisal of the bill's merits by the Commission would be required to reach a determination that the licensee had misconstrued its duties and obligations as a person licensed to serve the public interest. The Commission has observed, in considering this general problem that "the duty to operate in the public interest is no esoteric mystery, but is essentially a duty to operate a radio station with good judgment and good faith guided by a reasonable regard for the interests of the community to be served." Northern Corporation (WMEX), 4 Pike & Fischer, R.R. 333, 339. Of course, some cases will be clearer than others, and the Commission in the exercise of its functions may be called upon to weigh conflicting evidence to determine whether the licensee has or has not made reasonable efforts to present a fair and well-rounded presentation of particular public issues. But the standard of reasonableness and the reasonable approximation of a statutory norm is not an arbitrary standard incapable of administrative or judicial determination, but, on the contrary, one of the basic standards of conduct in numerous fields of Anglo-American law. Like all other flexible standards of conduct, it is subject to abuse and arbitrary interpretation and application by the duly authorized reviewing authorities. But the possibility that a legitimate standard of legal conduct might be abused or arbitrarily applied by capricious governmental authority is not and cannot be a reason for abandoning the standard itself. And broadcast licensees are protected against any conceivable abuse of power by the Commission in the exercising of its licensing authority by the procedural safeguards of the Communications Act and the Administrative Procedure Act, and by the right of appeal to the Courts from final action claimed to be arbitrary or capricious.

19. There remains for consideration the allegation made by a few of the witnesses in the hearing that any action by the Commission in this field enforcing a basic standard of fairness upon broadcast licensees necessarily constitutes an "abridgement of the right of free speech" in violation of the First Amendment of the United States Constitution. We can see no sound basis for any such conclusion. The freedom of speech protected against

governmental abridgement by the First Amendment does not extend any privilege to government licensees of means of public communications to exclude the expression of opinions and ideas with which they are in disagreement. We believe, on the contrary, that a requirement that broadcast licensees utilize their franchises in a manner in which the listening public may be assured of hearing varying opinions on the paramount issues facing the American people is within both the spirit and letter of the First Amendment. As the Supreme Court of the United States has pointed out in the Associated Press monopoly case:

It would be strange indeed, however, if the grave concern for freedom of the press which prompted adoption of the First Amendment should be read as a command that the government was without power to protect that freedom. * * * That Amendment rests on the assumption that the widest possible dissemination of information from diverse and antagonistic sources is essential to the welfare of the public, that a free press is a condition of free society. Surely a command that the government itself shall not impede the free flow of ideas does not afford nongovernmental combinations a refuge if they impose restraints upon that constitutionally guaranteed freedom. Freedom to publish means freedom for all and not for some. Freedom to publish is guaranteed by the Constitution, but freedom to combine to keep others from publishing is not. (Associated Press v. United States, 326 U.S. 1 at p. 20.)

20. We fully recognize that freedom of the radio is included among the freedoms protected against governmental abridgement by the First Amendment. United States v. Paramount Pictures, Inc., et al., 334 U.S. 131, 166. But this does not mean that the freedom of the people as a whole to enjoy the maximum possible utilization of this medium of mass communication may be subordinated to the freedom of any single person to exploit the medium for his own private interest. Indeed, it seems indisputable that full effect can only be given to the concept of freedom of speech on the radio by giving precedence to the right of the American public to be informed on all sides of public questions over any such individual exploitation for private purposes. Any regulation of radio, especially a system of limited licensees, is in a real sense an abrigement of the inherent freedom of persons to express themselves by means of radio communications. It is, however, a necessary and constitutional abridgement in order to prevent chaotic intereference from destroying the great potential of this medium for public enlightenment and entertainment. National Broadcasting Company v. United States, 319 U.S. 190, 296; cf. Federal Radio Commission v. Nelson Brothers Bond &

Mortgage Co., 289 U.S. 266; Fisher's Blend Station, Inc. v. State Tax Commission, 277 U.S. 650. Nothing in the Communications Act or its history supports any conclusion that the people of the nation, acting through Congress, have intended to surrender or diminish their paramount rights in the air waves, including access to radio broadcasting facilities to a limited number of private licensees to be used as such licensees see fit, without regard to the paramount interests of the people. The most significant meaning of freedom of the radio is the right of the American people to listen to this great medium of communications free from any governmental dictation as to what they can or cannot hear and free alike from similar restraints by private licensees.

21. To recapitulate, the Commission believes that under the American system of broadcasting the individual licensees of radio stations have the responsibility for determining the specific program material to be broadcast over their stations. This choice, however, must be exercised in a manner consistent with the basic policy of the Congress that radio be maintained as a medium of free speech for the general public as a whole rather than as an outlet for the purely personal or private interest of the licensee. This requires that licensees devote a reasonable percentage of their broadcasting time to the discussion of public issues of interest in the community served by their stations and that such programs be designed so that the public has a reasonable opportunity to hear different opposing positions on the public issues of interest and importance in the community. The particular format best suited for the presentation of such programs in a manner consistent with the public interest must be determined by the licensee in the light of the facts of each individual situation. Such presentation may include the identified expression of the licensee's personal viewpoint as part of the more general presentation of views or comments on the various issues, but the opportunity of licensees to present such views as they may have on matters of controversy may not be utilized to achieve a partisan or one-sided presentation of issues. Licensee editorialization is but one aspect of freedom of expression by means of radio. Only insofar as it is exercised in conformity with the paramount right of the public to hear a reasonably balanced presentation of all responsible viewpoints on particular issues can such editorialization be considered to be consistent with the licensee's duty to operate in the public interest. For the licensee is a trustee impressed with the duty of preserving for the public generally radio as a medium of free expression and fair presentation.

Appendix B
[FCC 64–612]

THE HISTORY OF THE FAIRNESS DOCTRINE

A. *Legislative History.*

The fairness doctrine was adopted pursuant to the public interest standards of the Federal Radio Act of 1927 and the Communications Act of 1934, and in light of the expressions of Congress as set forth in legislative history.

From the inception of commercial radio broadcasting, Congress expressed its concern that the air waves be used as a vital means of communication, capable of making a major contribution to the development of an informed public opinion. It was to encourage these capabilities within the American institutional framework that Congress legislated in this field.[1]

Both the Federal Radio Act of 1927 and the Communications Act of 1934 established that the American system of broadcasting should be carried on through a large number of private licensees upon whom rested the sole responsibility for determining the content and presentation of program material. But the Congress, in granting access to broadcast facilities to a limited number of private licensees, made clear from the beginning that the responsibility which licensees held must be exercised in accordance with the paramount public interest. Thus, the legislative history is clear that the Congress intended that radio should be maintained as a medium of free speech for the general public, rather than as an outlet for the views of a few, and that the responsibility held by broadcast licensees must be exercised in a manner which would serve the community generally and the various groups, whether organized or not, which made up the community.

As early as 1926, in the Congressional debates which led to the enactment of the Radio Act of 1927, Congressman (later Senator) White stated (67 Cong. Rec. 5479, March 12, 1926):

"We have reached the definite conclusion that the right of all our people

[1] S. Rept. No. 994 (Part 6), 87th Cong., 2d Sess., p. 1.

to enjoy this means of communication can be preserved only by repudiation of the idea underlying the 1912 law that anyone who will, may transmit and by the assertion in its stead of the doctrine that the right of public to service is superior to the right of any individual to use the ether. This is the first and most fundamental difference between the pending bill and present law."

"The recent radio conference met this issue squarely. It recognized that in the present state of scientific development there must be a limitation upon the number of broadcasting stations and it recognized that licenses should be issued only to those stations whose operation would render a benefit to the public, are necessary in the public interest or would contribute to the development of the art. This principle was approved by every witness before your committee. We have written it into the bill. If enacted into law, the broadcasting privilege will not be the right of selfishness. It will rest upon an assurance of public interest to be served."

Similarly, the view that the public interest is paramount to the private interest of particular licensees was emphasized again on June 9, 1948, in a unanimous report of the Senate Committee on Interstate and Foreign Commerce on S. 1333, S. Rept. No. 1567, 80th Cong., 2d Sess., pp. 14–15; and, more recently on April 17, 1962, in S. Rept. No. 994 (Part 6), 87th Cong., 2d Sess., pp. 1–4, with particular reference to the Commission's fairness doctrine, in which the view was expressed that the public interest requires that a fair cross-section of opinion be presented with respect to the controversial issues discussed, regardless of the personal views of the licensee.

Indeed, since 1959 the Communications Act has affirmed the fairness doctrine with respect to the broadcast licensee who permits the use of his facilities for the presentation of controversial public issues. In the 1959 Amendment to Section 315 of the Act, Congress specifically affirmed the fairness doctrine by providing that:

"Nothing in the foregoing sentence [i.e., exemption from equal time requirements for news-type programs] shall be construed as relieving broadcasters, in connection with the presentation of newscasts, news interviews, news documentaries, and on-the-spot coverage of news events, from the obligation imposed upon them under this chapter to operate in the public interest and to afford reasonable opportunity for the discussion of conflicting views on issues of public importance."

The legislative history of this amendment establishes that this provision "is a restatement of the basic policy of the 'standard of fairness' which is imposed on broadcasters under the Communications Act of 1934" (House Rept. No. 1069, 86th Cong., 1st Sess., August 27, 1959, p. 5). As shown by the use of the word "chapter" rather than "section" and also by the legislative history (ibid., Sen. Rept. No. 562, 86th Cong., 1st Sess., pp. 13, 19; 105 Cong. Rec. 16310, 16346–47; 17778, 17830–31), Congress made clear that the obligation of fairness is applicable to all broadcasts dealing with controversial issues of public importance. Thus, just as Section 315 prior to 1959 imposed a specific statutory obligation upon the licensee to afford "equal opportunities" to legally qualified candidates for public office, since 1959 it also gives specific statutory recognition to the doctrine that requires the licensee "to afford reasonable opportunity for the discussion of conflicting views on issues of public importance," i.e., to be fair in the broadcasting of controversial issues.

B. *The History of the Fairness Doctrine Within the Commission.*

The administrative history of the fairness doctrine dates back to some of the first decisions of the Federal Radio Commission, operating under the authority of the Federal Radio Act of 1927[2] and seeking to implement the public interest requirement of that Act.

One of the first responsibilities of the Radio Commission was to assign the frequencies and hours of operation to the numerous radio stations which had begun operations prior to the enactment of the Radio Act. The means through which the Radio Commission carried out this responsibility was primarily by the adoption of a general reallocation program which became effective on November 1, 1928, and pursuant to which, the frequencies and hours of operation of every radio station in the country were specified.[3]

Following the adoption of the general reallocation plan, the Radio Commission received numerous applications, many of which were mutually exclusive, for modification of the licenses which had been issued pursuant to the plan. Many of the applications were from organizations which had been using their facilities primarily for the promotion of their own viewpoint. While the Commission generally

[2]44 Stat. 1162 (1927).
[3]See 2 F.R.C. Ann. Rept. 17–18, 200–214.

adopted the principle that, as between two broadcasting stations with otherwise equal claims for privileges, the station with the longest record of continuous service would have the superior right for a license, one exception to the principle of "priority" was made in the case of stations which served as outlets for the presentation of only one point of view.

Thus, in *Great Lakes Broadcasting Company* (reported in 3 F.R.C. Ann. Rep. 32), the Commission denied an application for modification of license of a station which broadcast only one point of view, stating that (at pp. 32, 33):

Broadcasting stations are licensed to serve the public and not for the purpose of furthering the private or selfish interests of individuals or groups of individuals. The standard of public interest, convenience, or necessity means nothing if it does not mean this.

It would not be fair, indeed it would not be good service, to the public to allow a one-sided presentation of the political issues of a campaign. Insofar as a program consists of discussion of public questions, public interest requires ample play for the free and fair competition of opposing views, and the commission believes that the principle applies not only to addresses by political candidates but to all discussions of issues of importance to the public. The great majority of broadcasting stations are, the commission is glad to say, already tacitly recognizing a broader duty than the law imposes upon them.

In explanation of this view, the Radio Commission pointed out that in the commercial radio broadcasting scheme (*Id.* at p. 34):

* * * there is no room for the operation of broadcasting stations exclusively by or in the private interests of individuals or groups so far as the nature of programs is concerned. There is not room in the broadcast band for every school of thought, religious, political, social, and economic, each to have its separate broadcasting station, its mouthpiece in the ether. If franchises are extended to some it gives them an unfair advantage over others, and results in a corresponding cutting-down of general public-service stations. It favors the interests and desires of a portion of the listening public at the expense of the rest. Propaganda stations (a term which is here used for the sake of convenience and not in a derogatory sense)

are not consistent with the most beneficial sort of discussion of public questions. As a general rule, postulated on the laws of nature as well as on the standard of public interest, convenience, or necessity, particular doctrines, creeds and beliefs must find their way into the market of ideas by the existing public-service stations, and if they are of sufficient importance to the listening public the microphone will undoubtedly be available If it is not, a well-founded complaint will receive the careful consideration of the Commission in its future action with reference to the station complained of.[4]

And, in the Chicago Federation of Labor case (reported in 3 F.R.C. 36, affirmed, Chicago Federation of Labor v. F.R.C., 41 F. 2d 422, the Commission again denied a modification of license on the ground that:

Since there is only a limited number of available frequencies for broadcasting, this commission was of the opinion, and so found, that there is no place for a station catering to any group, but that all stations should cater to the general public and serve public interest as against group or class interest.[5]

These principles received early and unequivocal affirmation by the Federal Communications Commission operating under the authority of the Communications Act of 1934. Thus, in 1938, the Commission denied an application for a construction permit primarily because of the applicant's policy of refusing to permit the use of its broadcast facilities by persons or organizations wishing to present any viewpoint different from that of the applicant.[6] Similarly, in 1940, in its Sixth Annual Report, the Commission stated (6 F.C.C. Ann. Rep. at 55):

---

[4]Although the Commission's decision was reversed on other grounds, Great Lakes Broadcasting Co. v. Federal Radio Commission, 37 F. 2d at 993, in discussing the above holding, the Court stated (37 F. 2d at 995): "It is our opinion that [the] application was rightly denied. This conclusion is based upon the comparatively limited public service rendered by the station * * *."

[5]In affirming the Commission's decision, the Court of Appeals found that the radio station which would be adversely affected by a grant of the labor-organization's application "has always rendered and continues to render admirable public service. The station has consistently furnished equal broadcasting facilities to all classes in its community." Chicago Federation of Labor v. F.R.C., 41 F. 2d at 423.

[6]Young People's Association for the Propagation of the Gospel, 6 FCC 178.

"In carrying out the obligation to render a public service, stations are required to furnish well-rounded rather than one-sided discussion of public questions."

Again, in 1941, in Mayflower Broadcasting Corp., 8 FCC 333 at 340, the Commission stated:

"Freedom of speech on the radio must be broad enough to provide full and equal opportunity for the presentation to the public of all sides of public issues. Indeed, as one licensed to operate in the public domain the licensee has assumed the obligation of presenting all sides of important public questions fairly, objectively and without bias. The public interest—not the private—is paramount."

In that same case, however, it was also stated at p. 340: "In brief, the broadcaster cannot be an advocate." This statement was widely accepted as an outright prohibition of broadcast editorializing, and, in view of the reaction to such policy, the Commission, on September 5, 1947, initiated a proceeding in Docket No. 8516 to study and reexamine the role of broadcast editorializing and the fairness doctrine, in general. This study culminated in the Report on Editorializing, supra, as will be set forth more fully below.

Concurrently with it study in Docket No. 8516, however, the Commission continued the process of defining and applying the fairness doctrine to the various problems which were presented to it. Thus, the Commission made clear its belief that not only did the public interest require broadcast licensees to affirmatively encourage the discussion of controversial issues, but that, in presenting such programs, every licensee had the responsibility to afford reasonable opportunity for the presentation of contrasting viewpoints. See e.g., United Broadcasting Co., 10 FCC 515 (1945); Johnston Broadcasting Co., 12 FCC 517 (1947), reversed on other grounds, Johnston Broadcasting Co. v. F.C.C., 175 F. 2d 351 (1949); Laurence W. Harry, 13 FCC 23 (1948); WBNX Broadcasting Co., 12 FCC 805, 837. In the WBNX case the Commission also stated (12 FCC at 841):

"The fairness with which a licensee deals with particular racial or religious groups in its community, in the exercise of its power to determine who can broadcast what over its facilities, is clearly a substantial aspect of his operation in the public interest."

C. *The Commission's Report on Editorializing.*

The Report on Editorializing by Broadcast Licensees, supra, which was issued by the Commission in 1949 in Docket No. 8516, sets forth most fully the basic requirements of the "fairness doctrine" and remains the keystone of the Commission's fairness policy today. The Report was the result of a two-year proceeding in which members of the public, the broadcasting industry, and the Commission participated. In essence, the Report established a two-fold obligation on the part of every licensee seeking to operate in the public interest: (1) that every licensee devote a reasonable portion of broadcast time to the discussion and consideration of controversial issues of public importance; and (2) that in doing so, he be fair—that is, that he affirmatively endeavor to make his facilities available for the expression of contrasting viewpoints held by responsible elements with respect to the controversial issues presented. While concerned with the basic considerations relevant to the expression of editorial opinion by broadcast licensees, the Report also dealt with the relationship of licensee editorial opinion to the general obligations of licensees for the presentation of programs involving controversial issues, and, accordingly, set forth in detail the general obligations of licensees in this area.

First, the Report reaffirmed the basic responsibility of broadcast licensees operating in the public interest to provide a reasonable amount of broadcast time for the presentation of programs devoted to the discussion and consideration of controversial issues of public importance. Because of the vital role that broadcast facilities can play in the development of an informed public opinion in our democracy, the Commission noted that it:

"* * * has consequently recognized the necessity for licensees to devote a reasonable percentage of their broadcast time to the presentation of news and programs devoted to the consideration and discussion of public issues of interest in the community served by the particular station."[7]

The Commission further determined, however, that the "paramount" right of the public in a free society to be informed could not truly be maintained by radio unless there was presented to the public "for acceptance or rejection the different attitudes and viewpoints concerning these vital and often controversial issues which are held by the various groups which make up the community." Consequently, the Commission stated that:

"* * * the licensee's obligations to serve the public interest can[not] be met merely through the adoption of a general policy of not refusing to broadcast opposing views when a demand is made of the station for broadcast time * * * it is evident that broadcast licensees have an affirmative duty generally to encourage and implement the broadcast of all sides of controversial public issues over their facilities, over and beyond their obligation to make available on demand opportunities for the expression of opposing views. It is clear that any approximation of fairness in the presentation of any controversy will be difficult if not impossible of achievement unless the licensee plays a conscious and positive role in bringing about balanced presentation of the opposing viewpoint."[8]

At the same time, the Report made clear that the precise means by which fairness would be achieved as a matter for the discretion of the licensee. Thus, the Commission rejected suggestions that licensees be required to utilize definite formats, and stated:

"It should be recognized that there can be no one all-embracing formula which licensees can hope to apply to insure the fair and balanced presentation of all public issues. Different issues will inevitably require different techniques of presentation and production. The licensee will in each instance be called upon to exercise his best judgment and good sense in determining what subjects should be considered, the particular format of the programs to be devoted to each subject, the different shades of opinion to be presented, and the spokesman for each point of view."[9]

[7]Paragraph 6, Report on Editorializing, supra.
[8]Paragraph 9, Report on Editorializing by Broadcast Licensees.
[9]Paragraph 10, Report on Editorializing by Broadcast Licensees.

A limitation on this exercise of discretion is where a personal attack occurs in a program involving controversial issues of public importance. Here the Commission stated:

"* * * for elementary considerations may dictate that time be allocated to a person or group which has been specifically attacked over the station, where otherwise no such obligation would exist * * *."[10]

In determining in an individual case whether or not a licensee has complied with the fairness doctrine, the Commission looks solely to whether, in the circumstances presented, the licensee acted reasonably and in good faith to present a fair cross-section of opinion on the controversial issue presented. In making such a determination, an honest mistake or error in judgment will not be condemned, so long as the licensee demonstrates a reasonable and honest effort to provide a balanced presentation of the controversial issue. The question of whether the licensee generally is operating in the public interest is determined at the time of renewal on an overall basis.

Further, the above procedure does not require the Commission to consider the merits of the viewpoint presented. As stated in the Report:

"The question is necessarily one of the reasonableness of the station's actions, not whether any absolute standard of fairness has been achieved. It does not require any appraisal of the merits of the particular issue to determine whether reasonable efforts have been made to present both sides of the question * * *."[11]

It was against this background that the Commission approached the question of editorialization, stating that:

"Considered, as we believe they must be, as just one of several types of presentation of public issues, to be afforded their appropriate and nonexclusive place on the station's total schedule of programs devoted to balanced discussion and consideration of public issues, we do not believe that pro-

---

[10]Paragraph 10, Report on Editorializing by Broadcast Licensees.
[11]Paragraph 18, Report on Editorializing by Broadcast Licensees.

grams in which the licensee's personal opinions are expressed are intrinsically more or less subject to abuse than any other program devoted to public issues."[12]

Thus, the Commission concluded that while licensee editorialization was not contrary to the public interest, the overriding question was not whether a licensee could present his own viewpoint, but whether in presenting any viewpoint the licensee was fair.

Finally, the Report set forth the basic "fairness" considerations in the presentation of factual information concerning controversial issues, stating:

"The basis for any fair consideration of public issues, and particularly those of a controversial nature, is the presentation of news and information concerning the basic facts of the controversy in as complete and impartial a manner as possible. A licensee would be abusing his position as public trustee of these important means of mass communication were he to withhold from expression over his facilities relevant news or facts concerning a controversy or to slant or distort presentation of such news. No discussion of the issues involved in any controversy can be fair or in the public interest where such discussion must take place in a climate of false or misleading information concerning the basic facts of the controversy." [13]

[F.R. Doc. 64–7327; Filed, July 24, 1964; 8:45 a.m.]

[12]Paragraph 14, Report on Editorializing by Broadcast Licensees.
[13]Report, Par. 17.

Appendix D

A PROPOSAL TO INCREASE THE DIVERSITY OF POLITICAL AND ECO-
NOMIC ANALYSIS AND THEORY IN THE CULTURAL AND PUBLIC
AFFAIRS PROGRAMMING OF NATIONAL EDUCATIONAL TELEVISION
(NET) AND PUBLIC TELEVISION.*

Specifically: to seek ways to counteract the present preponderance of leftist and liberal thought in NET and PTV.

INTRODUCTION

The Leftist and Liberal Bias

During the past few years there has been mounting criticism
of NET and PTV (or educational television) for an *observable
leftist and liberal (progressive) bias in cultural and public affairs
programming.* Critics have pointed to the *lack of diversity* exhibited by NET in the political and economic opinion, theory,
and analysis that it presents. Especially, since National Educational Television claims to provide an alternative program service to the American public, it must present a *wide range of
responsible political and social thought to its viewers.*

John F. White, NET President, indicated that "when public
television really disturbs its viewers to the point where they
think for themselves and begin to do something about what it
is that disturbs them, then we will have succeeded." But, what

*Presented to the NET by Thomas Petry, president and general manager of WCNY-TV of
Syracuse, New York.

we see, are NET's disturbed producers addressing disturbed viewers, both of whom are on the same wave length, while the great audience has tuned out the message because they are tired of hearing the same old tune over and over again. They have despaired of complaining because they feel it is as useless to try to influence this new Public Television as it has been frustrating to make commercial television see the errors of its ways.

Arthur Krock, former *New York Times* columnist, as interviewed in *U.S. News & World Report,* commented:

What has happened, I think, to the press in general that might influence its objectivity—and sometimes unknowingly—is that the so-called "liberal" political philosophy has become very general in the management of the press; the editorial echelon of the press. It seems to me this has had the natural *effect of leaning communications too much to one side.*

PTV should seek out diversified controversy—no matter how difficult to deal with. John White has indicated that "NET can never win the 'balance' battle or the 'position' debate because no small or large group of interested parties can agree on where the fulcrum is on a given issue." Nor should we want NET to maintain a precarious and perhaps, spurious balance, but, only suggest that it spread its imbalance around a bit more.

As to the effects of such imbalance, it is relevant to note sociologist, Irving Janowitz' conclusion that:

Available research knowledge suggest that the mass communications can be decisive in moments of crises and tension, but that, in general, the influence is limited and has effect gradually, over a long period of time. The influence of mass media, reported by networks and inter-personal contacts among opinion leaders, is not a dramatic conversion to public opinion, but rather, in *setting limits within which public debate and controversial issues takes place.*

In the period from July, 1967 through June 30, 1968, NET produced 258 one-half-hour units in public affairs, and of these programs, only eight one-half-hour units were devoted to economics or finance; five half-hour units on the Soviet Union and the problems in Communist countries; four half-hour units on Southeast Asia, other than Vietnam; four half-hour units on the operations of government and diplomacy; three half-hour units on Middle East tensions; and two-and-one-half units on United States foreign policy, other than Vietnam. This would seem to indicate some serious "limits" on the treatment of these urgent matters.

THE NON-LIBERAL MAJORITY

A recent Lou Harris survey (December, 1968) indicated that 70% of American adults classify themselves as either conservative or middle-of-the-road, while only 17% consider themselves to be "liberals." NET most frequently appeals to that 17%, while exhorting the other 70% to mend its ways. Unfortunately, by now, *many in that majority audience are no longer watching.* For them, PTV is hardly presenting an "alternative"; for them, NET is no longer "relevant."

Since there is, at the moment, only one national program service, it would seem obvious that NET has an even greater obligation to provide not so much internal balance (within any given program), but an overall diversity in its expression of opinions, ideas, policy, and analysis, (even in regard to tendentious cultural presentations) commensurate at least, with the diversity existing in our present society.

Media Personnel - the "Eastern Establishment"

On a recent *PBL* broadcast on the national PTV network ("The Whole World is Watching," December 22, 1968) Frank Reynolds of ABC, stated, "Sure, I suppose maybe there is an Eastern Establishment, left wing bias. But that just happens to be because the people who are in, feel that way." On the same program, Blaine Littell, in response to a question as to how hard the networks look for conservative guest commentators or panelists:

> We look hard, and what seems to—to be true, is that most people who write well are in the arts, in the business of communicating, tend to be liberal. Conservatives tend to be businessmen, and businessmen do not tend to write well.

A need for Conservative Television Journalists - "The New Breed"

In discussing this general indifference of conservatives to the field of communications, Lee Edwards (*You Can Make the Difference,* Arlington House, 1968) makes the following observations:

> A young conservative would more often become a professional man or a businessman than he will a writer, a broadcaster, or a public relations consultant. Perhaps the most important reason is that *a liberal domination* of the media has discouraged young conservatives. Nevertheless. . . . *more young conservatives should and must be encouraged to enter a communications media and begin to tip the philosophical scales the other way.*

Does Anyone Care?

Thomas Petry, President and General Manager, WCNY-TV, Syracuse, recently addressed a position paper on the "Liberal-Conservative Debate" to NET and each PTV general manager, calling attention to the problem and making concrete recommendations for improvements. Enthusiastic responses were received from over fifty PTV stations, fairly evenly distributed throughout the country. The many controversial points raised in this paper were widely publicized in the *New York Times* by TV critic Jack Gould, and in such trade publications as *Variety* and *ETV Reporter.* The issues raised quickly became the subject for numerous regional network and other PTV meetings as well as an agenda item for the NET Affiliates Council and the NET annual board meeting. A number of newspapers throughout the country picked up the argument and carried it to their local public television stations who in turn, made the controversy the subject of further analysis on their own air. In response to these programs and articles, Petry received many letters from viewers, broadcasters, legislators and FCC commissioners, applauding the fact that someone had finally sought to question the apparently irresistible tide of "liberalism" on the PTV airways.

WHAT CAN BE DONE?

If one accepts these observations, then one is faced with a matter of serious concern. One needs to ask *what can be done about it?*

The Public Television Network, consisting of over *180 stations,* is growing rapidly in terms of service and audience. It cannot and should not be ignored by conservatives, particularly, since in many communities, it is an effective conduit to reach the opinion leaders in the various political, educational, and cultural elite groups. One should not regard prevailing influences and conditions in PTV as inevitable. It is possible by a concerted effort to develop a *greater diversity of opinion, personnel, and subject matter* than is currently available on Public Television.

How Can we Help?

A surprising number of station managers, community leaders, and viewers, wrote to ask: "What can we do to help? Where do we go from here? What can actually be done?"

The following proposals represent an *outline for an action program* designed to develop in PTV greater diversity, *a broader range of political and economic thought,* a *new breed of personnel,* and an *effective method for the majority viewer to assert himself* and demand his share of the TV action.

This should however, not be interpreted as a clarion call to radical reaction. On the major issues facing the American people, liberalism and conservatism are far closer together than either are to the left and right wing forces of revolutionary radicalism or reaction—nevertheless, *their differences are significant.* Nothing is served by ignoring a major and perfectly respectable political philosophy and code of practice, nor by revealing it only in its most distorted and exaggerated forms: the caricatures of radical reaction; the black magic of fascism. (The cause of liberalism is also ill served by spicing up its image; by lending undue respectability to the anarchists, new leftists and revolutionary radicals of any hue or misguided persuasion).

It is with this understanding—that we speak of responsible and moderate reform—that the following proposals are presented.

PROPOSALS

Index of Videotape and Film Programs to Provide Balance and Diversity in National PTV Programming

Patterned after the National Strategy Information Center, "Major

Sources of Films, Videotapes and Film Series on Communistic Ideology, Objectives, Capability, Strategy and Tactics—a Partial Index," it would be possible to compile an *annotated index listing existing programs to provide balance and diversity* under various subject categories; as well as information regarding distributors, producers, and costs.

In addition, such an index could contain information on a variety of responsible anti-communist, non-liberal, conservative organizations which have resources useful to producing stations in the production of local programs designed to provide a desired balance.

A list of informed articulate speakers, panelists, subject experts and other resources persons could also be included in the index to assist producers of local and regional programs who need aid in locating program participants to provide alternate points of view.

Much of this information is already available and would only require collating and distribution in loose-leaf form, permitting periodic updating.

(A responsible national advisory committee would screen out all extremist and lunatic fringe organizations, individuals, and materials).

National PTV Alternate Program Production Fund

In addition to the distribution of information concerning existing available programming and program resources, stations and regional networks should be encouraged to *develop and produce programs which would provide satisfactory alternatives or an adequate balance to NET and other liberally oriented productions.*

This could be accomplished by seeking the broad support of a coalition of concerned foundations who would initiate a joint production fund for this purpose. PTV stations and independent producers would then submit proposals to the alternate program production fund (as they do now to Ford, Carnegie, and other similar foundations who are financing the current liberal programming).

This alternate production fund makes possible the creation of programs in two categories: (a) those chiefly or wholly "non-liberal" or conservative philosophically (and in regard to participants) to be used as a *counterbalance* to existing liberal programs, and (b) specials or series which would seek to *integrate responsible conservative spokesmen and ideas* into more general documentary, news analysis, or discussion programs.

Such programs would be made available to regional networks and for national syndication for use on PTV (and secondarily commercial television).

Promotion Fund

Funds should also be provided to adequately promote alternate and balance programs. Since most PTV television stations have limited advertising budgets, this kind of support would be necessary to compete effectively with other programming promotion. This support could be provided on a matching basis similar to the monies currently being made available to promote NET, Ford Foundation, and Carnegie Foundation sponsored programs.

An important contribution also could be made by responsible national, regional, and state conservative, anti-communist, and other non-liberal magazines, newspapers, and newsletters, by *promoting the availability of such programs* to their readerships. Reduced advertising rates in such publications would also stimulate further advertising in these specialized channels.

Far greater initiative should be taken by all such publications to publish *critical reviews of NET and other PTV programs* when they deal with political, economic and social issues. Such attention given to these programs, favorable and unfavorable, will serve to stimulate network, stations, and citizen concern, and would also encourage a broader viewing audience to watch what is being shown on their PTV channel.

Personnel Development, Orientation, and Information Seminars

A continuing series of *"information and reorientation seminars"* aimed at general managers, program managers, executive producers, producers, directors, writers, and newsmen, would, perhaps, be the most telling method of bringing a long-range change in the communications climate.

Through the cooperative sponsorship of such organizations as the

Intercollegiate Studies Institute, Young Americans for Freedom, *Human Events,* and the non-partisan, Institute for American Strategy, (all of whom have previous experience in sponsoring such seminars and internships) a series of regional or national information seminars should be organized to provide full and effective discussion on political, economic, educational, and cultural issues, trends and interpretations, for communications personnel. It would be the objective of these high level seminars to bring key PTV communications specialists into intimate contact with a wide range of sophisticated and articulate conservative (as well as the usual liberal) spokesmen in order to exchange ideas and information, for a thoughtful analysis of the major issues of the day, and to stimulate fresh thinking.

Conservative and non-liberal academicians, government leaders, and writers would meet, informally and formally, with the PTV personnel providing a unique opportunity for informed discussion and dialogue.

These conferences would examine, for example, the responsibility of the media in informing (and forming) public opinion; their responsibility for education (and capability for indoctrination); the need for political, social, and economic literacy; awareness of cultural indoctrination through tendentious literature and dramatic productions; and a variety of similar issues. These seminars would serve to clearly define the basic difference between the liberal or progressive, and conservative points of view in terms of philosophy, methods, and ends. Major issues would be considered from a variety of points of view, through a series of formal papers, debates, and small group discussions.

Internships, Scholarships, "Patronships" and Awards

Business and industry and foundations should be encouraged to provide funds for a variety of internships, scholarships, and "patronships" for both short-term and long-term academic studies for students intending to make a career in Public Television as well as those seeking mid-career training and stimulation. These awards would be so structured as to select (on the basis of written applications and personal interviews) such applicants as lean toward a non-liberal orientation in regard to social, political, and economic thinking. Furthermore, the potentially conservative journalists could be directed to an educational institution where he would come under the direct tutelage of one or more conservative professors in the field of his choice who would participate in such a program. These awards could be patterned along the lines of the Nieman Fellowships, the CBS News and Public Affairs Fellowships, the Ford Foundation sponsored communications Fellowships at Stanford, as well as those sponsored by the American Political Science Association—but with a more specific direction and intention.

Finally, *apprenticeships* could be established at certain selected *public television stations* throughout the country where the host-management would furnish a solid grounding in the medium and at the same time, would arrange for related academic work at a nearby college or university.

Appropriate subjects for such special studies as mentioned above might be in the area of political philosophy, political science, public law, governmental institutions, economics, history, sociology, national and international relations, public administration, ethics and comparative religion. These, and similar subjects, would give the television journalist a sound basis for later analysis, interpretation and editorial judgment.

Special awards could also be established for scripts or program proposals, (or other publications adaptable for TV presentation) that would tend to support a general conservative point of view.

Publication and Distribution of an "Early Warning" Newsletter

A newsletter could be sent to all PTV stations providing: (1) information on upcoming controversial programs; (2) encouraging special promotion of positive programs (from a non-liberal conservative point of view); (3) program critiques; (4) information regarding "alternate program" availability; (5) and general information and news of interest to conservative minded managers, producers, and writers.

The main purpose of the newsletter would be to keep leaders in the

PTV communications media and conservatively inclined opinion leaders informed as to media opportunities (and storm clouds) on local and national PTV (as well as commercial television, and for audio-visual use).

Such a newsletter would also be of use to *conservative clubs and campus organizations* by calling attention to television programs and audio-visual materials available to them.

Information provided to such clubs and organizations could also provide them with ammunition with which to contact local PTV (or if none exists, local commercial stations) urging their consideration of available programming favorable to a conservative position.

This newsletter would serve as an effective *interface between the PTV station and those responsible organizations seeking to disseminate conservative and anti-communist educational and informational materials.*

Content, Participants, and Program Balance Analysis Studies

Since PTV is largely supported by foundations, school tax monies or government grants, and contributions from individuals and business and industry, the public obviously has an important stake in how PTV channels are used and what is presented on them.

A two year university (or research institute) based *study might profitably analyze PTV station* programs in regard to subjects, content and participants.

This kind of interpretive study has not been attempted and the lack of solid data creates an unfortunate vacuum.

Such information, once compiled, would also be of use to station personnel and to those congressmen and state legislators who are concerned with the development of this important new communications medium.

Summary

This outline proposal suggests several ways in which the problem of leftist and liberal or progressive bias in Public Television could be countered.

By taking constructive action, it should be possible to:

(1) Take full advantage of available "alternate" programs and

production resources as well as creating entirely new "balance" programs for national distribution.

(2) Disseminate information about programs, personnel, and organizations relevant to the creation of an alternate service with which to balance the existing PTV diet.

(3) Attract new audiences to PTV by adequate promotion of alternative programming and by using existing publications to promote this new channel.

(4) Reorient existing key PTV personnel and develop a new breed of PTV journalists and manager.

(5) Study and document existing trends and practices in PTV programming.

By taking such affirmative action and joining with those in Public Television trying to influence this medium, existing anti-communist, conservative, and non-liberal organizations can effectively reach a far greater potential audience than is presently possible. Available resources and talent could be more effectively tapped and exploited.

A new generation of articulate, conservative communicators might then be encouraged to take their position in the ranks of a growing and more influential Public Television Network.

These recommendations presume:

(1) that there is observable leftist and liberal bias in much of PTV programming;

(2) that many key managerial and creative personnel active in PTV are sympathetic toward this bias;

(3) that given only one PTV network (and in any given community, one PTV station) the question of bias becomes particularly acute—especially when appearing under the auspices of the educational, cultural, and informational establishment;

(4) that what is needed to correct this condition is not censorship and tight controls, but greater diversity in regard to both personnel and points of view represented on PTV.

Conclusion

Many of the world's problems lie in the ideological sphere. Psychological weapons should be the most powerful in the American arsenal. We live in a world where small groups of highly dedicated individuals can overcome conventional armies by the deep belief in a cause. We, in the United States, are not mustering sufficient belief in our own cause to counterattack in the realm of ideas and idealism. We are deficient in the art of "consolidation propaganda" designed to close ranks behind our own cause, to reaffirm beliefs in our own ideals and purposes, and to bring moral courage and dedication to things genuinely essential to our way of life.

Unfortunately, our mass communications all to frequently do not help us to consolidate, but rather, harp on the negative aspects of our society to a degree that even the faithful doubt their cause and forget the heritage of our Western Civilization.

Finally, in the words of David Lawrence's recent editorial in *U.S. News and World Report* (October 28, 1968):

> As we look over the pages of history we do not find 'liberalism' or 'conservatism' defined in just the same way each decade.
>
> The true conservative is not opposed to change, but he is anxious to avoid plunges into the dark—policies that are risky and can do more harm than good. Government, to be sure, must move into unexplored fields and enact reforms—to meet the needs of a growing population, but the exigencies of American politics vary with the epoch and the particular issues that arise.
>
> What we may be witnessing . . . is a normal reaction of the electorate when it is disturbed by the failure of government at all levels to deal with some of the major problems . . .
>
> So the time has come to recognize that 'conservatism' and 'liberalism' are not today—and never have been—inflexible philosophies. For government rests not merely on consent of the governed, but on the effectiveness of its leadership in maintaining stability in the economic system. What is needed is not more ideology but a greater respect for feasibility.
>
> Whether in the international or national field, we can hardly define the demand for a safe society as 'conservatism' or 'liberalism'. It is just 'common sense'.

Appendix E

*Hearings Before a Subcommittee of the Committee on
Appropriations
House of Representatives*
NINETY-FIRST CONGRESS—FIRST SESSION

Subcommittee on Department of Agriculture and Related Agencies
Appropriations

Jamie L. Whitten, Mississippi, *Chairman*

William N. Natcher, Kentucky.   Odin Langen, Minnesota
W. R. Hull, Jr., Missouri   Robert H. Michel, Illinois
George E. Shipley, Illinois   Jack Edwards, Alabama
Frank E. Evans, Colorado

Ross P. Pope, *Staff Assistant to the Subcommittee*

THE COLUMBIA BROADCASTING SYSTEM TELEVISION PROGRAM
ON "HUNGER IN AMERICA"

You might refer to page 64 of the report concerning the CBS
broadcasts. This is what the investigators say on this subject:

"The Columbia Broadcasting System (CBS) featured a television program on May 21, 1968, entitled 'Hunger in America,' which program was shown again on June 16, 1968. According to the script of the broadcast, CBS News spent 10 months investigating hunger in America, and four areas of the country were selected for 'close examination of hunger conditions.' The geographical locations illustrated in the filmed program were San Antonio, Tex.; Loudoun County, Va.; Tuba City, Ariz,; and Hale County, Ala.

"The staff visited the geographical areas selected by CBS for its program and talked to the people interviewed on the program. The staff also attempted to develop additional background information pertaining to these people to determine the cause and extent of their hunger as alleged on the CBS program. The statements made by representatives of CBS about the conditions of persons interviewed on the program and the results of the staff's investigation are set forth for each of the four geographical locations.

"A. SELECTED AREAS USED BY CBS TO ILLUSTRATE 'HUNGER IN AMERICA'

"1. *San Antonio, Tex.*

"San Antonio was described on the program as a city celebrating its 250th birthday with an international exposition, Hemisfair 68, that had foreign pavilions, restaurants, amusements, and exhibits. It was stated that Texas Governor John Connally claimed the Hemisfair had 'turned the downtown area 'from slum to jewel box.' The announcer for the CBS program, Mr. Charles Kuralt, stated that '* * * the jewels don't glitter very brightly on the other side of town where 400,000 Mexican-Americans live, half the city's population. Most ot them are crowded into what city officials refer to as 'poverty tracks' [sic]. Mexican-Americans face a language barrier, and like most poor people, they suffer from lack of skills and unemployment. A hard time earning means a hard time eating. A quarter of San Antonio's Mexican-Americans, 100,000 people, are hungry all the time. CBS News correspondent David Culhane found out how hungry from a woman with six children and an unemployec husband.'

"*a. Interview with Mrs. Esther Medrano*

"Mrs. Medrano was questioned by Mr. Culhane, who asked her if she had food in the house. She replied, 'No, sir. I haven't got anything.' Mr. Culhane then asked her what she told her children when they came home and there was no food in the house. Mrs. Medrano replied, '* * * we haven't got anything to eat and they just have to lay down like that until the next day and see if we can find something to eat.' She further commented that her children '* * * just come in and drink some water and go to bed.'

"Mrs. Esther Medrano, 203 Mirasol Place, San Antonio, was interviewed by the staff on October 1, 1968. She advised that she had eight children, two of whom were married and were living away from home. Her husband was blind in one eye and had only 50 percent vision in the other eye. He had been a victim of eye trouble since he was 17 years old and, due to his eye condition, was limited in the type of work he could perform. Mrs. Medrano advised that her husband was able to find work only 2 or 3 days a week and earned approximately $5 a day, and she formerly did domestic work about the same number of days each week for which she was paid $5 a day.

"Mrs. Medrano advised the staff that Dan Medina, a social worker for 'Wesley House,' a private organization, brought the CBS representatives to the house where she was residing at the time the program was filmed. The house was located at 808 South Leona, San Antonio. She recalled that her electricity and gas had been turned off for nonpayment at the time, and it was necessary for CBS to obtain electricity from a neighbor to operate the camera equipment. She agreed to be interviewed and photographed for which CBS paid her $15, the amount she would have earned as a domestic during the 3 days she stayed at home waiting for the CBS crew to arrive.

"Mrs. Medrano advised that her family had been on the USDA commodity distribution program but the children did not like the powdered milk and beans which were distributed. However, they ate them in order to have enough food to eat. At the time of the CBS interview she was receiving food from the 'Wesley House' because the family had been dropped from the commodity distribution program for some reason unknown to her. She stated that the family did not have food in the house when she was interviewed by CBS.

"Soon after her appearance on the CBS program, the Medrano family was placed on the welfare program of San Antonio for a temporary period, after which it was placed on the State welfare program. Under the present program the family received $135 a month until September 1968, at which time the monthly payment was reduced to $123 consistent with a statewide reduction in all welfare payments. The Medrano family now participates in the food stamp program and receivies $132 in stamps for a purchase price of $86 a month. The family rents a three-bedroom house in a public housing project for which it pays $42.70 a month. Mrs. Medrano advised that the family was able to get along very well at that time through the income received from welfare checks and by working a few days each week. She said that prior to being placed on welfare there were times when the children did not go to school because they had no food. Now two of her children receive free lunches at school.

"Mr. Dan Medina, coordinator, Wesley Community Center, San Antonio, advised the staff on October 3, 1968, that he was contacted by CBS representatives in October 1967, and requested to identify known cases of hunger. He told them there were cases of hunger in San Antonio as evidenced by the number of people who came to the Wesley Community Center for food and other help. He had personally confirmed the lack of food many times by making spot checks in the homes and cupboards of those seeking help. He advised that instances of hunger were usually temporary and were generally more frequent during the winter months due to a slack period in employment. He remarked that CBS personnel appeared disappointed to find that the hunger he described was not obvious in the appearance of the people they met. He pointed out to the CBS representatives that because of their diets the poor people appeared fat and well-fed but actually they were victims of malnutrition because of starchy diets. Mr. Medina advised that families which experienced temporary hunger conditions usually had other problems. For example, in the Medrano family, Mr. Medrano 'drinks a lot and at times would stay away from home 3 or 4 weeks at a time.'

"b. Interview with 'Jerry'

"A young boy, identified only as 'Jerry' on the CBS program, was interviewed by Father Ralph Ruiz, a Catholic priest. The boy said that he attended Southside Junior High School but had nothing to eat for lunch because he did not take his lunch nor did he have the 35 cents to buy lunch. He also said that he had only beans for breakfast.

"Father Ralph Ruiz was interviewed by the staff on September 30, 1968, and he advised that he was the contact in the west side slum area of San Antonio for hearings held by the Citizens Board of Inquiry and the CBS-TV crew that filmed 'Hunger in America.' He selected and produced witnesses at the hearings and led the CBS-TV crew to the poverty people. Father Ruiz refused to make known to the staff the identities of witnesses he produced for the hearings or the poverty people that were filmed by the CBS-TV crew. His reason for refusal was based on his belief that these people were living in misery and had been badgered enough by both the 'do-gooders and the curious.'

"Jerry was identified by the staff in October 1968 as Jerry Cantu, 16 years of age, who resided with his parents, Larry and Rose Cantu, at 1630 Santa Rita Street, San Antonio, at the time of the filming by CBS. Mr. Raymond G. Cheves, regional director, State welfare department, San Antonio, determined for the staff on October 3, 1968, that Jerry Cantu left school shortly after he was interviewed by CBS and was employed as a civilian at the Brooks Air Force Base, San Antonio. He was reported to be living at 1407 San Rafael Street, San Antonio, with a sister.

"According to Mr. Cheves, the records of the State welfare department disclosed that on July 25, 1968, the Cantu family made application for participation in the food stamp program but the application was denied because of excess resources. The welfare files disclosed that Larry Cantu, the father, was employed as a dishwasher at a restaurant in San Antonio and his income from this employment was $247 a month. He was purchasing a house at 1639 Santa Rita Street which cost $2,950 and in which he had an equity at $1,680. He was also purchasing the house in which he lived at 1630 Santa Rita Street.

This house also cost $2,950. Neither Mr. Cantu's income nor the ownership of the house in which he lived would disqualify him for food stamps; however, his equity in the additional property at 1639 Santa Rita Street exceeded the allowable maximum of $600 in other resources and was the basis for which he was denied food stamps.

"On October 3, 1968, it was ascertained by the staff that Jerry Cantu had recently moved to 1410 San Rafael Street. At the 1410 San Rafael Street address, a young girl identified herself to the staff as Martha Cantu. She advised she was 14 years of age and was living with Jerry Cantu, the father of her 6-week-old baby. She said that they were not married because Jerry had only turned 16 years of age on September 30, 1968. They planned to be married when Jerry received his next paycheck.

"Jerry Cantu was interviewed on October 3, 1968, at Brooks Air Force Base, where he was employed as a dishwasher for a private contractor. He recalled that some TV men were at his parents home about 1 year ago and Father Ralph Ruiz, who was with them, asked him to appear on TV. Jerry Cantu claimed he answered Father Ruiz questions truthfully and explained he never had enough to eat at home. There were 15 children in the family (ages 8 months to 24 years) and when he lived at home with his parents he usually had only one meal a day, which was in the morning. He could not remember having had anything to drink at home other than water. He did not eat lunch at school because he did not have the money to buy lunch and there was not enough food for his mother to prepare a lunch for him. Jerry Cantu remarked that since he was employed at Brooks Air Force Base 9 months ago, he gained 45 pounds and gets all the food he wants to eat. His 'wife' and baby also have plenty of food to eat. He stated he is buying the property where he lives at 1410 San Rafael Street for $4,000 and made a downpayment of $90 from his last paycheck. He was obligated to make monthly payments of $40. Jerry Cantu introduced his brother, Larry Cantu, age 19, who also was employed as a dishwasher at the Brooks Air Force Base. Larry Cantu advised the staff that on many occasions food was scarce at home and as soon as he could find another place to live, and when he could afford to move, he would leave his parents' home.

"C. Interview With Mary Garcia, a Social Worker

"The CBS program showed an interview with a social worker, identified as Mary Garcia, who was with a young girl, aged 11. The announcer opened the interview with Miss Garcia with the following statement:

" 'Hunger is never so devestating as in a child. Never so horrifying as in what it may drive a child to do. Social worker Mary Garcia sees many such children.'

"Miss Garcia explained on the program that the girl had been picked up for soliciting for prostitution and she had quite a number of girls involved in this activity. She remarked that the reason the girls gave for soliciting was that they needed money to buy food because they did not have food at home.

"Miss Mary Garcia, assistant probation officer, Bexar County Probation Officer, Juvenile Division, San Antonio, was interviewed by the staff on October 3, 1968. She stated that for 2 years prior to her employment as a probation officer (her employment as a probation officer began in June 1967), she taught physical education and special education in a San Antonio high school. She further advised that very little of her college work or her previous employment had prepared her for a position as a probation officer and therefore she had had limited experience with cases similar to the one she discussed on the CBS program.

"Miss Garcia advised that the case of the 11-year-old girl, shown on the CBS program with her, had been referred by the juvenile court to the child welfare department before she could complete her investigation to locate and interview the parents to determine the true family circumstances. At the time of the interview on the CBS program the child had been placed in a home by the child welfare department but had been brought to the juvenile court hearing room specifically to be displayed on the program.

"Miss Garcia stated that the 11-year-old girl filmed by CBS had a 14-year-old sister, and both girls had been arrested in July 1967 when they solicited a San Antonio detective for prostitution. They claimed they had solicited in order to get money to buy food. Miss Garcia's records disclosed the two girls had been referred previously

to the juvenile authorities in May 1967, after the father had complained they had run away from home. They were referred a second
time, in June 1967, to the same agency on suspicion of soliciting and
released when no witnesses appeared against them. The third referral
occurred with their arrest in July 1967.

"Miss Garcia advised that her investigation disclosed that the
girls' mother died in 1963 and they had a stepmother for a short
period of time. She said that during her investigation of the case she
went to the girls' home and found a 12-year-old brother alone in the
house. None of the neighbors could furnish information concerning
the whereabouts of the father. She searched the house and could find
no food. She was unable to find anything concerning the father's
employment. Miss Garcia stated that tests given the girls disclosed
that both were mentally retarded.

"Through the child welfare department, San Antonio, it was
learned by the staff on October 4, 1968, that the family had consisted
of the parents, three girls, and two boys. The mother died in 1963,
after which the father brought another woman into the house to live
with him. The father, who was illiterate, mentally retarded, and
addicted to liquor, was suspected of making his living by stealing. He
had been apprehended with one of his sons for breaking, entering,
and theft. The son was subsequently arrested for shoplifting, after
which he was declared a delinquent and placed on probation. The
third sister was declared a delinquent in 1963, put on probation, and
placed in a foster home. In 1964, she was sent to a State school for
the retarded. The records of the child welfare department disclosed
that on September 26, 1967, after the 11- and 14-year-old sisters were
transferred to the child welfare department, they were placed in a
foster home. On October 14, 1967, the girls ran away and were
located on October 19, 1967. On October 20, 1967, the 14-year-old
girl was placed in a foster home, from which she ran away on
October 21, 1967, but she was soon located. All three sisters are
presently in State-controlled schools.

"The records of the child welfare department disclosed that during
August and September 1967, the father left the 12-year-old son, who
also was mentally retarded, alone in an apartment. The father paid

the rent but did not furnish his son with food. The boy, fed by the neighbors, was afraid to stay in the apartment at night and slept on the neighbors' porches. When the father was finally located he was in possession of a late model pickup truck and was performing odd jobs. The father refused to attend his children's hearings in juvenile court and refused assistance in being taught a trade.

"d. Interview with Commissioner A. J. Ploch

"Commissioner A. J. Ploch, one of four county commissioners, Bexar County, which includes San Antonio, was interviewed on the CBS program and was asked about the children in San Antonio who were not receiving enough food and their possible inability to learn properly because of an inadequate diet. Commissioner Ploch replied that the problem was actually caused by the fathers who would not work and, as far as education was concerned, he did not believe that education, other than an eighth-grade education, was needed. Commissioner Ploch also remarked on the CBS program that 'You'll always have hunger * * *' and '* * * you've got to have Indians and chiefs.'

"Commissioner Ploch was interviewed by the staff on October 3, 1968, and he advised that portions of his interview by CBS were cut from the film in an effort to portray him as a villain and as one not concerned about the poor people of San Antonio. He stated that the full text of his interview would have disclosed that he also remarked that there were many people with only an eighth-grade education who were successfully working as plumbers, carpenters, and tradesmen, and they were earning more money than some college professors. He contended that too much emphasis was placed on a college education and, as a result, training as a craftsman was neglected. Commissioner Ploch maintained that contractors in the San Antonio area were begging for laborers and, because some 'lazy fathers' would not work, the contractors were 3 months behind their schedule on jobs. He said he would stand by his statements that there will always be Indians and chiefs and some degree of hunger in Baxar County because of ignorance and indolence.

"Commissioner Ploch advised that when he was interviewed by

representatives of CBS, he was led to believe that San Antonio would not be portrayed in its worst light. He further stated that because his interview was reported out of context and he was made to appear as an enemy of the poor, he received a number of threatening telephone calls at his home. In the interest of personal safety to his family and to himself, and at the suggestion of the chief of police, he was forced to vacate his home for approximately 10 days until interest in the program had subsided.

"e. A Dying Baby

"Probably the most touching portion of the film, and one which CBS later said, 'moved the Nation to tears,' was the scene of a baby being given resuscitation in the hospital after which it appeared motionless. The CBS narrator, Charles Kuralt, made the following statement with respect to the scene:

" 'Hunger is easy to recognize when it look like this. This baby is dying of starvation. He was an American. Now he is dead.'

"Mr. Jack E. Coughlin, director of community relations, Bexar County Hospital District, which includes the Robert B. Green Memorial Hospital, San Antonio, advised on October 2, 1968, that the hospital scenes shown on the CBS program for the San Antonio portion were filmed at the Robert B. Green Memorial Hospital. Arrangements for the filming were made by Mrs. Vera Burke, former director of social services at the hospital, who had requested permission from the hospital authorities. Mr. Coughlin advised that when permission was granted to Mrs. Burke, it was generally understood that the filming would be confined to the pediatrics ward if she could obtain the concurrence from the doctors in that ward. Mr. Coughlin stated that after viewing the CBS program, he determined that Mrs. Burke had permitted the CBS crew to take photographs in the premature nursery, an area which is off limits to visitors.

"Mr. Coughlin stated that after a local newspaper had published a news article which indicated that the baby shown on the CBS program was a premature baby and did not die from starvation, the hospital administration made an independent investigation. The results of that investigation were stated by Mr. Coughlin to be as follows: 'The male baby involved was born at the hospital at 8:15 a.m. on October 24, 1967, and expired at 3 p.m. on October 29, 1967, in the premature nursery. The baby's weight at birth was 2 pounds, 12 ounces, and the gestation period was 28 weeks (approximately 7 months). The hospital records disclosed that Dr. Luis Rey Montemayor, the doctor on duty, recorded on the baby's chart that the child had a cardiac arrest and respiratory arrest on October 27, 1967, and two additional attacks on October 29, 1967, the last when he was pronounced dead. The death certificate, filed by the hospital on the baby, disclosed the baby died from septicemia, meningitis, and peritonitis, with the underlying cause being 'prematurity.'

"Mr. Coughlin produced copies of releases CBS had obtained from the parents of a number of children photographed in the pediatrics ward. Each indicated a payment of $5 had been paid to a parent for the release. He advised that he had no evidence that CBS had obtained releases from the parents whose children were photographed in the premature nursery.

"Dr. Luis Ray Montemayer, who had entered private practice in San Antonio, was interviewed by the staff on October 3, 1968. He advised that he had obtained his education in Mexico and performed his intern work at the Robert B. Green Memorial Hospital. He recalled on occasion when he was attending a baby in the premature nursery in the hospital and was summoned by a nurse who said another baby in the same nursery was in distress and required immediate attention. He stated he rushed to the isolette to attend to the baby. He observed at the time that there were CBS cameramen and equipment in the premature nursery and learned that filming of babies had taken place. He stated that as soon as he started attending the baby he noticed the CBS camera crew move into his area and commence filming his efforts. He said that the baby had suffered a cardiac and respiratory arrest, one of several the baby had suffered since birth, and he administered resuscitation. For a short period of time it appeared that the baby would not respond, but he continued to work with it and it did respond. He said the baby died 2 days later when it suffered another series of attacks and could not be saved.

"Dr. Montemayor remarked that CBS was wrong in depicting that the baby died of starvation, that there was no evidence of malnutrition, but rather the baby was premature and the prognosis for survival at the time of birth was not good. He recalled that one of the CBS representatives questioned him concerning the 'malnourished babies he saw in the nursery.' Dr. Montemayor advised that he informed the CBS representative that the babies he saw in the premature nursery were small because they were born prematurely and the chances of survival for many of them were questionable. He said that the CBS representative, for some unknown reason, wanted him to say that the mothers of the babies gave birth to premature babies because they were malnourished. Dr. Montemayor advised that while it was possible that malnutrition could be a contributing factor to a premature birth, there was no such evidence in the case of the baby photographed by CBS and shown on the program. Dr. Montemayor positively identified the baby he attended and which was filmed by CBS in his presence as the same baby identified by Mr. Coughlin from hospital records. Identification was also made by the head nurse in the premature nursery and by a student nurse, both of whom were witnesses to the CBS filming.

"The parents of the baby were interviewed by the staff on October 4, 1968, in San Antonio, and they positively identified the baby shown on the CBS-TV program as their baby. The mother was in the hospital and witnessed the filming of her baby by CBS from the hall leading to the glass-enclosed isolette where she knew her baby was being cared for. The father had visited the baby on a number of occasions and saw the program broadcast. The parents claimed that CBS did not contact them for permission to use the film and the statements in the program about starvation were definitely untrue. The mother advised that she had fallen when she was in her 7th month of pregnancy and began experiencing pains, at which time she was taken to the hospital by her husband, and she gave birth prematurely. She stated that the availability of food had been no problem for her because she not only ate at her home but at her mother's home and the home of her mother-in-law. The father advised that he had won acclaim for his athletic abilities in high school and exhibited several trophies awarded to him in track and basketball competition. He is presently in his second year of college and has expectations of making the varsity basketball team. Upon graduation he plans to teach physical education.

"The grandmothers of the baby advised on October 3, 1968, that they both had steady jobs and felt that they had provided well for their children's health and did not believe they were ever malnourished. They advised that the daughter had recently lost her second child at 28 weeks of pregnancy, the cause of death being prematurity. They said the second child weighed approximately the same as the first child.

"On October 2, 1968, Mr. Kemper Diehl, a reporter for the San Antonio Express, advised he first brought to the attention of the people of San Antonio the facts concerning the baby that was reported to have died during the filming of the CBS program. Initially, another reporter for the newspaper, Arthur Moczygemba, had been informed by Mrs. Vera Burke at the Robert B. Green Memorial Hospital that the baby shown on the CBS program was a premature baby and there was no starvation involved. As a result of this information the editor of the San Antonio Express assigned Mr. Diehl to determine the facts. Mr. Diehl searched the records of the hospital and death certificates on file at the City Health Department which disclosed that three recently born infants had died during the period CBS was in San Antonio filming the program. Investigation disclosed that one of the babies was a girl, which was ruled out because CBS referred to the baby as a male. Of the two remaining babies, both were males; one weighed 7 pounds and 11 ounces and the other weighed 2 pounds and 12 ounces. Only the smaller baby was confined to the premature nursery. Mr. Diehl interviewed hospital personnel and was advised that the hospital background which appeared in the film clearly showed that the filming of the baby occurred in the premature nursery. The size of the baby was determined to be approximately two pounds, based on a pathologist's calculation of the approximate size of the baby as compared to the size of the hands of the doctor who was holding the baby at the time it was filmed. Mr. Diehl stated that after the baby was identified he interviewed the parents who also confirmed that the baby filmed by the CBS crew was, in fact, their baby.

"f. CBS Statement Concerning the USDA Commodity Program

"Mr. Charles Kuralt made the following comments concerning the commodity distribution program of the USDA during the narration of the portion of the film on San Antonio. He stated that San Antonio's answer to hunger for the last 14 years had been surplus commodities. Surplus commodities were foods that farmers could not sell and nobody else wanted. The USDA bought surplus crops from farmers and got rid of them by giving them to the poor. For farmers and the Government, commodities were a convenience; for the poor they were simply an inadequate dole. The commodity distribution program consisted largely of dumping excesses rather than providing essentials. The program had not changed since it was conceived in the 1930's.

"Secretary of Agriculture Orville L. Freeman publicly denounced the statements made on the CBS program. According to Secretary Freeman, the commodity distribution program had changed radically in that, as late as 1960, USDA offered only five items of food for distribution, namely, lard, rice, flour, nonfat dry milk, and cornmeal, which foods had a value of $2.20 per person per month, but, in 1961, the number of commodities and the amount of food for distribution were doubled. The program was improved still further by offering additional foods, and at the time of the showing of the CBS program a total of 16 items were offered to recipients. During the late summer of 1968 an additional six items were added, making a total of 22 items offered to the needy. An official of USDA advised that the dollar value of commodities now being distributed for each person per month was $12.70 and, as of November 1, 1968, the commodities included dry beans, bulgur, butter, cheese, whole canned chicken, corn grits, cornmeal, scrambled egg mix, flour, fruit and vegetable juice, lard or shortening, chopped canned meat, evaporated milk, nonfat dry milk, peanut butter, dry split peas, instant potatoes, raisins or prunes, rice, oats or rolled wheat, corn syrup, and canned vegetables, with many of these foods having been nutritionally fortified.

"In rebuttal to the charge that the commodity distribution program consisted largely of dumping excesses rather than providing essentials, Secretary Freeman said that some of the foods distributed were items which were in oversupply but certainly could not be classified as foods 'nobody else wants' because they were identical in content and purity to foods purchased by millions of Americans in local supermarkets. He submitted that these foods currently provided the following percentages of full daily allowances recommended by the National Research Council: protein, 127.7 percent; calcium, 158 percent; iron, 91.4 percent; vitamin A, 69.5 percent; thiamine, 143.9 percent; riboflavin, 165.7 percent; vitamin C, 92.4 percent; and food energy, 77.6 percent.

"g. Filmed Scenes and Interviews Not Included in Program
"Mr. John E. Bierschwale, director of the San Antonio City Welfare Department, advised on September 30, 1968, that at the time the CBS crew was in San Antonio, the city operated a commodity distribution program for the needy. The city has since changed to a food stamp program. He said the CBS crew wanted to film a typical commodity distribution office and made arrangements to set up the cameras at one of the offices. CBS waited for a long line to form outside the office, but when this did not occur the CBS crew requested that the doors to the office be closed to allow a line of people to form. Mr. Bierschwale stated that he cooperated with CBS by closing the office without realizing that CBS intended to discredit the commodity distribution program. The doors were closed for 1 hour and 45 minutes to permit a line of about 20 people to form before the filming took place.

"Dr. Ramiro P. Estrada, a private physician and member of the staff at the Robert B. Green Memorial Hospital, advised on October 2, 1968, that he was asked to take part in the CBS program but the filmed portion relating to his interviews was not used in the televised program. He said he met with CBS representatives and Mrs. Vera Burke prior to the actual filming. At the meeting, the CBS representatives indicated that they were interested in showing only advanced cases of malnutrition. They visited several homes where he examined the children while CBS filmed the interviews. Dr. Estrada stated the CBS representatives wanted him to say some of the cases of malnutrition were severe, whereas they were actually relatively minor cases. He advised that he told the CBS representatives he 'would not bend the truth' and they accused him of being evasive. Dr. Estrada indicated that it was apparent to him the CBS representatives were interested only in sensational-type material and they wanted him to say things with a more sensational impact than what he was willing to say.

"*2. Loudoun County, Va.*
  "The CBS narrator reported that:
  " 'Loudoun County, Va., is anything but a poverty pocket. It is headquarters for the so-called horsey set. The county contains hunt clubs, private schools, and aristocratic race meets that mingle the pedigree of the horses with those of their owners. The trappings of wealth are everywhere. Loudoun County is only 25 miles outside Washington, D.C. It is the home of distinguished legislators like Senator Everett Dirksen, celebrities like Arthur Godfrey. Society here is studded with American nobility—names like du Pont, Mellon and Whitney.
  " 'Hunger is the last thing an outsider would expect to find; indeed it might be the last thing he would find. Yet hidden away in Loudoun County are thousands of shacks where tenant farmers lead a marginal existence. Loudoun County, like one-third of the counties in America, has no Federal food program.'
  "Mr. Kuralt introduced Dr. Stephen Granger, Loudoun County Medical Officer, as a man who knew and treated many of the tanant families.

  "a. Remarks by Dr. Stephen Granger
  "Dr. Granger mentioned on the program that the diet of tenant families was heavy on starch and light on protein. Because of the diet the children had a '* * * kind of a hollow lifeless look—stringy hair, a pasty complexion, a dead look about their eyes. There is a hopeless feeling that springs almost physically from these children.' Continuing, Dr. Granger said a poor diet affected brain tissue and the child's ability to think and to learn, a condition that was not

reversible, 'Not by Christmas baskets, not by hot lunches when he starts school, or anything else, 1 year from now or 5 years from now." Following the interviews with two tenant farmers in Loudoun County, Dr. Granger commented on people among his patients who looked old prematurely. He said premature aging may be caused by a number of medical problems, but malnutrition certainly played a big part. He claimed there were about 7,000 households in the area that had severe nutritional problems and that the people in these households rarely, if ever, ate a complete meal.

"Dr. Granger asserted that such people '* * * with no past to be proud of and no hope for the future, seek immediate forms of employment.' With this statement he justified the presence of a late-model television in the house, empty pint bottles in the yard, and a late-model baby in the crib.

"Mr. Charles F. Turner, executive secretary, Loudoun County Board of Supervisors, Leesburg, Va., advised the staff on October 10, 1968, that Dr. Granger initially informed him about the plans for CBS to make a film in Loudoun County. Prior to the actual filming he met with CBS representatives who assured him that the program would be an objective analysis of malnutrition, that the subject matter would be handled in a general way, and that CBS would not be critical of Loudoun County. Mr. Turner stated he felt that CBS misrepresented the conditions in Loudoun County and, further, misrepresented the program objectives as stated to him.

"Mr. Turner stated that Dr. Granger's remark that 'There are about 7,000 households in the area that have severe nutrition problems' was inaccurate. A recent county survey, by actual count, disclosed the existence of 10,086 homes in the county, and Dr. Granger's estimate would indicate that 7 out of every 10 households in the county were suffering severe nutritional problems. Mr. Turner advised that he challenged Dr. Granger on his estimate after he saw the program and Dr. Granger, in a succession of attempts to clarify his comment, first said that he meant individuals instead of households, and then expanded his statement to include individuals in Loudoun and Fauquier Counties. Finally, he included individuals in Loudoun, Fauquier, and Prince William Counties.

"Dr. Stephen Granger, Children's Hospital, Washington, D.C., former Loudoun County Health Officer, was interviewed by the staff on November 20, 1968. Dr. Granger said he was contacted by Mr. Martin Carr of CBS who explained that the CBS film would depict hunger and malnutrition in the United States and Mr. Carr requested to meet with some white tenant farmers in Loudoun County who were believed to be suffering from malnutrition due to economic deprivation. Dr. Granger advised that a list of approximately 20 households was compiled and discussed with Mr. Carr. Mr. Carr was shown some of these households and the ultimate selection of households filmed was made by CBS.

"Reflecting on his comment on the CBS program relative to 7,000 households in the county having severe nutritional problems, Dr. Granger advised the staff that if he had it to do over again he would say 7,000 people in Loudoun County rather than 7,000 households. When he was questioned further concerning this estimate he said that the figure applied to the 'area' rather than the county, but refused to describe in a geographic sense his use of the term 'area.' He acknowledged that he had no statistical basis for his use of the figure 7,000, whether it be households or people. Dr. Granger was of the opinion that the program accurately depicted conditions in Loudoun County. He regarded the film as being of high quality—an excellent presentation showing a good balance in placing the responsibility for malnutrition on the county, State, and Federal Governments. Dr. Granger advised that his resignation as county health officer from Loudoun County was only coincidental with the release of the CBS program and the critical reaction the program received in the county.

"b. Interview with Mrs. Franklin Hopkins

"During the CBS program an interview with a Mrs. Franklin Hopkins was conducted by Mrs. Pauline J. Barrett, a Loudoun County Public Health Nurse, in which Mrs. Hopkins was questioned concerning the eating habits of her children. The questioning disclosed that Mrs. Hopkins had not decided what to prepare for lunch, that she had no baby food in the house for her baby, and that another child had only gravy for breakfast that morning.

"Mrs. Pauline J. Barrett, public health nurse, Department of Public Health, Leesburg, Loudoun County, advised the staff on October 11, 1968, that arrangements for her participation in the interview with Mrs. Hopkins were made by Dr. Granger with CBS. She was asked by CBS to conduct the interview in the same manner as she would in any home visit. The interview commenced with a discussion of the children's diet and continued with a discussion of family supervision, care of teeth, and immunization shots. CBS used only that portion of the interview which dealt with the children's diet, because that was their primary interest. Mrs. Barrett was of the opinion that CBS neglected to bring out that fact that it was not normally the lack of food so much as not knowing or caring how to prepare an adequate diet which was responsible for the dietary deficiencies of many poor people. She did not consider Loudoun County unique nor was it better or worse than other counties she knew about. Mrs. Barrett noted that in her 6 years as a public health nurse in Loudoun County, the few cases of hunger she had seen were the result of parental neglect.

"Mrs. Helen C. Shorey, superintendent, Loudoun County Department of Public Welfare, Leesburg, advised the staff on October 10, 1968, that Franklin Roosevelt Hopkins had asked the welfare office for assistance in September 1967, when his wife was expecting their fifth child. He was employed at the time, with a monthly income of $277.33. He was not eligible for assistance because of his income, but the welfare department paid the hospital bill for Mrs. Hopkins' maternity care pursuant to a ruling which permitted such payment for a family of six with an income under $300 a month.

"Mr. Roland Hope, a dairy farmer who resided in Loudoun County, near Purcellville, Va., advised the staff on October 11, 1968, that Claude Hopkins and his family were tenants on another farm operated by him, also near Purcellville, at the time CBS filmed the program in Loudoun County. He identified the Mrs. Hopkins interviewed on the program as Mrs. Franklin Hopkins, the daughter-in-law of Claude Hopkins, his tenant, with whom the Frankin Hopkins family lived. He said that Claude Hopkins had sons living with him at the time he as a tenant. He thought Franklin Hopkins had been working on a highway crew in the neighborhood of Hamilton, Va., at the time of the filming of the program. Mr. Hope advised that his basic pay for tenant farmers, including the Hopkins family, was $200 a month, and in addition he furnished a house, electricity, firewood, a gallon or more of milk a day, and between one fourth and one half of a beef twice a year. He stated that the better farmhands received the larger portion of beef. He also provided garden space but commented that it had been his experience that tenants seldom planted a garden even after he prepared the land for them. Mr. Hope stated he had a constant need for farmhands but was only able to get Franklin Hopkins and his brothers to work occasionally. He advised that all of the Hopkins men had a drinking problem and Franklin Hopkins frequently did not show up for work for a couple of days after receiving his pay.

"Mrs. Franklin Hopkins was interviewed by the staff on October 11, 1968, at Lovettsville, Va. The Hopkins family moved to this location following the filming of the CBS program. Mrs. Hopkins stated that the farm where she now resided was owned by Mr. Asbury Smith. Her husband, Franklin Roosevelt Hopkins, worked for Mr. Smith and was paid $90 every 2 weeks. In addition, they were furnished a house which had indoor plumbing, electricity, and furnace heat. They were provided the fuel for winter months, milk every day, two hogs and feed necessary to raise them, and a quantity of beef. Mrs. Hopkins said she had received clothes for her daughter from a relative of Mrs. Smith. When asked if she had enough food for the family, Mrs. Hopkins stated she did but could always use more.

"With respect to her appearance on the CBS program, Mrs. Hopkins advised that Dr. Granger and Mrs. Barrett arrived at her home with the CBS film crew without making prior arrangements with her. Mrs. Hopkins explained that her comment about not having baby food in the house was due to the fact the baby was only 2 weeks old and not old enough for solid food. She said she had the money to buy baby food if the baby had been old enough for solid food. Relative to her statement that one of her children had only gravy for break-

fast, Mrs. Hopkins said the family had gravy and biscuits for breakfast, a standard breakfast for them because they preferred it. Mrs.
Hopkins advised the staff the family had everything it wanted in the
way of food at the time her interview was filmed, including meat
remaining from a side of beef previously given to the family by the
landowner. She said the CBS film crew was aware of the food because
one of them opened the refrigerator during the visit and saw the food.

"3. *Tuba City, Ariz.*

"CBS reported that 'The deserts of Arizona and New Mexico are
nice places to visit, but the Navajo Indians have to live there. Living
in a desert, just staying alive, is very hard for the 125,000 members
of the largest tribe in the United States. The West was theirs once.
They were nomads and their home was vast. Now they have an arid
reservation. Dr. Jean Van Duzen of Tuba City, Ariz., has practiced
among the Navajo Indians for the past 14 years. She continually
faces the medical problems caused by lack of food.'

"Dr. Van Duzen commented that the people she saw every day
appeared as though they ate mostly starches. The older people
tended to be rather fat and dumpy and the children were just plain
undernourished. She stated that surplus commodities only provided
40 percent of the caloric needs of the people and did not make any
allowance for protein, vitamin, and mineral needs.

"Scenes filmed at Tuba City, Ariz., included unidentified Indian
hogans and a visit to the Public Health Service hospital for the
Navajo Reservation. Dr. Van Duzen exhibited several children in the
hospital who allegedly had Kwashiorkor, which she described as
'* * * the most severe form of protein calorie malnutrition. This is
a disease that was seen first in South America and Africa. It's not
supposed to exist in the United States, but it does.' She also exhibited
children who allegedly had Marasmus, which she described as a
'* * * total calorie and protein malnutrition. She said children who
had Marasmus became that way because they had '* * * nothing,
practically nothing but water, and very quickly they get into great
trouble and frequently they die.' She went on to state that one-third
of the children admitted to the hospital for Marasmus die.

"Dr. Van Duzen, chief of pediatrics, Tuba City Hospital, advised the staff on September 24, 1968, that she did not know why Tuba City was selected by CBS for its program but she cooperated with CBS after permission had been granted by her superiors. The Navajo families contacted by CBS were selected by her and Wilson Grey, a health education aid and formerly a driver-interpreter at the time CBS visited the hospital. She stated that they visited five or six Navajo camps on the reservation and at each camp filmed one hogan. She also conducted the CBS camera crew through the Public Health Service hospital and exhibited several children who had been admitted to the hospital for various illnesses, most of whom had been underfed.

"Dr. Van Duzen advised the staff that when the CBS representatives visited the hospital there were several cases of Kwashiorkor and Marasmus, but at the time of the staff's visit she had no cases of Kwashiorkor and had only two cases of Marasmus. Dr. Van Duzen stated that usually the cases of Marasmus involved babies 2 to 2 ½ months of age where the mothers had been breast feeding the babies, the milk had dried up, and they were not getting any food. The babies were brought to the hospital only after a considerable period of time had elapsed and it was difficult to save them. She stated that the Navajo mothers were reluctant to bring their babies to the hospital when their milk dried up because to admit this fact was an admission that they were incapable of functioning as a mother. She advised that within the past 5 years, she had 28 cases of Marasmus in the hospital and, of these, 14 died. The death rate was exceptionally high because the babies were in poor health, including almost total dehydration, when they were admitted.

"Dr. Van Duzen stated that Kwashiorkor appeared in children from 1 to 2 years of age. In most cases the children had been weaned and were given whole milk after which they developed diarrhea. The mother thought the milk caused the diarrhea and the child was then taken off milk. Consequently, the child received little nourishment. Another factor to be considered in Kwashiorkor cases is that in the Navajo families the children traditionally eat after the adults and receive what food is left, if any. If the family ate together, the children had to fend for themselves. She advised that the typical Navajo mother was totally unknowledgeable about nutritional and medical needs and would bring a child to the hopsital only after the illness had continued for a substantial length of time.

"Mr. John P. Sipe, agency social worker, Bureau of Indian Affairs, Tuba City, advised the staff on September 23, 1968, that the day after the CBS program appeared on television he received a telephone call from his superiors instructing him to make a report on the Navajo families shown on the program. Mr. Sipe advised that the CBS program was not shown in Tuba City and he had not seen the film. After considerable investigation, including interviews with Dr. Van Duzen and Wilson Grey, he identified four families visited by the CBS representatives but he could not say if they were included in the televised program. Information concerning the four families was furnished by Mr. Sipe as follows:

"a. Mr. and Mrs. Jimmy Kerley

"In 1967, the Kerley family lived at Cameron, Ariz. Mrs. Kerley was formerly married to the brother of Jimmy Kerley, first name not known, who was an alcoholic. She left the brother to live with Jimmy Kerley, also an alcoholic. There were four children by the two fathers in the home. In November 1967, when CBS was filming the program in Tuba City, the Kerley's infant child was in the hospital. At the time of the filming the parents were separated, but Mr. Kerley was working in Flagstaff, Ariz., and contributed to the support of the children. The mother and children received surplus commodities, but the family did not receive welfare assistance because there was no financial need.

"In December 1967, Mr. Kerley was in jail, and Mrs. Kerley, who also had a drinking problem, was placed on general assistance by the Bureau of Indian Affairs and was given $178 month. During the period of separation the Bureau of Indian Affairs worked with the family in an effort to bring about a reconciliation. In January 1968, Mr. and Mrs. Kerley were reconciled and married. On March 26, 1968, Mr. and Mrs. Kerley enrolled in training programs at the Bureau of Indian Affairs Employment Center, Roswell, N. Mex., where they resided and reportedly were progressing well.

"b. Mr. and Mrs. Yodell Billah

"Mr. and Mrs. Yodell Billah, who live in the area of Red Lake, Ariz., had 10 children. One child was married and resided away from home; one was in Vietnam; two were in a Bureau of Indian Affairs boarding school; two resided at home and attended Red Lake Day School; two were in foster homes under the Indian placement program sponsored by the Church of Jesus Christ of Later-day Saints; and one was of preschool age. The other child was unaccounted for. The husband was a shepherd, but performed odd jobs and participated in tribal work projects. The husband had 2 years of education but had no job training. At the time of the filming by CBS in November 1967, the family did not receive assistance because the husband was working and had not applied for assistance. The family had since commenced receiving surplus commodities and, because of a recent injury, the husband applied to the Bureau of Indian Affairs for general assistance. The social services agency, Bureau of Indian Affairs, had no information that indicated there was any malnourishment in the family.

"c. Mr. and Mrs. Andrew Woody

"Mr. Andrew Woody and his wife were 63 and 42 years of age, respectively. They had eight children, ranging in age from 6 months to 20 years. Their eldest daughter, along with her husband and infant child, lived with them. At the time they were filmed by CBS in November 1967, the Woody family received social security and aid to families with dependent children totaling $220 monthly, the maximum paid under the Arizona State statutory grant. The daughter's husband was employed by the branch of plant management, Tuba City agency, Bureau of Indian Affairs, where he earned over $2 an hour. According to Mr. Sipe, there was no malnutrition in this family.

"d. Mr. and Mrs. Boyd Nez
"Mr. and Mrs. Boyd Nez were grandparents, who lived in a family camp at Cow Springs, Ariz. Their daughter Anna Nez, her husband, and their child lived in the same camp but in a different hogan. CBS first filmed Anna Nez with her child and then filmed the grandpar-

ents with Anna's child. Boyd Nez and his wife were 68 and 66 years of age, respectively. Both received old-age assistance totaling $128 a month. Anna Nez' husband had an income from odd jobs and livestock which ranged from $2,000 to $2,500 per year. The grandparents also received surplus commodities at the time they were filmed by CBS. The family reportedly ate as a group and there was no apparent hunger problem. The grandparents advised Mr. Sipe that they received a total of $40 for posing for CBS and were promised more money and some lumber which they never received.

"Mr. Sipe advised that the Navajo families he was able to identify as having been filmed by CBS had in common the fact that they resided in traditional dwellings, namely hogans, and spoke little or no English. Mr. Sipe stated that the families had a limited education and no job training. He further said that they were well known to the Bureau of Indian Affairs and were receiving services from various Federal and State programs.

"4. *Hale County, Ala.*

"CBS reported that:

" 'It has never been easy to be a Negro in Alabama. Times have often been bad, and they've never been good. But there's always been cotton—to plant, to chop, to pick, and to plough. Cotton has been a misery, but at least it's been a meal ticket. Now it's not even that. The machines have taken over, and a field that once needed 100 Negroes today barely supports three. Ten years ago machines harvested only 2 percent of Alabama's cotton. This year they will harvest more than 80 percent.

" 'The Negroes must look elsewhere for jobs, and the jobs are not in Alabama. Some go North. Many others remain, often because they are so poor, so tired, and so hungry that they can't even get up and go. In the long history of Black Belt deprivation there have never been times as bad as these.

" 'Last spring the Field Foundation sent six prominent doctors to investigate hunger in Mississippi. One of these was Dr. Raymond Wheeler, who has lived and practiced in the South all his life.'

"Dr. Wheeler was asked by CBS to visit Hale County, Ala., during the filming of the segment of that area and he conducted the interviews with local participants.

"*a. Interview with Mrs. Louise Zanders*

"The interview of Mrs. Zanders conducted by Dr. Wheeler, as set forth in the transcript of the program, was as follows:

" 'Dr. Wheeler. You have how many children to feed?

" 'Mrs. Zanders. Ten.

" 'Dr. Wheeler. Ten children.

" 'Mrs. Zanders. Yes.

" 'Dr. Wheeler. Are there times when you don't have enough food in the house to go around?

" 'Mrs. Zanders. Yes, sir; lots of times.

" 'Dr. Wheeler. There are times when——

" 'Mrs. Zanders. I just have to make out with what I have. Give each one of them a little of what I have.

" 'Dr. Wheeler. What did you have for dinner today?

" 'Mrs. Zanders. I didn't have any dinner.

" 'Dr. Wheeler. You're going to have a baby before long?

" 'Mrs. Zanders. Yes, sir.

" 'Dr. Wheeler. What kind of food do you eat?

" 'Mrs. Zanders. Rice, chicken sometimes.

" 'Dr. Wheeler. What else do you eat?

" 'Mrs. Zanders. That's all, and water.

" 'Dr. Wheeler. Mrs. Zanders, what does your husband do for a living?

" 'Mrs. Zanders. He gets jobs in hayfields.

" 'Dr. Wheeler. In hayfields?

" 'Mrs. Zanders. Yes.

" 'Dr. Wheeler. How much does he make when he's working?

" 'Mrs. Zanders. From $3 to $4 a day.

" 'Dr. Wheeler. $3 to $4 a day?

" 'Mrs. Zanders. Yes, sir.

" 'Dr. Wheeler. And he hasn't worked now in 3 or 4 weeks?

" 'Mrs. Zanders. Yes.

" 'Dr. Wheeler. Do you get food stamps?

" 'Mrs. Zanders. No, sir; because I'm not able to get them.

" 'Dr. Wheeler. Why not?

" 'Mrs. Zanders. I ain't got them this month. They cost $70 and I don't have it.

" 'Dr. Wheeler. Have you asked for any help from anyone in raising the money to buy those stamps?

" 'Mrs. Zanders. No, sir; there ain't no need.

" 'Dr. Wheeler. Why?

" 'Mrs. Zanders. They ain't going to give it to you.

" 'Dr. Wheeler. Have you been down to the welfare department and talked to them, or has your husband?

" 'Mrs. Zanders. No, sir; the last time I went to welfare the lady told me—said if you have a living husband that they can't give you no help.

" 'Dr. Wheeler. Even if he's not working?

" 'Mrs. Zanders. Yes, sir.'

"Following the interview of Mrs. Zanders by Dr. Wheeler, Mr. Charles Kuralt, the CBS narrator, remarked that 'Three weeks after talking to Dr. Wheeler, Mrs. Zanders gave birth to a severely malnourished baby. Two days later the baby died.'

"The staff interviewed Mrs. Louise Zanders on September 27, 1968, at her farmhome near Faunsdale, Ala. She advised that in the fall of 1967 a 'white person' stopped at her home and asked some questions about hunger and asked to take pictures for a TV program. In November 1967, a camera crew accompanied by Dr. Wheeler, arrived and took pictures inside and outside her home for 3 days, working from approximately 8 a.m. to 7 p.m., with only a break for lunch. During this time, Dr. Wheeler asked her many questions while the camera crew took pictures, and the interview with Dr. Wheeler was recorded several times. The CBS crew gave her $39 while they were at her home.

"Mrs. Zanders stated that her husband, her mother, and 11 children resided on 4 $\frac{3}{10}$ acres of land they rent. They paid $189 per year rent, payable 'when the crop comes in.' She claimed to have purchased food stamps on and off since September 1967. The food stamps were very helpful and her family had enough food and did not go hungry. She said her husband planted corn, cotton, okra, peanuts, and potatoes, but the only crop they sold was cotton as they used the other products themselves. It was observed by staff members that the house where the Zanders resided was in extremely poor condition and appeared on the verge of collapse. Two lean hogs were observed enclosed in an area near the house and Mrs. Zanders said the hogs belonged to them and would be killed during the winter, if they could be fattened. The Zanders also owned two mules, a calf, and a few chickens. She was asked about her water supply and pointed to a well about one-half mile away as being the closest source. It was noted during the interview that four or five children were in and about the house and upon inquiry Mrs. Zanders advised that they were not in school because they did not have the proper clothes and she needed them to carry water. Her husband obtained occasional work in the fields and her mother received $26 a month in old-age assistance payments as well as $70 a month from the Veterans' Administration. An older son, who was married but did not live with his wife and child, paid her from $10 to $20 a week from the wages he received from a packinghouse.

"Mrs. Zanders had not seen the CBS program and the transcript of her interview was read to her. She remarked that if the CBS program said her baby died from malnutrition it was not true, and she would tell it like it is.' According to Mrs. Zanders, at about 3 p.m. on December 23, 1967, she experienced labor pains and was admitted to the Hale County Hospital at Greensboro, Ala., by Dr. Chester Singleton, her doctor. Sometime after admittance, the doctor told her that the baby was very large and was in a breech position. Around midnight she was transferred to Druid City Hospital, Tuscaloosa, where Dr. William Standeffer performed an operation and delivered the child. She continued that she never saw the baby but was informed that the baby was stillborn and that it weighed about 12 pounds. According to Mrs. Zanders, many of her children were large at birth.

"The death certificate on file at the Bureau of Vital Statistics, Montgomery, Ala., disclosed that the birth was a stillbirth, with delivery made by a cesarean section operation by Dr. Standeffer on

December 24, 1967. The weight of the female child was 12 pounds 5 ounces; the length of pregnancy was 40 weeks; and death was due to prolonged labor at another hospital.

"Dr. Standeffer advised the staff on September 26, 1968, that Mrs. Zanders was admitted to Druid City Hospital around Christmas 1967. She had been in labor a long time and had been admitted from another hospital. Upon examining Mrs. Zanders he determined that the baby had already died so he removed the body by a cesarean section operation. The baby was very large and showed no signs of malnutrition. It was his opinion that death was due to prolonged labor. He said that Mrs. Zanders did not show any signs of being malnourished.

"The records of the Druid City Hospital disclosed that Mrs. Zanders was a patient in the hospital for a total of 25 days; she was seen by two obstetricians and one urologist, and received five X-rays and numerous medications. Her hospital bill of $1,284.40 had not been paid.

"Mrs. Virginia Glass, director of pensions and security, Greensboro, Ala., advised on September 26, 1968, that her records disclosed that Mrs. Zanders inquired in November 1965 about welfare assistance but did not make application as she was informed that she was ineligible because Mr. Zanders had a small income and there were two able-bodied people in the household.

"Mrs. Barbara Drury, supervisor, food stamp program, Hale County, Ala., advised that the Zanders family first applied for food stamps in July 1967, at which time the family income was $181 per month, making it eligible for $128 in stamps at a cost of $70. In view of the fact that this was the first month for the family to participate, the cost was only half price, $35. Mrs. Drury stated that the Zanders family had been recertified a total of nine times since it was first certified in July 1967. The recertifications were caused by changes in the monthly income earned by the family and changes in the number of people in the household. Food stamp costs for the family had ranged from a low of $22 a month in February 1968, when the family only had an income of $60, to a high of $102 in June 1968, when the family income was $317.42. Mrs. Drury stated that Mr. Zanders reported on August 19, 1968, he had lost his job due to lack of transportation. His income for August 1968 had been $132.40. In September 1968, he was entitled to purchase food stamps, valued at $130, for $58, but he received a voucher from OEO for the $58 and the food stamps did not cost the family any money for the month. Mrs. Drury advised that the purchase price for food stamps was paid by OEO for a number of families in Hale County during September 1968 in order that poor families could use their money to purchase school clothes for their children.

"b. Interview with Mrs. Sally Lee Carlisle

"Mrs. Sally Lee Carlisle of Faunsdale, Ala., was also interviewed on the CBS program by Dr. Raymond Wheeler. Prior to introducing Mrs. Carlisle, Mr. Charles Kuralt,CBS narrator, stated that Dr. Wheeler 'talked to a woman whose family has been sharecroppers ever since they stopped being slaves. The woman and her husband and 14 children and grandchildren still live on the farm, but it does not support them any more.' In response to questioning by Dr. Wheeler, Mrs. Carlisle indicated that she had a garden in which she raised okra and other things, but could not raise corn to feed hogs, chickens, and turkeys because the landowner had sold the corn acres to the Government. She was unable to buy food stamps every 2 weeks because she did not have the $33 necessary for the purchase price. Her husband worked for the city and earned only $3.50 a day. Mrs. Carlisle concluded with general comments dealing with her thoughts that they are not treated as well as they were formerly treated, probably because of school integration and increased voting by members of her race. She spoke of the young people moving to the North where they were getting better jobs and better treatment.

"Mrs. Sally Lee Carlisle was contacted by the staff on September 26, 1968, at her home near Faunsdale where the family had resided since 1964. The home was a run-down cabin located in the middle of a cotton field and had no electricity or plumbing. The family had no toilet because the one they had formerly used had rotted and fallen down. Water was carried from a spring located approximately one-fourth mile from the house.

"When Mrs. Carlisle was contacted by the staff there were 10 children residing at home, four of which were her own, and six belonged to her daughter Ruby, who was residing either in New Jersey or New York and worked as a domestic. Mrs. Carlisle's husband had a steady job working for the city of Uniontown, Ala., and, according to her, earned $3 a day. Mrs. Carlisle received approximately $25 each week from Ruby for support of the children and $20 each week from two grown sons who lived at home and worked in town. Mrs. Carlisle stated that she and some of her children picked cotton occasionally and earned a little over $2 a day.

"Mrs. Carlisle advised that the family had purchased food stamps since November 1967, and paid $46 for $128 in stamps. The family had three hogs, which they intended to butcher during the winter months, and were raising 10 pigs for later use or sale. She advised that they had not raised a garden in recent years because the weather had been too dry. The family attempted to grow some cotton but the yield was not good.

"Mrs. Carlisle advised that since the family had been on food stamps her children had not been hungry. She was able to purchase 4 gallons of milk each week and two of her children received free lunches at school. For the others, she packed peanut butter sandwiches and a 'little sweet cake' and gave each a nickel for milk.

"Mr. John Turpin Vise, the Carlisle's landowner, advised the staff on September 27, 1968, that at the time he purchased the farm in 1966, the Carlisle family was a tenant. He told the Carlisles they could plant all the cotton they wanted, for which he would receive one-third of the yield as his share. He also told the Carlisle family they could plant any other truck crop, such as okra, and there would be no charge for the land use. Mr. Vise said that okra can bring approximately $200 an acre in a good year.

"Mr. Vise stated that in 1967 the Carlisle family planted 15 acres of cotton but only produced one bale of cotton for the entire field. Average cotton yield for this type of soil ranged from ½ to 1 ½ bales per acre. Mr. Vise stated that the Carlisle family did not pick all the cotton that was raised. Mr. Vise stated that as a result of the cotton crop experience, he told Wade Carlisle that he should give up farming and stick to his job in town. He agreed to permit the Carlisle family to stay on the property for a monthly rent of $5 but he has yet to receive his first payment. Mr. Vise advised that he found employment for the two grown sons at a local poultry plant at $1.65 an hour, and when they work they are good workers but they do not report for work regularly.

"Mrs. Virginia Glass, director of pensions and security for Hale County, Ala., advised the staff on September 26, 1968, that Mrs. Carlisle applied for welfare in 1966 for seven grandchildren living with her and received aid to families with dependent children assistance until Ruby, her daughter, returned from the North where she had gone to seek employment. Mrs. Carlisle was notified that because Ruby had returned to Hale County, the mother of the children would have to apply for assistance, but Ruby never applied. As a result, payments to Mrs. Carlisle were discontinued.

"On September 26, 1968, Mrs. Barbara Drury, supervisor, food stamp program in Hale County, advised the staff that Mrs. Carlisle first applied for food stamps in July 1967, at which time the income for the family was reported to be $166.16 a month. She was certified to purchase $142 in food stamps at a cost of $66. The certification continued until January 1968. On February 5, 1968, the Carlisle family was recertified for the purchase of $146 in food stamps at a cost of $74, based on a monthly income of $208.66. On March 5, 1968, the family was recertified for the purchase of $150 in food stamps at a cost of $82, based on an income of $234.66. The family purchased food stamps for only one-half of March 1968, and did not reappear at the food stamp office until July 17, 1968. Mr. Carlisle was out of work at the time due to an illness; Ruby had another child which had been added to the household; and a son had entered the Job Corps. During July 1968, the family was recertified for $120 in food stamps, at a cost of $32 but purchased only one-half of this amount because it was after the 15th of the month. On August 2, 1968, the Carlisle family was recertified for $128 in food stamps, at a cost of $46, based upon a monthly income of $109.77. For the month of September 1968, the $46 purchase price of food stamps was paid by OEO, which enabled the family to use its money to help outfit the children for school.

"On September 27, 1968, Mrs. Jeanette R. Hinton, town clerk, Uniontown, Ala., advised the staff that Wade Carlisle, Jr., who resides near Faunsdale, had been employed as a handyman by the Uniontown Utilities Board since April 1967. His starting salary was $4 per 8-hour day, and, about 5 months ago, he was given a raise to $5 per day. Mr. Carlisle claimed six withholding exemptions, and his wages averaged between $22.50 and $27.50 per week.

"Relative to Mrs. Carlisle's statement on the CBS program concerning their inability to grow corn because the landowner sold the corn acres to the Government, and her consequent inability to raise hogs, chickens, and turkeys without the corn, the Secretary of Agriculture has observed that the records of the Agricultural Stabilization and Conservation Service disclosed that the Carlisles never did grow corn on the land they rented from Mr. John Turpin Vise. The records confirmed the fact that Mr. Vise had diverted his corn acreage under the feed-grain program, but met with his tenants, and, as required, offered to share with them the payments received under the feed-grain program. Actually, Mr. Carlisle was not eligible to share in this agreement, because he had never grown corn on his rented land. Mr. Vise voluntarily offered, in lieu of sharing the Government payment under the feed-grain program, to give land, rent-free, to the Carlisle family for the commercial production of vegetables, and they accepted the offer. The Secretary of Agriculture has stated that the Carlisle family could have grown sweet corn without violating the Government agreement, if they had wished to do so."

Report on Federal Food Programs for Needy Persons

I have read this part of the report to indicate the complete lack of objectivity in these TV programs on alleged hunger conditions.

The balance of the report will be included in the record at this point. [Deleted—author.]

Mr. Whitten. Now, I will turn to the other members for any questions they might have. Mr. Michel.

Mr. Michel. I think the report pretty well speaks for itself.

Mr. Whitten. Mr. Edwards, do you have any questions?

Mr. Edwards. No; not concerning this report.

Mr. Whitten. I repeat again, members of the committee will have a chance, after they have studied it more thoroughly, to ask such questions or make such statements as they might wish.

I mention this problem to you, and read from our investigator's report, Mr. Lennartson, because I believe that this subcommittee can take a share of the credit for all of the things that are being done in this general area now. Every bit of it is being done under the appropriations that originated with this committee.

It is a difficult thing when you find, as this record will show, feeble-minded cases or cases where, because of drunkenness or negligence, parents don't look after their children. It is tragically true that in many rural areas, and in many of the big cities, it is possible for people to exist under circumstances which the general public is unaware of.

We have enough stir-up in this country to last us a good long time. It is my opinion, for what it is worth, that the way to do anything, and I was district attorney about 8 ½ years, where you hear reports and see evidences and when the public gets worked up, is to go out and try to find out what the facts are. With the facts you know what to do. This report that I put in the record includes the bad with the good, prepared and delivered by a professional staff working under a system that the Appropriations Committee has had in existence for 30 or more years. As I say, this is one of probably 35 or 40 studies made last year.

A copy will be made available to you, Mr. Lennartson, so that we may all work together, trying to find some solution. By putting it in the record it becomes available to the public, which needs to know the facts.

I point out again, as a lawyer, I am a strong believer in freedom of speech. It is essential. We don't want Government control, nor do we want control by Government threat. But we also have about reached the point, in my judgment, where there must be some way found to get the news media to accept responsibility for the objectivity and the soundness of that which they publish for public consumption.

This is a rather strong statement—but someone has said that we are rapidly reaching the place where we could have government by public clamor, and television is an instrument that could well create public clamor.

I need not name all the incidents, all the riots, all the burnings, the Chicago convention or other things, to make us realize that we need the industry's help in trying to see that those things that are lifted out of context are so identified, so that the public may judge the true facts.

This is a touchy subject. It's one where, as I said, I have been vilified and revilified, and you can't ever catch up with that kind of thing.

But I had an idea, that when they started hitting at me, 60 days ago, they were bound to suspect what any investigator was bound to find out. But I didn't know it, so I didn't say anything.

I believe in finding out the facts first, making them public, and then taking corrective action.

For that reason all of this has been placed in the record. I hope it will have your close study, you and the folks in the Department. I hope it will have the close study of the Department of Health, Education, and Welfare, and of the committees on both sides of the Capitol, that we may look at this matter judiciously. We ought to see that these, hunger or malnutrition, don't exist. But, at the same time, we must try to save our country's economic position and place some degree of responsibility on the parents, who, after all, we must look to to develop the kind of children that this country must depend upon in the future. It is tragic that any of this could happen, but while we are trying to get the parents to meet their responsibilities, certainly I agree with others that we can't see anybody suffer from hunger, malnutrition, or anything else if it is humanly possible to prevent it.

Appendix F

Code of Broadcast News Ethics of the Radio Television
News Directors Association

The following Code of Broadcast News Ethics for RTNDA was
adopted January 2, 1966.

*The members of the Radio Television News Directors Association
agree that their prime responsibility as newsmen—and that of the
broadcasting industry as the collective sponsor of news broadcasting—
is to provide to the public they serve a news service as accurate, full
and prompt as human integrity and devotion can devise, To that end,
they declare their acceptance of the standards of practice here set
forth, and their solemn intent to honor them to the limits of their
ability.*

Article One

The primary purpose of broadcast newsmen—to inform the public
of events of importance and appropriate interest in a manner that is
accurate and comprehensive—shall override all other purposes.

Article Two

Broadcast news presentations shall be designed not only to offer
timely and accurate information, but also to present it in the light
of relevant circumstances that give it meaning and perspective. This
standard means that news reports, when clarity demands it, will be
laid aganst pertinent factual background; that factors such as race,
creed, nationality or prior status will be reported only when they are
relevant; that comment or subjective content will be properly iden-

tified; and that errors in fact will be promptly acknowledged and corrected.

Article Three

Broadcast newsmen shall seek to select material for newscast solely on their evaluation of its merits as news. This standard means that news will be selected on the criteria of significance, community and regional relevance, appropriate human interest, service to defined audiences. It excludes sensationalism or misleading emphasis in any form; subservience to external or "interested" efforts to influence news selection and presentation, whether from within the broadcasting industry or from without. It requires that such terms as "bulletin" and "flash" be used only when the character of the news justifies them; that bombastic or misleading descriptions of newsroom facilities and personnel be rejected, along with undue use of sound and visual effects; and that promotional or publicity material be sharply scrutinized before use and identified by source or otherwise when broadcast.

Article Four

Broadcast newsmen shall at all times display humane respect for the dignity, privacy and the well-being of persons with whom the news deals.

Article Five

Broadcast newsmen shall govern their personal lives and such nonprofessional associations as may impinge on their professional activities in a manner that will protect them from conflict of interest, real or apparent.

Article Six

Broadcast newsmen shall seek actively to present all news the knowledge of which will serve the public interest, no matter what selfish, uninformed or corrupt efforts attempt to color it, withold it or prevent its presentation. They shall make constant effort to open doors closed to the reporting of public proceedings with tools appropriate to broadcasting (including cameras and recorders), consistent with the public interest. They acknowledge the newsman's ethic of protection of confidential information and sources, and urge unswerving observation of it except in instances in which it would clearly and unmistakably defy the public interest.

Article Seven

Broadcast newsmen recognize the responsibility borne by broadcasting for informed analysis, comment and editorial opinion on public events and issues. They accept the obligation of broadcasters, for the presentation of such matters by individuals whose competence, experience and judgment qualify them for it.

Article Eight

In court, broadcast newsmen shall conduct themselves with dignity, whether the court is in or out of session. They shall keep broadcast equipment as unobtrusive and silent as possible. Where court facilities are inadequate, pool broadcasts should be arranged.

Article Nine

In reporting matters that are or may be litigated, the newsman shall avoid practices which would tend to interfere with the right of an individual to a fair trial.

Article Ten

Broadcast newsmen shall actively censure and seek to prevent violations of these standards, and shall actively encourage their observance by all newsmen, whether of the Radio Television News Directors Association or not.